IRISH POETRY: POLITICS, HISTORY, NEGOTIATION

Irish Poetry: Politics, History, Negotiation

The Evolving Debate, 1969 to the Present

Steven Matthews

First published in Great Britain 1997 by
MACMILLAN PRESS LTD
Houndmills, Basingstoke, Hampshire RG21 6XS and London
Companies and representatives throughout the world

A catalogue record for this book is available from the British Library.

ISBN 0–333–64335–6 hardcover
ISBN 0–333–64336–4 paperback

First published in the United States of America 1997 by
ST. MARTIN'S PRESS, INC.,
Scholarly and Reference Division,
175 Fifth Avenue, New York, N.Y. 10010

ISBN 0–312–16436–X

Library of Congress Cataloging-in-Publication Data
Matthews, Steven.
Irish poetry : politics, history, negotiation, the evolving
debate, 1969 to the present / Steven Matthews.
p.   cm.
Includes bibliographical references and index.
ISBN 0–312–16436–X (cloth)
1. Political poetry, English—Northern Ireland—History and
criticism.   2. Politics and literature—Northern Ireland–
–History—20th century.   3. Literature and history—Northern
Ireland—History—20th century.   4. English poetry—Northern
Ireland—History and criticism.   5. English poetry—Irish authors–
–History and criticism.   6. English poetry—20th century—History
and criticism.   7. Northern Ireland—Intellectual life—20th
century.   8. Northern Ireland—In literature.   I. Title.
PR8781.P64M38   1996
821'.914099416—dc20   96–9649
                                                              CIP

This book is printed on paper suitable for recycling and made from fully managed and
sustained forest sources.

10   9   8   7   6   5   4   3   2
06   05   04   03   02   01   00   99   98

Reprinted and bound
in Great Britain by
Antony Rowe Ltd, Chippenham, Wiltshire

Contents

Acknowledgements

My deepest gratitude is to Elleke Boehmer for her wonderful help and support, and for her telling conversation about the book – in short, for making everything possible.

My discussions with Hugh Haughton have always been inspirational and enlivening, and I owe him a great debt. I have also enjoyed important discussions with Shirley Chew, Ian Fairley, Alan Marshall, Alistair Stead, Ashley Taggart, Loreto Todd and John Whale. I would like to thank my Mum, Dad and sister for their backing in some difficult times. I am grateful to the School of English, University of Leeds, for providing me with a travel grant for a research trip to Ireland.

Thanks also to our newly born son Thomas, whose equability created the time to complete this book which would otherwise not have been available.

The author and publishers are grateful to the following for permission to reprint copyright material:

W.H. Auden – Faber & Faber for extracts from *The English Auden* and *Collected Poems*.

Eavan Boland – Carcanet Press for extracts from *Selected Poems, Outside History, In a Time of Violence* and *Object Lessons*.

Ciaran Carson – The Gallery Press for extracts from *First Language* and *Letters From the Alphabet*.

Brian Friel – Faber & Faber for an extract from *Selected Plays*.

Seamus Heaney – Faber & Faber and Farrar Straus & Giroux Inc. for extracts from *Wintering Out, North, Field Work, Station Island, The Haw Lantern, The Cure at Troy, Seeing Things, Preoccupations, The Government of the Tongue, The Redress of Poetry*; The Scholar Press for extracts from *The Place of Writing*.

John Hewitt – The Blackstaff Press for extracts from *Collected Poems* and *Ancestral Voices*.

Thomas Kinsella – Thomas Kinsella for extracts from *Poems 1956–1973, New Poems 1973, One and Other Poems, Fifteen Dead, Blood and Family* and *From Centre City;* Carcanet Press for extracts from *The Dual Tradition.*

Michael Longley – Jonathan Cape for an extract from *The Ghost Orchid.*

Medbh McGuckian – The Gallery Press for an extract from *Captain Lavender.*

Paul Muldoon – Faber & Faber for extracts from *Mules, Quoof, Meeting the British, Madoc: A Mystery* and *The Annals of Chile;* Farrar, Straus & Giroux Inc. for extracts from *Madoc* and *The Annals of Chile;* The Gallery Press for extracts from *Six Honest Serving Men* and *The Prince of the Quotidian.*

Eiléan Ní Chuilleanáin – The Gallery Press for extracts from *The Magdalene Sermon* and *The Brazen Serpent.*

Tom Paulin – Faber & Faber for an extract from *Walking a Line* and *Minotaur.*

1

Introduction: Making History?

On 1 September 1994, the complete cessation of violence in the North of Ireland announced by the Provisional IRA came into effect. It was followed shortly afterwards by parallel announcements from other paramilitaries on both sides of the religious divide. With these events, 25 years of more-or-less continuous conflict were broken, and the hopes of finding a lasting peace greatly intensified in both communities.

The new situation was greeted two days later by the appearance in the *Irish Times* of a sonnet by the Belfast poet Michael Longley called 'Ceasefire'. Drawing on an incident in Book XXIV of the *Iliad*, 'Ceasefire' recounts the visit of the old Trojan king, Priam, to Achilles' camp in order to beg for the return of his dead son's body. Achilles weeps on seeing Priam, who reminds him of his own father, and his tears are in their turn echoed by Priam himself. Achilles makes sure that the corpse of the dead warrior, Hector, is washed and made ready for return, 'Wrapped like a present', to Troy at daybreak. The two sit to eat, and then after the meal admire each other's physical beauty 'as lovers might'. 'Ceasefire' ends by recounting that Priam had now grown garrulous, Priam who had earlier sighed:

'I get down on my knees and do what must be done
And kiss Achilles' hand, the killer of my son.'[1]

Longley's poem is a subtle, moving and timely intervention, suggesting that the inevitable way forward for the two traditions in the North is through mutual understanding and, vitally, through forgiveness. What is striking here is that aesthetic appreciation plays a crucial part in that move towards reconciliation and conversation between the two sides. It is the homoerotic appreciation by each man of the other's 'beauty' which brings them together almost as

1

lovers, suggesting that new terms between the hitherto opposing sides must be founded upon admiration by each for the beauties of the other. The poem claims, then, a deciding role for the aesthetic within the larger continuum of understanding between the warring sides.

Crucially, of course, 'Ceasefire' itself represents a lull, a nurturing and quiet space against the backdrop of larger historical action. Longley's brilliant and delicate seizing upon this incident as exemplary is itself an act of recuperation, an assertion of wholeness and coherence against larger processes. Longley's 14 lines are culled from some two hundred of Homer's. In the final couplet, the graceful unifying of an acknowledgement of the fated with the enormous courage of the act of reconciliation, is won out of, and asserted against, the epic sweep towards the destruction of Troy which Homer narrates at the end of the *Iliad*.

Longley's poem is both a celebration and a warning – a warning that the new reconciliation between the Catholic and the Protestant sides must itself step outside of the hitherto seemingly 'fated' sweep of Irish history and achieve a formal ratification like that both described and exemplified in the poem. The sonnet form provides a salutary model for the balances and loving-harmonies which might be attainable in the North of Ireland should the moment of ceasefire be carried to its next logical stages of forgiveness, sitting down together, admiring the graceful strengths of the other side and talking. Longley's form here is itself something of a compromise – between the long line produced through the retention of something like Homer's hexameters for this version, and the traditional virtues of the sonnet in the English tradition. Through such formal compromise, Longley recognizes the cultural and historical distance of his subject from his own tradition, while simultaneously asserting its continuing relevance and the urgency of its message. Yet that form in itself carries the salutary reminder that without this new process being entered into, the epic spiral towards destruction of the city will necessarily work itself through.

'Ceasefire' exemplifies the fact, therefore, that under pressure of historical event, a poem's adaptation of even the most seemingly abstruse and ancient subject matter, and of one of the most transhistorically complete forms, does not alter the urgency of its pertinence, its possibility or its warning. The poem's allusion to the aesthetic enforces its own claim to attention, while alerting us also to the fact that its beauties, despite its measured perfection, might only be temporary. The poem's virtues remain contingent upon the history towards which it forms both a response and a salutary model of possibility.

Longley has carved here a lyric poem out of an epic one. Yet it would be inadequate to read the poem solely *as* a lyric, to accept its consolations without in turn reading them back into the public world from which, as the title and publication of the poem suggest, it received its instigation. In literary terms, Longley's adoption here and elsewhere in his poetry of the 1990s of the seemingly extraneous matter of Homer's epic to suit his particular circumstance suggests a Joycean approach to capturing his times. Joyce discovered in *The Odyssey* a structuring myth for the portrayal in his novel *Ulysses* of a day in modern Dublin's life. That discovery was famously envied by T.S. Eliot, who sought and failed to apply a similar continuous parallel between antiquity and his contemporary London in *The Waste Land*. Through his use of Homeric material, Eliot claimed, Joyce had triumphantly succeeded in 'controlling...ordering...[and] giving a shape and a significance to the immense panorama of futility and anarchy which is contemporary history.'[2]

Longley's own adaptation of Homeric material to describe the fragile moment of understanding in 'Ceasefire' seems to arise out of a similar impulse to Joyce's as Eliot perceived it. Times which are tragically contradictory and anarchically lacking in direction, which could lead to irreversible destruction, need to find an ahistorical correlative before they can be adequately contained poetically. The history of sectarian division and violence has rendered all harmonies, and all aesthetic solutions, such as that envisaged in 'Ceasefire', vulnerable.

It is from the violence and sense of futility in the First World War that many commentators – and most vividly Paul Fussell in *The Great War and Modern Memory* – have seen the poetic modernism of Eliot and his mentor Ezra Pound as arising, a modernism which had correlative impact on Joyce's own work for other reasons. That war brought the breakup of traditional ways of life and of social and national order. It also led to a foregrounding in literature of formal issues, since the traditional unities of narrative in the realist novel and of poetic form and rhythm were all thrown into question by the horrors witnessed at, and reported from, the Front. Eliot's attention to the structuring principle of Joyce's novel rather than to its content is symptomatic of the ways in which when (as Wilfred Owen put it in 'Dulce et Decorum Est') the 'old lie' of heroism and glory had been exposed, all notions of order, social, national and aesthetic, were thrown under scrutiny and new solutions sought.

In this book I describe and discuss the similar formal self-consciousness and disjunctiveness present in poetic responses to the violence in the North of Ireland from 1969 to 1996, responses both from there and from the South of the island. Through concentrating on that modernist formalist approach as one which also establishes continuities between historical event and poetic practice, I hope to challenge what seems an internally divisive and polarizing tendency in international criticism of that poetry. That tendency reads the poems in terms of their aesthetic coherence, and so sees all other readings as narrowly ideological or politically partial. In challenging this approach, I want to set the poetry uneasily between the two poles of the aesthetic and the public or political. I want to show, rather, how poetry uncertainly mediates between them, and how that mediation leads poets to review the formal choices which underlie their poetic practices. Out of this emerges, I want to suggest, a sense that in Ireland North and South there has been, in response to the renewed violence, an emergence of a late, local modernism, one in which poetry has been forced to break up traditional form from within and to adapt itself to terrible and shocking circumstance.

Further, I will describe how that modernity which is directly reflected in poetic form is mirrored in – and exacerbated by – the progression in the two economies in the North and South of the island during the 1960s towards late capitalism: one in which, as I describe it below, the arrival of international commercial pressures led to a perhaps overly rapid and pressurized modernization of life. This had tragic effects in the North, where the inequality between the two communities, Protestant and Catholic, was heightened and dramatized by the sudden arrival of new economic growth; traditional sectarian antagonisms and eventually violence were reawakened. In my chapters on the poetry below (and particularly those on the poets who have most openly embraced the literary tenets of modernism, Thomas Kinsella and John Montague), there often emerges a tension between a modernist *poetic* which seeks to reflect and describe both the contemporary violence and its historical roots, and an awareness of economic and social change which further throws that aesthetic accommodation into doubt.

So the book's approach is twofold. On the one hand I will describe how poets have both consciously and unconsciously adapted their poetics to the situation of renewed violence in the North since 1969. In order to do this I have always set their responses against the perspective of their poetic careers as a whole. On the other hand, I want to set that formal emphasis against the economic and social change out of which it arises, suggesting that poetry's local, lyric struggles for order always occur within and against those other preoccupations. Out of this dual focus emerges a sense that history partly determines the progress of a poetic and a poetic career, but also that poetry answers back by adapting itself to the altering contexts of its creation.

Having established these as the terms of my reading of that poetry, however, I am forced to admit its own partiality and un-adaptibility. As Peter Nichols has argued, that complex of disorientation and desire surrounding the First World War which included a desire for order among the so-called 'Men of 1914' – the first generation of modernists which included Pound, Eliot and Joyce – was an essentially male one which sought male solutions to poetic and cultural dilemmas: 'For the "Men of 1914" a renovated culture often carried a paternal sanction, with resulting forms of "filial" emulation actually providing the condition of an authentic modernism.'[3] My paradigm for reading poetic responses post-1969 describes a similar sanction and emulation operating within this later context, and so consciously registers the difference between, and limitedness in, this model and one which could explore the other emphases and priorities within the history shared by women poets, for example, in Ireland North and South. As I show later in this chapter, the work of Medbh McGuckian and Eavan Boland sets their response to the situation in the North alongside a further attention to the nature and practice of women's writing itself. Boland in particular has shown a strong scepticism for the kinds of limited masculinist modernism which she feels are practised around her. The new priorities which she brings to poetics are ones which, as a male reader, I feel only inadequately able to describe, but which raise important questions about the paradigms which exist in male poetry across this time and therefore about the terms of this book.

MODERNISMS IN THE NORTH AND SOUTH OF IRELAND

The Dublin-based philosopher Richard Kearney has claimed that Ireland has been undergoing in this century a 'crisis of culture':

This has often been experienced as a conflict between the claims of tradition and modernity. Such an experience of residing between two worlds...has given rise to a crisis of consciousness. How is one to confront the prevailing sense of discontinuity, the absence of a coherent identity, the breakdown of inherited ideologies and beliefs, the insecurities of fragmentation? Is it possible to make the *transition* between past and future... ?[4]

Kearney's all-Ireland view is perhaps confirmed by the fact that that crisis was accelerated in the 1960s with the sudden and abrupt imposition of a modern international economics both South and North. In the Republic, as Taoiseach between 1959 and 1966, Sean Lemass instigated Ireland's first industrial revolution. His lift on trade tariffs lured foreign firms into the country and established it as part of an international marketplace; as a result, manufacturing output rose by 5 per cent yearly from 1959 to 1972. When Terence O'Neill became prime minister in the North in 1963, he instigated a similar plan for economic revolution to that taking place in the South, whose programme he envied. As more traditional industries like linen manufacture and shipbuilding went into decline, he encouraged (through incentives offered by the Ministry of Commerce) many foreign multinationals like Grundig and ICI to set up factories. Although the new jobs gained barely offset the losses of those in traditional industries, there was a striking improvement in living standards throughout the 1960s, although the North of Ireland remained well behind the mainland in this respect.

O'Neill's plan was, though, applied in ways which alienated the minority Catholic population; all the areas of growth were in Protestant heartlands. This palpable unfairness exacerbated the sense of disparities between the two communities, and led to the growth of the Civil Rights movement in the late 1960s, which (as I describe it below) in its turn led to the breakdown of communication between the two sides and the outbreak of the so-called 'Troubles'.[5] Both parts of Ireland, therefore, entered the 25-year period of civil strife in the North on the back of economic and political moves which brought the island more into line with other modern capitalist societies.

In terms of the literary aesthetics which have emerged in the island during that period, there has been a similar sense of transition between a more settled and inward-looking past, often based upon rural ideals, and a rebarbative and absolute present which is contingent upon modern change and the opening of aesthetics itself to broader, questioning contexts. The Dublin poet Thomas Kinsella has famously recognized the inevitable partiality with which any writer in Ireland or beyond now operates: 'Every writer in the modern world – since he can't be in all literary traditions at once – is the inheritor of a gapped, discontinuous, polyglot tradition.'[6] Kinsella's answer to the kinds of question posed by Kearney is simply to pragmatically accept discontinuity as a fact, and to adapt his poetic to that recognition. Seamus Heaney from the North has sought to describe a complexity in the relation between past and present which makes the issue of transition itself crucial, and which defines it as establishing the relevance of past poetry in the present.

In his 'Introduction' to a selection of the poems of the Catholic nationalist poet Francis Ledwidge who was killed in the First World War, Heaney has made an argument for modernity which recognizes its association with historical urgency. He challenges the view of Ledwidge's biographer that the earlier poet's work represents a traditional, domesticated, pious picture of an Ireland which had become inward-looking in the years before independence. Rather:

> ...Ledwidge's fate had been more complex and modern than that. He very deliberately chose not to bury his head in local sand and, as a consequence, faced the choices and moral challenges of his times with solitude, honesty and rare courage. This integrity, and its ultimate gratifying effects upon his poetry, should command the renewed interest and respect of Irish people at the present time: Ledwidge lived through a similar period of historical transition when political, cultural and constitutional crises put into question values which had previously appeared as ratified and immutable as the contours of the land itself.[7]

Heaney's poem, 'In Memoriam Francis Ledwidge: Killed in France 31 July 1917', is not itself free of sugary piety. The Catholic poet killed while fighting as a British soldier is, in the poem's final lines which ghost Wilfred Owen's 'Strange Meeting', said to 'consort' in death with those 'true-blue' Protestants who would seem more at home in the British army. Yet the progress across Heaney's traditional quatrains in this elegy is juddery and regressive, leaping from the present time of writing, to his own holidays with his aunt in 1946–7, to the years of the first World War. In the event, however, the use of the familial as a link to the War and to

Ledwidge's death only serves to exaggerate the awkward distance between the domesticity of certain views of Ireland and the actualities of modern war:

> It's summer, nineteen-fifteen. I see the girl
> My aunt was then, herding on the long acre.
> Behind a low bush in the Dardanelles
> You suck stones to make your dry mouth water.
>
> It's nineteen-seventeen. She still herds cows
> But a big strafe puts the candles out in Ypres:
> 'My soul is by the Boyne, cutting new meadows....
> My country wears her confirmation dress.'

In this second stanza, Heaney wittily alludes to wartime cliché ('puts the lights out') in order to undermine Ledwidge's pious, nostalgic conflation of religion with nationalism. Yet by juxtaposing his own voice against Ledwidge's in the stanza which follows this, Heaney proves the immediate contemporary relevance of his elegy; by implication he links death in the war, which is often seen as instigating modernism, with the sectarian violence in his country continuing in the present ('You were rent/By shrapnel..."I am sorry/That party politics should divide our tents"').

Ledwidge emerges from the elegy as a reminder of the 'uselessness' of equilibrium when viewed against such times of crisis and division; writing in his own time of violence, Heaney says 'I hear again the sure confusing drum' which Ledwidge followed into battle (echoing the drums to be heard in Orange parades, presumably), 'But miss the twilit note' which he should hear in Ledwidge's work.[8] It is almost as though the violence which broke out in the North in 1969 has made him more sceptical of nationalist pieties, but also more attentive to the brutal note of modernity to be heard beneath the traditionally sanctified sounds in Ledwidge's work. Ledwidge's story makes him more aware of similar resonances in his own times, and of their barren futility.

Seamus Heaney's transitional recognitions form something of a presiding note over the debates in this book and for the terms I use in describing them. From the late 1980s onwards, he has used the forums of lectures, essays and reviews to conduct the most extensive discussion by any poet writing in Ireland North and South about the relations between poetry, politics and history. Further, he stands at a mediational and mediatory point within the genealogy of poetry which I seek to establish; in such discussions, he has frequently drawn upon examples from the work of those poets from the generation above him – Hewitt, Kinsella and Montague – and his stance has proved crucial to the more expansive and contingent writing of the generation below him, a generation including Carson and Muldoon. Heaney's own poetry exemplifies those mediatory but also 'crisis' and conflictual qualities which reflect the transitional phase towards modernity which Ireland North and South has undergone since the 1960s. As poems like 'The Swing' and 'Tollund' from his 1996 collection *The Spirit Level* confirm, Heaney continues to strive to negotiate between, on the one hand, a more modestly traditional, formally balanced mode and, on the other, a modern and improvisatory mode responsive to the historical moment. In the mediation between the two lies a paradigm for the kinds of modernism which emerge in much of the poetry responsive to 'the Troubles'.

It remains true, however, that, like Heaney, few poets from North or South have written poems which directly register the transitional effects of this modernity and its correlative cosmopolitanism on their island or their work. The new economics in the South had, as I will show in my chapter upon him, a crucial impact upon Thomas Kinsella's development of a modernist poetic in the 1960s; Brendan Kennelly's writing often shows the urban deprivation in Dublin which has been brought about by an economic expansion which has only benefited part of the population; and Ciaran Carson's work, discussed in my last chapter, reveals a deep involvement with Belfast past and present. Moreover, Derek Mahon's cosmopolitan poetry has had, as I show in Chapter 6, an important influence within Heaney's move towards a greater modernism in his work.

However, the poetry, and particularly that from the North, mainly centres upon more traditional and often pastoral subjects, and derives its origin, energy, command and strength from them. As Heaney enjoins someone, presumably one of his children, after revealing a bird's nest in a well in 'Changes':

> ...Remember this.
> It will be good for you to retrace this path
>
> when you have grown away and stand at last
> at the very centre of the empty city.[9]

John Hewitt's Glens of Antrim, Montague's Garvaghey and Muldoon's Armagh countryside all form similar experiential and poetic resources to Heaney's Co. Derry. This sense is confirmed in a *Krino* article which claims that Ulster poetry has reached an impasse because of its failure to experiment with ways which would allow it to articulate most people's experience of the modern world around them. Tom Clyde laments that 'you will search in vain in recent volumes for anything which speaks to the contemporary statelet, the Ulster of both BMW and Volvo's busiest British dealers, of child prostitution on the streets of Derry ...'.[10]

Only among poets from the South, poets physically removed from the duress of the situation in the North, is there emerging a poetry which reflects modern city life. Eavan Boland's earnestly suburban poetic will figure prominently in the last section of this chapter; Thomas McCarthy has constantly castigated contemporary political life there; in his collection *The Bottom Line*, Dennis O'Driscoll has written 50 11-liners in various voices revealing the stresses and boredoms of modern office life. In his previous collection, *Long Story Short*, O'Driscoll presented a modern world end-stopped by disease, a modern world in which Ireland appears as part of a European continuum, and several poems in the collection focus upon the 1989 revolutions there.[11]

The frequent retreat into the countryside in poetry which emerges from a more direct engagement with the history of violence in the North is surprising and striking therefore. Yet it remains true that, as an aspect of the modernity which I describe in each of the poets below, such pastoralism marks a particular and difficult response to the situation rather than a retreat into a safe, sanctioned, aesthetic fastness. In response to the renewed violence in the North, Hewitt actually questions the validity of the nature poetry which he has written all his career; at the end of *The Rough Field*, Montague shows that, in the light of incidents like 'A New Siege' of Derry, pastoralism is itself passing away. As part of the increasing historical contingency in his later poetry, Heaney has recognized that 'The places I go back to have not failed/But will not last'.[12] In response to the changing public situation, therefore, the poets find themselves consciously or unconsciously revising the origins of their poetic inspiration.

In each of the chapters below, it will emerge that the poets' modernist response to the historical disorders and violence in the North is itself the source of the duress which the poetry suffers, a duress from both external circumstance and from the internal uncontainability of much of its extreme subject matter. The modernity of the poetry provides its true picture of historical and contemporary reality *through* its very questioning of traditional themes like pastoralism and of stable formal structures. I now want momentarily to return to discuss how these pressures operated in the first modernist poets in order also to show how they exert an immediate, particular and local formal duress upon an earlier poet in Ireland itself, a poet with whose terms the later poets inevitably have to negotiate.

POUND, ELIOT, YEATS AND HISTORY

Those very issues of response, relation and negotiation form the central instigation for Ezra Pound's reading of the historical imperative behind, for instance, the orchestration of his epic 'containing history', *The Cantos*. That work is formed by juxtaposing particulars from one historical moment or phase with particulars from another phase, without any mediational, explicatory matter between the two. This is because, as Pound claimed:

> We do NOT know the past in chronological sequence. It may be convenient to lay it out anaesthetized upon a table with dates pasted on here and there, but what we know we know by ripples and spirals eddying out from us and from our own time ...A man does not know his own ADDRESS (in time) until he knows where his own time and milieu stand in relation to other times and conditions.[13]

As the allusion here to T.S. Eliot's early poem 'The Love Song of J. Alfred Prufrock' indicates, Pound is arguing similarly but more generally for the necessary historical perspectives which Eliot had given classical critical formulation to. For Eliot, history itself often became conflated with literary tradition, as in the essay on Joyce, in the diagnosis of a 'dissociation of sensibility' in England after 'The Metaphysical Poets' or, equally famously, in his 1919 essay 'Tradition and the Individual Talent'.

Tradition, for Eliot, does not mean merely accepting what is handed down from the previous generation (he favours 'novelty' over 'repetition'); rather it involves a great deal of labour to acquire a true 'historical sense', 'a perception, not only of the pastness of the past, but of its presence'. Tradition only falls 'simultaneously' into place with the creation of each new work of art, and each new work alters, 'if ever so slightly', the *whole* existing order' – the whole of the literature of Europe from Homer and the whole literature of the writer's own country. Tradition, therefore, does not serve to provide the writer with a secure sense of continuity; rather, it is 'what makes a writer most acutely conscious of his place in time, of his own contemporaneity.'[14] In Eliot's *The Waste Land*, the form is constructed from a mosaic of fragments from different phases of literary history which partly seeks both to diagnose and unsuccessfully to bring order to the diffuse and decentred world after the First World War. In the laying down of this mosaic, history as changing process falls away across the poem; there is no progression between the sections but rather a simultaneity of effects within a frozen present where all the fragments are shored against the ruins of the modern world.

There is a similar and more conscious attempt to freeze history and to exclude its process from poetic form in the work of the poet whose impact is more directly felt in all three of the generations of poets I will be discussing. And it is here that the issue of form and its relation to a violent contemporary history finds a surprising, immediate and literal application, as it is mediated through the negotiations which these poets have transacted with their ambiguously modernist, ambiguously national forebear, W.B. Yeats. Yeats's later poetry reacts against the marginalization of his own Anglo-Irish tradition in the legislation of the early years of the Republic, against the bourgeoisification of the Catholic middle classes and against the internecine strife during the Civil War in 1922–3 by making a magnificent retreat behind the walls of the Norman tower, Thoor Ballylee, which he had purchased in 1917. In the poems recalling the Civil War from the 1928 collection *The Tower* on, we see Yeats pacing his battlements and creating in resonant, sonorous stanzas poetic equivalents of the platonic, noble and enduring structure he envisaged the Thoor to be. Such stanzas serve both to contain and to resist the 'mere anarchy' into which he, like Eliot, felt the world had descended:

Now days are dragon-ridden, the nightmare
Rides upon sleep: a drunken soldiery
Can leave the mother, murdered at her door,
To crawl in her own blood, and go scot-free;
The night can sweat with terror as before
We pieced our thoughts into philosophy,
And planned to bring the world under a rule,
Who are but weasels fighting in a hole.[15]

Even when describing a contemporary nightmare from which there seems little chance to awake, then, Yeats's stanzas retain their aloof, resonant magnificence. The resounding rhymes and the four-squareness of the stanzas stand as the stone blocks of the Thoor also stand, rebutting the violence which rages at its walls.

Throughout each of the chapters in this book, my discussion of the formal constructions of recent poetry from Ireland North and South and its relation to history and politics involves the negotiations which later poets are forced to make with Yeats's architectural solution, negotiations which in their turn release those poets into a closer involvement with events since 1969.

Seamus Heaney, who has himself written magnificently of the significance of the Thoor in Yeats's later poetry and its effect upon his political ideas (with, as my chapter on him below argues, important implications for his own work), has also recognized the challenge and imaginative stalemate such noble intransigence has exerted for later writers in Ireland and for their negotiations with history. Introducing the poems of Padraic Fallon, poems themselves often concerned with building and with architecture, Heaney has argued that Fallon's 'Yeats's Tower at Ballylee' reveals 'one of the big dynamics of Irish literary history in the post-Yeatsian era':

> Fallon indeed cannot get an equal footing upon [his own] ground until he breaks up his Yeatsian lines and stanzas...to admit also the vertiginous disjunctions between himself as aspiring schoolboy, nose pressed to the big sweetshop window of classical learning, and the remote, apotheosized sage of Ballylee.[16]

In his later work, Fallon sporadically uses a Poundian poetic to help him with this dismantling; later poets like Kinsella and Montague have also found in Pound a useful model for registering the disjunctions between the history which they are living through in Ireland and that noble dream envisaged for the fledgling country by Yeats. It is these models and formal issues which will form the substance of my discussion in this book.

With the outbreak of the religious and communal but also historically conditioned violence in the North of Ireland in 1969, writers from the whole island inevitably reviewed their relations to history and its presence. And, for both sides of the religious divide, that history is not generated by any necessary sense of continuity but is rather dependent upon some symbolic dates which must be continually reread: 1690, 1798 or 1916.[17] There is a similar emphasis upon fragmented, frozen moments of time in modernist poetics. As a counter-strain within Pound's historical 'relation', and also within the 'not only...but' construction of Eliot's sentence above on the relation of past to present, there operates a fully felt force of division, of the intransigence of those historical materials which need relating. Once history is no longer a continuum, the 'labour' to relate historical materials within the present becomes an urgent, difficult and contingent one.

In Ireland post-1969, not only the division of the violent present from the possibilities involved with symbolic historical dates, but the divisions within the present itself: both receive full and inevitable recognition within the poetry through its adoption of something close to such modernist thinking. Yet, paradoxically, it is the irreconcilable, fragmented poetic which is contingent upon that history that is most misread and resisted by its international critics, some of whose ideas I wish to review now in order to further clarify my own approach.

'AESTHETIC CRITICISM', MATERIALISM AND MODERNISM

Anglo-American discussions – as well as some Irish discussions (from both North and South of the border) – of the poetry which has focused on the North of Ireland since the renewed violence there from 1969 have inevitably also focused upon the relations between the poetry and the traumatized history out of which it arises. But those discussions have not always readily granted that work its continuities and contingencies between historical event and poetic form. Rather, those discussions have celebrated the formal beauties emanating from the poetry for their universalizing impact, and have neglected the context out of which those beauties have arisen. In the process, the historical urgency, the critical force of the poetry and the nature of its political intervention have often been obscured.

To take but the example of readings of Seamus Heaney, whose receipt of the 1995 Nobel Prize for Literature confirmed his popular and academic international standing: a welter of criticism championing his work has sought to prove the poetry's transhistorical and transcultural importance. Helen Vendler, Heaney's primary advocate in America, opens her book *The Music of What Happens* (the title of which is derived from a line in one of Heaney's poems in *Field Work*) with a complex argument for what she calls 'aesthetic' as opposed to 'ideological' criticism. Aesthetic criticism, in Vendler's version of it, seems very much of a piece with earlier attempts to see a poem as a universal icon; it is a criticism which recognizes the uniqueness of the individual work of art and its internally balanced elements. Vendler involves Heaney's poem 'Song' with her discussion of the practicalities of this approach:

> The first rule of thumb is that no significant component can be left out of consideration. A critic must notice not only... 'what happens', but also 'the music of what happens' and must perceive the pertinence of both 'the mud-flowers of dialect/And the immortelles of perfect pitch.' And the second rule of thumb is that the significant components are known as such by interacting with each other in a way that seems coherent, not haphazard.

Against this assertion of the organic wholeness and separateness of the single poem, Vendler claims that 'ideological criticism' is only interested to conflate it 'with other works sharing its values'.

Yet a kind of conflation is surely what Vendler is herself guilty of when it comes to her actual chapter on Heaney in the book, one which seeks to describe the 'unique' qualities of his writing. She objects to the attempt to see Heaney as an Irish poet, something which, she argues:

> ...distorts the beauty and significance of his work: he is as much the legitimate heir of Keats or Frost as of Kavanagh or Yeats, and the history of his consciousness is as germane to our lives as that of any other poet...Heaney's may be an extreme sequence, but a similar passage from a sequestered childhood to a forcibly

socialized adulthood happens to us all: we are constrained to acknowledge evil, violence, and our individual helplessness in history.[18]

Despite her eloquent disavowals in both the 'Preface' and in the later chapters of her book discussing recent literary theory, then, Vendler emerges as, on her own terms, an *ideological* critic, one who conflates Heaney's poetry with values which she (and, she argues, everyone) can recognize and share. What is significant within Vendler's polemic on behalf of 'aesthetic' criticism is the ease with which she establishes her readings upon the secure ground of the poem as *lyric*, as the expression of the poet's personal feelings or 'consciousness'. She thereby wrenches the literary space away from the cultural and historical background of its origin towards a universal humanism. Having established that lyric tradition, Vendler can then override issues of cultural authenticity or 'uniqueness'. In the process, it remains unclear as to why Heaney, who after all writes in the English language, cannot indeed be the 'legitimate heir' of Keats or Frost, and yet not remain an *Irish* poet. Vendler's 'aesthetic criticism' is a kind of cultural imperialism writ large.

While not wanting to deny that, as critics – and particularly critics in Ireland – have argued, Heaney's *critical* writing (if less so the poetry) sometimes seems to itself further such aestheticized interpretation,[19] it is striking how often non-Irish critics are ready to remove the work from its context, or at least to see 'the Troubles' as some kind of rude intervention into the privileged, harmonious space of the poems. Heaney does indeed mainly write in lyric forms, but the question remains as to whether it is best to read them solely in that light. This issue becomes pertinent in the extreme terms which such a view of the poem-as-lyric forces on another critic.

Tony Curtis, in his own contribution to a pioneering collection of critical essays on the poet which he edited, does allow that Heaney 'wants to involve himself...directly with the facts of life around him in Ireland.' But in his readings of Heaney's 1979 collection *Field Work*, the space of the poem appears as a space of almost mystical wholeness upon which those awkwardly put 'facts of life' awkwardly impinge. On the collection's opening poem, 'Oysters', Curtis writes that:

> There are many indications in Heaney's writing that his personal, family life is settled and a source of happiness for him. Images of

the Troubles, the problems of the country as a whole, intrude themselves into the context.

Aside from the historical blindness which allows Curtis to slip in his essay between 'Ireland' and violence in the North as though they were interchangeable, the angle of his approach, like Vendler's, suggests that the poetic space as he sees it in Heaney is primarily lyrical. His presumption is that the poems express directly the poet's personal and emotional completeness in contrast to the divisive and 'impinging' 'facts of life'. The solution which the poetry offers, the something which it wants to '*do* about Ireland' is, therefore, to project such personal unity onto the national political sphere and to thereby 'alter' it. Dangerously and ludicrously, Curtis claims that 'Poetry works as positively as the gun, but on a different level.' This raises the iconic sphere of poetry's internal coherence and of the poet's magisterial self-knowledge to the status of angry gods presiding over a perverse history: '...Heaney is pointing to the warped perspective of sectarian divisions as the essentially unnatural distorting force in his country.'[20] In his use of 'unnatural' here and of similar terms elsewhere, Curtis is sustaining the organicist model of lyric poetry which is essential to Vendler's reading also, a model which is at least superficially under question in Heaney's and other poets' own self-consciousness about their nature poetry which I described above.[21] In Curtis's reading, then, the aesthetic has become so far unstuck from its literary, historical and political context that the context itself only seems to be an annoyance.

In order to challenge such Anglo-American aesthetic, placeless and timeless views of poetry from both North and South of Ireland written in response to events post-1969, I have always in this study taken as my instigation for the discussion of individual poets critical arguments and debates about poetry which have been published in newspapers, books and magazines from both parts of Ireland itself. This is not to claim that the mode of proceeding in most of the writing from the island as a whole differs in any radical way from that to be found in, say, British or American publications. Reviewers of new collections of poetry in the North and the Republic are as generally concerned to separate 'good' poems and collections from 'bad' ones as reviewers overseas are. What I would want to claim, however, is that by setting the poetry against the responses which it has received in more local publications, it is possible to receive a fuller awareness of the kinds of political, historical and linguistic pressures exerted upon the poetry itself; that, given historical and contemporary division, the poetry takes on a greater urgency and immediacy for its readership as its responses (and sometimes its imagined solutions) to the divisions are weighed within that more immediate context.

'We Still Believe What We Hear', urges Robert Johnstone in his review in the Belfast journal *Fortnight* of Heaney's *Field Work*. Johnstone then asks a series of questions of the collection's final poem, a version of a passage in Dante which Heaney calls 'Ugolino', questions which register the kind of immediacy and relevance within poetic symbolism sought after by critics writing in the poet's own part of Ireland: 'Is Ugolino's incarceration a veiled comment on H-Block [the prisons in which paramilitary internees are held]? Are we meant to read "Ulster" for "Pisa"? Or is Ugolino's gnawing of Roger's head a symbol of England and Ireland?' Johnstone's review ends with scepticism about the kinds of magisterial note (the poet as 'acknowledged legislator') being struck by Heaney in making such literary parallels to the realities of contemporary history in the North: 'Are these the best tools to bring to a murderous, tangled, sensitive situation without simple rights and wrongs?'[22] Johnstone's is a radical and practical scepticism which inter-involves an assured sense of aesthetics – the slightly false note he detects in such parallels and the lack of clarity which results from it – with historical and political relevance, the notion that by using the wrong 'tools' Heaney is failing to express 'the Catholic experience in Ulster' as his style aims in every aspect to do. An artistic failure is inevitably a political failure here. From this perspective, the very godlike and judgemental relation to history which Curtis celebrates in *Field Work* is the cause of this local critic's greatest scepticism and of his heightened sense of the difficulty and of the divisive pressures with which the poetry involves itself.

This is not to claim, though, that aesthetic criticism is an alien critical approach in Ireland. The Belfast critic Edna Longley has striven to defend a similar division between the aesthetic and the political to that discussed in Vendler and Curtis, and I want to give some sense here of the arguments pursued to this end by this most important of all critics of the poetry North or South.

In an interview, Longley has attacked literary 'theory' in ways reminiscent of Vendler's dismissal of 'ideological criticism': 'It doesn't allow for the formal or the aesthetic.' She strongly defends poetry against the supposedly democratizing reduction by theorists of all language to 'discourse' by asserting that there *are* ways 'of using language with greater concentration or greater intensity or greater memorability.'[23] In her interventions into critical and literary debates in Ireland, similar recognitions have served to inform – but also to finally politicize – Longley's own fiercely polemical stance.

Longley's primary concern has always been to keep open some sense of the Protestant tradition in Ireland and of the continuities between Irish poetry and the English tradition – contentiously so, perhaps, in her readings of Yeats and MacNeice; valuably so in continuing to point out the fact that, despite the renewed polarization in the North in the 1960s, the poetry from both sides of the religious and cultural divide 'emerged in close proximity to English modes.'[24] Her anger at the exclusion of this tradition from most discussions, and her objection to the concurrent way in which, most notoriously by Field Day (which I discuss below), poetry was constantly being harnessed in the island to (invariably nationalist) political agendas, famously led Longley in 'Poetry and Politics in Northern Ireland' to assert that there must be a *cordon sanitaire* between the aesthetic and other ambitions:

> Poetry and politics, like church and state, should be separated. And for the same reasons: mysteries distort the rational processes which ideally prevail in social relations; while ideologies confiscate the poet's passport to *terra incognita*.[25]

Once again, a polarizing impetus establishes poetry as the site of the numinous, the mysterious and the unknown. At some level, Longley is operating with a spurious Manichaean division in which a Rousseauistic political rationalism counters poetry's more fugitive and metamorphic 'truths'. Yet in her modulation of these polarized terms in the long introductory chapter to *The Living Stream*, it is these latter qualities which emerge to undermine the nationalist language offered by Field Day.

In this later discussion, Longley harnesses poetry to the movement towards historical revisionism in Ireland. Revisionism has been concerned to question some of the homogeneity and orthodoxy within the Republic's sense of its own history, to question, initially, historical accounts which claimed that the Easter 1916 Rising and its particular aims formed a heroic, originating moment for the new Free State. Revisionism, in other words, seeks to reread and to revise earlier partial and narrowly political or bigoted historical accounts. Longley discovers a similar scepticism and polymorphousness of reading in post-1969 Northern Irish poetry, which is 'itself the product of multi-ethnic cross-fertilisation':

It draws on all the available literary traditions, cultural traditions, historical experiences – the world wars as much as 1690 or 1798 or 1916. Without evading political obstacles, it transgresses many supposed borders and breaks many imposed silences...The whole cognitive exercise shakes rigid concepts of identity built on the polarisations that occurred in the 1920s and the 1970s. Northern Irish poetry is revisionist (in more than one direction) because it exposes cultural phenomena and cultural permeations that political ideologies deny....[26]

This celebration of diversity is clearly the central counter in Longley's thought to what she sees as Field Day's monocular, ideological nationalist view. Yet within this setting up of poetry as a special space open to opposing cultures (something urged again in Michael Longley's 'Ceasefire'), it is the transformative effect that poetry has upon conventional expectation which Edna Longley most argues for. In the essay 'From Cathleen to Anorexia', she admits that within the polarized communities of the North of Ireland poets have been forced to become revisionists:

Writers born into the over-determined, over-defined environment, into a tension between political simplicities and cultural complexity, have felt impelled to redefine: to explore and criticise language, images, categories, stereotypes, myths. Northern writing does not fit into the binary shapes cut out by Nationalism and Unionism.

This allows a degree of social and historical determinism into the discussion, only to immediately limit it by establishing poetry once more as a place where such concerns are explored, criticized and, presumably, transcended or superseded. Under this freed-up revisionist aegis, poetry emerges because of the 'changes' which it effects upon language as an interventionist corrective of historical misreading. As she claims when discussing a poem by Paul Muldoon,

'Poetry, then, puts history (and literary history...) in its place...'[27] – a claim not unlike that made by Curtis for Heaney's work.

Poetry's function remains for Longley one of resistance, its aesthetic space one which counters and transcends what she sees as the simplicities of political debate, particularly in its Nationalist longings. Further, in its privileged and critical revisionist reading of such debate and of historical error, poetry for her finally stands over and against the circumstances of its making, its formal and aesthetic qualities ultimately secure against them.

Therefore, while arguing validly against what she perceives as an approach to analysis from Field Day which excludes the Protestant tradition in Ireland, Longley's remains ultimately a bounded and aestheticized reading as do those of the American Vendler and the British Curtis. It shares, in other words, in the critical tradition which her political arguments for keeping alert to continuities with Britain and other English-speaking Nations also promulgate. Longley, like other critics in that tradition, does not seek to theorize the relations between poetic and non-poetic language contemporary with it. She does not seek to articulate *how* the languages of the divided traditions might come to be reconciled in the revisionary language of poetry, how language makes the leap from one debilitated and sectarian place to the other transcendent one; or how, alternatively, the language of poetry might serve to permeate back down and perhaps influence and complicate the politics of its audience. She simply and unquestioningly accepts the aesthetic as a place where such changes rather mysteriously occur.

Longley in *The Living Stream* shares with Vendler an authorizing presence for the stance which her criticism takes: Theodor Adorno. For Vendler, Adorno is the twentieth-century critic who has been most faithful to the fact that within a work of art we can see 'its originating propositions and beliefs' necessarily subordinated 'to intrinsic efforts of form'. Art stands alone from 'other mimetic or expressive or discursive activities' in its formal integrity, and so the 'ideological content of the art work' is not alone intrinsic to it; Vendler sees Adorno's 'aesthetic base' in music criticism as having taught him that a reading of a work which simply confined itself to that work's '*meaning* or *value*' is 'foolish'.[28] For Longley, as for Vendler, the Adorno of *Aesthetic Theory* promotes the social process which she finds literature to be, a process in which the impulse behind the work of art and the form of that work meet and are transformed:

> For Adorno, all artistic transcendence is necessarily (and desir-
> ably) 'fragmented', as a result of its divorce from 'the magical
> and cult functions of archaic art'. But he allows this transcenden-
> tal residue a significant space ('breath'), threatened both by re-
> ductionist ideologies and by magic.[29]

But this, although it enters more sense of contingency ('threatened') than Vendler's exegesis, is in the end like Vendler's a partial
reading of Adorno's case in *Aesthetic Theory*. The process of transcendence is often the other way round for him, and it is not simply
aesthetic criticism's bugbear 'ideology' or 'magic' (which earlier
Longley had herself seemed to discover in art) which 'threatens'
art's space. Throughout the book, Adorno insists that *everything*, including aesthetic theorizing itself, is subject to the processes of historical change:

> All works of art, including those that pretend to be completely
> harmonious, belong to a complex of problems. As such they
> participate in history, transcending their uniqueness.[30]

Earlier he had claimed a special place for art as a signifying structure related to its time: 'History is constitutive of works of art.
Authentic ones give themselves over completely to the material
substance of their period, rejecting the pretence of timelessness.
Unbeknown to themselves, they represent the historiography of
their times.'[31] More specifically, both Longley and Vendler sup-
press the radical changes which Adorno feels modern times to have
enforced upon all aesthetics, and therefore upon the relation of the
work of art to its age, since 'Modernism negates tradition itself.'
Further, the demand for newness upon the modern work of art 'is
the aesthetic counterpart to the expanding reproduction of capital
in society.' In other words, modern works of art, in their fragmentedness and self-consciousness about their own value and meaning,
are reflections of the bourgeois principle of progress which underlies capitalist economies.

Adorno sees this as confirming what he calls the 'irritating abstractness' of many modern works, our uncertainty about how to
even begin to criticize them; this is due to their equivalence to the

empty exchange values of monopoly capitalism as distinct from the use-values of products in earlier economies. Drawing upon the ideas of his mentor Walter Benjamin, who in essays like 'The Work of Art in the Age of Mechanical Reproduction' had argued that the 'aura' or quiddity had – as Longley says – been taken from works of art, Adorno feels that it is difficult to establish grounds for aesthetic valuation any more. With the advent of techniques like photography, which could put into circulation hundreds of thousands of faithful copies of, for example, the *Mona Lisa*, the cultic value and mysterious power of Da Vinci's original are inevitably undermined. Once this happens, reproductions of the picture become commodities like all others, art enters the modern marketplace on a par with all other products and can claim no special status or use within it.

More importantly, for the purposes of my argument with the critical stances of Longley, Vendler and other critics, Adorno locates the difference of modern works of art from former works specifically in those issues related to form and to the response of form to social and cultural conditions:

> It would be wrong to ascribe the aspect of violence in modernism...to some kind of subjective orientation or to the psychological make-up of the artist. In a situation where there is no secure basis in terms of form or content, creative artists are compelled by force of circumstance to experiment....[32]

Artistic form itself emerges in modernity, then, as a contingent, compromised expedient – as it is in Michael Longley's carving of sonnet from epic in 'Ceasefire' – which pushes the traditional lyrical or subjective orientation into the background before the primacy of 'constructive methods'.[33]

It is therefore questionable whether Longley's, or that of international 'aesthetic' or practical critics, is a wholly adequate response to either the history or the poetry of the North or the Republic of Ireland from the 1960s to the present. As I argue in the other chapters, formal experiment which is consonant with that of the early international modernists Pound and Eliot is evident even within the writing and thought of such a seemingly 'traditional poet' as John Hewitt or in a seemingly traditional sonnet sequence like Brendan Kennelly's *Cromwell*, as it is in Heaney's later airy poetic architecture and in the racily vernacular sequences of Muldoon and Ciaran Carson. Indeed, it is true that the older generation of poets,

Kinsella and Montague (and to an extent Hewitt), poets who have more readily and explicitly experienced and embraced modernist formal practices than the younger generations, have been the ones who have most openly addressed specific events from the recent history of the North in their work. Kinsella's *Butcher's Dozen*, and parts of Montague's *The Rough Field* and Hewitt's *An Ulster Reckoning* are outspoken about specific events as the work of later poets has not so readily been. These are works which have often been neglected in criticism of the poet's work as a whole, presumably because they seemingly fall under the debilitating label of 'occasional poetry'; but it is my concern here to argue for the continuity between these works and the ways in which disjunctive, modernist formal thinking has underpinned their responses to the violent history of Ireland across their careers. By concentrating on the later work of Heaney, Carson and Muldoon, I hope to show that their increasing development of a contingent, fragmentary poetic form has also allowed for an openness to the element that Adorno sees as 'constitutive of works of art', history.

What emerges in all of the poetry (however much it explicitly partakes of modernist poetic experiment) is an extreme tension between the lyric moment and the processes of history out of which it emerges. Against the controlled and iconic sureties of the 'aesthetic critics' approach, I would want to argue that the modernism of these poems exemplifies a more urgent and adaptive *response* to the political and historical events in the North, one in which the aesthetic is by no means denied by a developed sense of the difficult negotiations which poetry enacts with context and circumstance.

In pursuing this approach, I use for their suggestive descriptive terminology the ideas of writers who have been concerned to theorize the relations of the modern work of art to modern economic, cultural and political movements within a historical perspective. Adorno, Frederic Jameson, Raymond Williams and M.M. Bakhtin have each striven to describe the various breaks with tradition consonant with modernity in ways that do not negate the historical context within which such breaks occur. Contiguously, in my final chapter, I discuss the work of Ciaran Carson and Paul Muldoon in terms of the ordinary language philosophy of Richard Rorty. Carson's and Muldoon's prioritization of language questions (witness the titles to Carson's collections *First Language* and *Letters from the Alphabet*, or Muldoon's wondrous welcoming of his daugh-

ter into the world/alphabet, 'the inestimable//realm of apple-
blossoms and chanterelles and damsons and eel-spears/and foxes
and the general hubbub...'[34]) have earned their poetry for the critics
a place within international discourses of postmodernism. Yet, I
would want to argue, postmodernism's emphasis upon the text, the
written word, seems curiously alien to a culture and a poetry which
constantly draws upon the intonations of the spoken word. Against
this, Rorty's philosophy highlights the historical, social and cultural
context within which such language games operate, while also emphasizing their presence and contingency, qualities which have been
increasingly to the fore in these two poets' work.

In deploying this range of theoretical and philosophical authority
I am aware that there exist differences between each writer's approach, particularly with regard to the degree of determinism they
are prepared to accord to history over literary texts. But my
primary concern is not with the theoretical debates raised by and
between these authorities. Rather, I have quoted from them in each
of my chapters simply because they raise the kinds of issue the
poets themselves raise, and because their terms open up an insight-
ful dialogue with those of the poetry itself. Throughout, my
method has been to draw upon the poets' own extra-poetic statements in interviews and essays in order to define the ambition
which underlies their poetry, and I have explored how this intent
manifests itself in practice. But I also want to suggest that historical
events and cultural debates do impinge upon poetic texts and alter
both their form and a reading of them. The theoretical arguments of
Adorno and others therefore provide partially useful *descriptive*
terms for how that two-way process between the poets' and
history's determining presence might occur.

Further to this, I have deliberately drawn upon those thinkers
who do not believe that a literary text is absolutely determined by
historical circumstance, but rather leave poetry something to say to
history. Poetry is a place where conscious and unconscious relations towards history interact and are questioned and transformed.
Poets who have adopted a consciously modernist approach, like
Kinsella and Montague set their poetic to delineate history, though
without establishing a totalizing vision over it. Yet other poets, like
Hewitt and Heaney, who promulgate a rhetoric of pattern and resolution, have across their careers written a poetry which has itself
changed in response to events. Lastly, those who have accepted a
degree of historical determinism, who have taken a rhetoric of

historical violence or contingency into their work, like Kennelly, Carson and Muldoon, find themselves uncertainly registering both the actual vagaries of historical event and also their fraught relation to economic and social modernisms on their home ground.

I now wish to go on to describe the ideas and literary productions of the group from the North of Ireland which for over a decade determinedly sought to establish and theorize the relations between the aesthetic and the political – the Field Day Theatre Company. Their attempted reconciliations on an aesthetic ground of the crisis they perceived in the North involves their terms in the kinds of dilemma and debate which I will be describing in relation to other writers' negotiations on these matters in later chapters, terms which are in themselves contingent upon and reflective of a particular historical moment.

FIELD DAY AND THE CIVIL RIGHTS MOVEMENT

Field Day was founded in 1980 by the playwright Brian Friel and the actor Stephen Rea, and later included upon its board of directors another playwright Thomas Kilroy, the critics and poets Seamus Deane, Seamus Heaney and Tom Paulin, and the musician and broadcaster David Hammond. For over a decade, the Company were responsible for producing a play each year which had its opening performances in the Derry Guildhall before touring the North of Ireland and the Republic. Field Day was also responsible for producing a series of pamphlets which, as the joint Preface to a collection of the first six claimed, aimed to 'explore' 'the nature of the Irish problem' and to 'confront it' more successfully than hitherto it had been possible to do. The Company's northern directors:

> ...believed that Field Day could and should contribute to the solution of the present crisis by producing analyses of the established opinions, myths and stereotypes which had become both a symptom and a cause of the current situation. The collapse of constitutional arrangements and the recrudescence of the violence which they had been designed to repress or contain, made this a more urgent requirement in the North than in the Republic, even though the improbability of either surviving in its present form seemed clear in 1980 and is clearer still in 1985.[35]

Claims like that overly optimistically made in the last clause here have simply served to confirm for Edna Longley that beneath the surface of Field Day's seemingly neutral 'analyses' there lurked a political ambition in the form of a romanticized Irish Nationalism which merely served its own ends. In her eyes, Field Day largely excluded Protestant traditions from its consideration, as well as all ideas which were antagonistic to its view of the future.

For, from early on, Field Day strove not only to diagnose or analyse the situation, but to turn that 'analysis' towards imagining the shape of a future, reconciled state on the island. That attempt to re-envisage the conditions was an integral part of the enterprise (an enterprise which initially also involved rereading and demytholo- gizing Yeats[36]), however partial that enterprise might in the end have been. Brian Friel, one of the Company's co-founders, has ad- mitted that a principle element in this attempt to re-envisage was the appropriation of the idea of a 'fifth province' as it had originally been defined by Richard Kearney and Mark Hederman in the first issue of a Dublin magazine, *The Crane Bag*:

> ...although Tara was always the political centre of Ireland, this middle or fifth province acted as a second centre which though non-political was just as important, acting as a necessary balance...[it was] the secret centre where all oppositions were resolved.[37]

The 'fifth province' established, then, a non-sectarian, non-preju- diced platonic imagined space to set against the violence in the North. Yet, for Field Day, writing from Derry within 'the political crisis in the North', that space was intensely political (and it is this of course which has attracted Edna Longley's attacks), a platonic counterweight which would redefine divided traditional rhetorics in order to promulgate a new possibility. 'Everything,' wrote Seamus Deane at the end of the fourth pamphlet, 'including our politics and our literature, has to be re-written – i.e. re-read. That will enable new writing, new politics...'.[38]

As Deane's seamless interweaving of the literary and the political here shows, the aesthetic played a strong part in the envisaging of a reconciled 'fifth province' in all of the Company's ideas.[39] Answering understandable objections that Field Day was peddling a not too well disguised nationalism, Friel said: 'I don't think it should be read in those terms. I think it should lead to a cultural state, not a political state. And I think that out of that cultural state, a possibility of a political state follows.'[40] Seamus Heaney, one of the Company's directors, has spoken of a similar continuum in which the experience of the individual artist becomes urgent within the political concerns of his or her country:

> It seems to me that the artist's struggle for growth equals or parallels the struggle of every other soul for growth... . Because there is a shared, impacted set of standards and beliefs in the moral and cultural sphere, his inner drama goes beyond the personal to become symptomatic and therefore political....
>
> What I am talking about is the transmitting power of art within the *polis*, its political reality to mean not sloganeering or the canvassing of topical themes but rather the address of art to a secret unspoken level of understanding that is intimate to a country or a language or a certain community. In that sense, the political quotient of art is alive and well in Ireland.[41]

Heaney's is a significant and self-justifying extension of the aesthetic into the *polis*, setting his own kind of writing, lyric poetry, at a centre of an address beyond the known and the polarized to some more human, but admittedly nationalist, level. Such statements by Heaney challenge the more limited aestheticization of his work by critics like Vendler and Curtis. Yet they also point to a potential difficulty within this 'continuity', one inadvertently and damagingly realized within the theatrical productions mounted by the Field Day Company; how does the new language, literature and politics in fact translate beyond the aesthetic bounds of the work of art to the 'community'? And how does the emphasis on the individual (Hederman's and Kearney's initial definition of the 'fifth province' had said that 'The constitution of such a place would require that each person discover it for himself within himself') or the lyric work of art figure within the rhetorics of that community as a whole? Such a lack of stable bases in debates around art had, of course, for Adorno underpinned modernist uncertainty and constructivism, as well as the difficult relation between the individual and the modernist work of art and that work's 'irritating abstraction' from its audience.

These uncertainties resound again through each of the poets' responses to the North after 1969 which I describe below. As such, they seem very much a part of a particular moment in the history of the North about which many of these issues cluster. Further, that moment involves an awareness of cultural possibility consonant with the revolution in economic conditions in the North. It would not be too extreme a reading of the ambitions and aesthetic dilemmas of Field Day and of those writers associated with it (as well as those other writers like Michael Longley and Derek Mahon who began publishing in the late 1960s) to see them as profoundly linked to the rise and later evolution of the Civil Rights movement there. The notion of the 'fifth province' itself reflects many of the qualities shared by the early stages of the movement, a place where tolerance between the two communities was the basis of a hope to bring about an alleviation of traditional prejudice and the furthering of social equality.

Heaney has claimed that with the Civil Rights movement at work, 'an evolution towards a better, juster internal balance might have been half trusted to begin.' With that trust and hope, Heaney justifies the frequent abstraction (to again deploy Adorno's word) of his and his peers' poetry from the specific and horrifying realities of the situation:

> I think the writers of my generation saw themselves as part of the leaven. The fact that a literary action was afoot was itself a new political condition, and the poets did not feel the need to address themselves to the specifics of the politics because they assumed that the tolerances and subtleties of their art were precisely what they had to set against the repetitive intolerance of public life.[42]

Since the Civil Rights movement and events around it form such a pivotal part of my later discussions, not only of Heaney himself but of each of the poets, I will give a reasonably detailed account of it here before returning to the issues which are raised by that historical moment for Field Day specifically. Many commentators have seen the origins of the movement in the 1947 Education Act, which allowed greater access to decent schooling for the Catholic population and hence created a more articulate and affluent body of opinion critical of the status quo which reached maturity in the mid–late 1960s. Seamus Heaney and Seamus Deane were both beneficiaries of the Act, attending St Columb's College in Derry. Brian Friel had left the College several years before, and the Social Democratic and Labour Party (SDLP) leader John Hume, an important figure in the Civil Rights movement as in subsequent moves to achieve a solution to the situation in the North, was a near contemporary.

But Jonathan Bardon has shown that dissatisfaction with the discrimination in housing and jobs which operated against the Catholic minority, and the gerrymandering in elections which ensured a huge Unionist majority in the Stormont parliament, had been growing throughout the decade. In 1965, in the predominantly Catholic Derry, these critical pressures led to the founding of the Derry Unemployed Action Committee and the Derry Housing Association; the latter was superseded by the more radical and actively interventionist Derry Housing Association Action Committee in 1967, which arranged several protests including an invasion of the city's Guildhall. These actions around housing inequality soon led to the founding of the Northern Ireland Civil Rights Association on 29 January 1967, a body which in the light of subsequent events was seen by loyalists as a front for nationalism, but which in its early years had also a significant number of Protestant supporters, including the Young Unionist Robin Cole who served on its executive committee. The Association had its first confrontation with the Royal Ulster Constabulary in August 1968 during a protest march from Coalisland to Dungannon, a march which, Bardon argues, felt similar for many of those who took part 'to demonstrations elsewhere against nuclear weapons or participation in the Vietnam War'. [43]

Another march, organized for Derry on 5 October 1968, was banned upon the threat of a counter-demonstration by the Apprentice Boys of that city. The leaders of the Association were reluctant to be drawn into further confrontation with the police, but upon persuasion from the more radical Derry Housing Action Committee, the march went ahead. It was violently broken up by police and led to brutal scenes which were beamed by television all over the world. William Craig, in charge of the police forces, appeared on television to bluster against the Civil Rights movement as a front for Republicanism and Communism, and so further exacerbated the situation in which the sectarian divisions in the North were re-awakened.

The Derry march is often seen as the defining moment which sparked the subsequent 25-year conflict in the North. The Civil Rights Association won a huge increase in membership, largely from the Catholic population. The students at Queen's University, Belfast, where Heaney was a lecturer at the time, formed People's Democracy, a body aimed to further the Civil Rights cause in that city (and so provided another direct echo of the student bodies rising up in Paris and America at the time).

The Prime Minister, Terence O'Neill, and Craig were summoned to London by Harold Wilson and forced to put into immediate effect a programme of reform which tackled the housing and vote-rigging issues. But the mass Civil Rights movement would not be stopped by these gradualist measures, which offered the setting-up of new committees and an ombudsman to hear complaints. Then, with the continuation of the campaign, and an increasingly obvious aim within it to provoke confrontation with the police and with the majority population, most Protestant and many Catholic moderates left the movement. A People's Democracy march was ambushed by Protestants aided by the police at Burntollet in January 1969. A march in Newry ran out of control. The original executive of the Civil Rights Association resigned in March 1969, leaving the way for more radical elements to take control. A series of bombs were planted and O'Neill resigned in April. Sectarian violence erupted in July and August, with Orange marching bands being pelted with bottles by Catholics in Belfast. In Derry, the annual Apprentice Boys parade led to what became called the 'Battle of the Bogside' from 12 to 14 August, in which the police openly fought alongside Protestants against the Catholics. The British Home Secretary, James Callaghan, sent in troops to restore order. This led to rioting among the Catholics and sporadic shots being fired with resultant casualties and fatalities. Protestants in turn burned Catholics out of their homes and the Provisional IRA began to emerge as a movement claiming to protect Catholics from their attackers.

The bombings and shootings continued unabated for the next couple of years, despite the presence of British troops on the streets. There was a further intensification of violence in August 1971 when internment was introduced, a policy which involved the rounding-up of hundreds of suspected terrorists. In practice the internees were a group including very few Protestants, and their imprisonment included brutal treatment and harsh conditions. Terrible violence followed, with over 440 explosions caused by the IRA in the subsequent three months. A single incident on Sunday 30 January 1972 formed a kind of tragic culmination of these events and of the confrontations between the Civil Rights movement and the security forces. In defiance of a government ban, the Civil Rights Association went ahead with their march in Derry. The British Army had hatched a plan to seize what they saw as the most violent of its supporters, using snatch squads of paratroopers as the march broke up. But in response to being stoned by Catholic youths the troops opened fire indiscriminately on the marchers, killing 13 men and injuring 13 others. The day has subsequently been known as Bloody Sunday. There were violent and angry protests the next day and Bernadette Devlin, a campaigner who had witnessed the 'Battle of the Bogside', physically attacked the new Home Secretary, Reginald Maudling, in the Commons. On 2 February 30 000 people marched on the British Embassy in Dublin and burned it down. The British Prime Minister, Edward Heath, took control of the situation by bringing an end to the Northern Ireland parliament at Stormont and ruling from Westminster with the aid of a Northern Ireland secretary. So were brought to an end the 50 years that Northern Ireland had been a self-governing part of the United Kingdom.

Bloody Sunday itself incited poems from, among others, John Hewitt and Thomas Kinsella, poems which I will be discussing below. Yet more generally, with the failure of the marchers' aims and the lapse into violence, that Civil Rights ambition found continued currency, but now upon an *aesthetic* level with uncertain transformative power in regard to the political realities, in the work of writers who variously responded to the situation. Hence, perhaps, the attempts to theorize the relation between art and politics and history by Heaney and the Field Day pamphleteers. Yet that shift to the aesthetic space in the absence of coherence within the political one more closely involves the poetry with the politics rather than removing the politics from aesthetics altogether.

With the provoked relapse of that Civil Rights ambition into sectarian violence, the hope given by that movement, with its parallels to other attempts to cast off the old order in the international students protests of 1968 in America and France, soon gave way to despair at the first wave of violence down to 1972. That dual emotion overshadows and haunts much of the poetry which I will be discussing in this book, as it does the appropriation by Field Day of the notion of an imaginary alternative to conditions in a 'fifth province'. In the process, the issue of the relation of the aesthetic artifact to 'reality' became a critical and urgent one (in Heaney's words, 'poetry moved from being simply a matter of achieving the satisfactory verbal icon to being a search for images and symbols adequate to our predicament'[44]), and this again resonates through all of these texts. The 'tolerances and subtleties' of art have come to seem increasingly false in relation to reality, and have taken on that modernist abstraction shared also by the older generation of poets like Kinsella, Hewitt and Montague when bringing their poetic to bear on the post-1969 violence.

With regard to Field Day itself, such questions have attracted criticism and scepticism about the success of their project. Reviewing one of the productions for *The Irish Review*, Shaun Richards complained that:

> These Field Day audiences were not being forced to confront their own political and sectarian differences, rather they were united by [the play's] 'liberal' message to which no-one could object as nothing was being fundamentally questioned....That the humanity of the 'self' has to be realized before the individual can respond to the humanity of others is the fundamental message; one which is inadequate as a response to a complex, but clearly materially and historically founded situation... .[45]

Friel's own plays produced by the Company in particular continually situate the imaginative possibilities of reconciliation and union between two opposing sides within the traditional and highly personal human motif of a love plot. This is true of the doomed relationship between Irish girl Maire and English soldier Yolland in Field Day's inaugural production *Translations*. Their love scene is one of gentle comedy which both concretizes the play's central notion that the difference between the two cultures is essentially one of language (Maire, speaking Irish, cannot understand Yolland's English) while also claiming that love transcends such differences and offers the possibility of a higher union beyond superficial difference. Friel's lovers come to a mutual apprehension of physical beauty which prefigures the role of the aesthetic in Longley's poem 'Ceasefire' with which I began:

> *Yolland*: I wish to God you could understand me...I would tell you how beautiful you are, curly headed Maire. I would so like to tell you how beautiful you are.
> *Maire*: Your arms are long and thin and the skin on your shoulders is very white.[46]

In an ending which reflects the killings of British soldiers who had become involved with Catholic girls in the 1970s, Yolland is himself killed by the mysterious proto-paramilitary Donnelly twins. Within the history of the play's larger action, this lover's lyric moment is overtaken by the inevitable violence with which such fragile unions are greeted in the play's historical and political context. Its possibility seems almost sentimental and naive in relation to the play's other concern with the complexity of the language issue in Ireland, and its terms curiously inadequate either to alter or to re-envisage the history of conflict between the two peoples.

The old schoolmaster Hugh's last speech, which is an attempt at a translation of a passage from Virgil, contains the possibility through its allegory that the British might be thrown out of Ireland: 'a race was springing from Trojan blood to overthrow some day these Tyrian towers.' But his memory of the original Latin passage fails, he ends up repeating himself and going astray, as he had in his earlier report of his experience of 1798 ('in Phelan's pub...we got homesick'). The possibility of understanding glimpsed in the union through love of Maire and Yolland breaks down, then, in a failed repetition of an asserted fated freedom which will emerge 'some day'; the history of Ireland as a whole here emerges as a mixture of ramblingly expressed hope and violent revenge and thwartedness.

Similar 'lyric' moments punctuate the Company's 1988 production, Friel's *Making History*, where the possibilities in the play of union between the two sides in Ireland are again represented in a love match, that which took place between the last of the Irish chieftains Hugh O'Neill and a Protestant English Planter's daughter Mabel. Again, Friel's *The Communication Cord*, Field Day's 1982 production, rewrites the traditional picture of Ireland presented in *Translations* as farce, but resolves itself into a momentary union of the lovers Tim and Claire before the house is (literally) brought down. Andrey, in his version of Chekov's *Three Sisters* (the Company's 1981 production), rather piously asserts that 'We have got to keep believing that all this squalor, all this degradation...it will end soon.'[47]

It is doubtful, at this level, whether Friel's plays for Field Day fulfil the translation between different orders of experience which Heaney, in writing more generally about him, has claimed they do. Heaney sets Friel in a modernist tradition coming down from T.S. Eliot, a tradition for whom the 'overwhelming question' is 'how does the fully conscious human life...navigate between...the allure of inherited affections and inexplicable meaningful memory, on the one hand, and on the other, the command to participate intelligently in the public world of historical process?' In answer to that question, Heaney claims that Friel has established his own personal myth on a Jungian model:

> The evidence is what we are all up against, and when Jung writes of telling a 'personal myth' which will be 'my fable, my truth', he is not proposing to enter the realm of fantasy or to shirk his responsibility to face facts. He is insisting rather that the evidence and the facts be confronted afresh, that the individual consciousness take the measure of reality in a first-hand, unmediated encounter, that the panaceas and alibis and stereotypes offered by convention be avoided... .[48]

Yet, beyond the stereotypical use of romance plots, Friel has little to offer in confronting the facts afresh and envisaging a different future beyond 'personal myth', individual experience or rather desperate expressions of hope. From the evidence of its drama, then, Field Day's exploration of the platonic 'fifth province' seems limited and despairing against the imprisoning terms of convention and of the violent history of the island. The 'overwhelming question' about the relation between personal potential and intransigent historical and political reality remains unanswered, and the fulfilment of personal desire is made to seem the more vulnerable in the light of that impersonal process. Rather than a continuity between the terms of the personal and the historical which Heaney envisages in Friel, many of the original plays commissioned by the Company serve to illustrate the confusion and disjunction between them. Such uncertain relevance of the play's familial and relational action to the 'political and cultural situation' resonates through Stewart Parker's *Pentecost* (the play criticized by Shaun Richards), and through Derek Mahon's version of Molière's *The School for Husbands*, *High Time*, which formed one half of a 1984 double bill with *The Riot Act*, Tom Paulin's version of Sophocles's tragedy *Antigone*, which in its turn represents the clash of familial with social and religious duties and ceremonies.[49] But, again, that uncertainty and disjunction between different orders of experience marks the modernist dilemma of the Field Day enterprise, its very exacting response to the circumstances of its founding moment.

OBJECT LESSONS

As I said above, women poets writing across this period have been interested in a different version of politics and history to that of their male counterparts. The modernist tendencies which I will discuss in male poets' responses to violence in the North are outside of the different poetic priorities shared by these women writers, priorities which, as a male critic, I feel some awkwardness and dilemma about describing. That constructivism which I shall be addressing in each of the male poets' responses looks very different and less persuasive from the perspective of the poetry and views of women writers like Eavan Boland, Eiléan Ní Chuilleanáin and Medbh McGuckian.

A salutary impatience with an essentially male, continuing but confusing attention both to the divisive past and also to lyric transcendence within modernist poetry has come from the Dublin poet Eavan Boland. Writing in the *Irish Times* on 'Young Poets', Boland wearily diagnosed what she saw as the same difficulties which recur for Irish poetry time and again:

> New poets inherit old problems and may waste a lot of their energy trying to come to terms with them. Some of these problems are historic. The relationship of Irish poetry to the great Modernist initiatives of this century has been troubled....Very often in the work of both new and established poets, the poem is written in a Modernist mode while the poetic stance remains deeply conservative, unquestioningly Romantic and therefore out of touch with the form in which the poem is written. Thus the poem and the poet fail to meet, and the result is unconvincing.[50]

Boland's argument registers something like the impact of that clash between the transcendent lyric moment and the intransigent conditions out of which it arises which I described in the male poets and in Field Day above. For all writers against that background, of course, the relation between personal experience and the modernity of the conditions, as well as the modernist demand to 'make it new' poetically and politically, is an uncertain and fraught one.

Yet, in another article for the paper, Boland sought to assert a solution to such problems which removes that uncertainty, a solution which maintains a distance between poetry and the 'division' wrought by the Northern Troubles:

...whatever the suffering, the shabby politics, the terrible happenings in the streets and the minds of people, poetry should remain clear of it and by that clarity show there was something worth salvaging, a common possession North and South. There may even have been a belief, however misguided and idealistic, that it was by such common interests in the end that a divided people would recognise their mutual identity.[51]

Poetry gains an exemplary status for Boland through its remoteness from the actualities of sectarian suffering, rather than through its translation of them into its own form. Corresponding to this criticism, and impelled by a strong feminist conviction of difference in position and interest, Boland's own poetry is placed largely outside of the problematic which conventionally has been dealt with by male poets and which I am studying in this book, a problematic which confronts the clash between modernity and tradition in the relations between poetry, politics and history in the light of events in the North of Ireland since 1969.

That self-conscious and political distance from the specifics of the violence in the North is something which Boland shares with another Dublin-based poet, Eiléan Ní Chuilleanáin, and also with the Belfast writer Medbh McGuckian. These poets, like Boland, place women's experience, an experience very often absent from standard (male) historical discourses, at the centre of their work – as they do also the struggles undergone by the woman poet in seeking to give voice to that experience. As Ní Chuilleanáin's poem 'History' puts it:

> ...Our history is a mountain of salt
> A leaking stain under the evening cliff
> It will be gone in time
> Grass will grow there –
>
> Not in our time.[52]

Women's history remains remote for Ní Chuilleanáin, not only from national history but even from its own past, from the 'lost art' of 'our grandmothers'. 'Her history is a blank sheet,' we are told of a woman in another of her poems, 'The real thing, the one free foot kicking/Under the white sheet of history.'[53] That history is awaiting the writing which will be its very matter, and remains blanked/blanketed by existing official history, including history as it has been interpreted by male poets. Under this aegis, 'reality' remains that which is not written, that which remains outside of 'legitimized' historical discourses. It is this recognition which Ní Chuilleanáin shares with other women poets from North and South.

Medbh McGuckian is the most established woman writer in the North at present. Her poetry has always tackled woman's experience of the unspoken by deploying a symbolist poetic which seeks to articulate that which lies beyond standard male public and traditional poetic rhetorics. It is a poetry intensely attentive to the obscure colours, moods and temperaments of personal relationship. That attention is manifested through such pressured and minute modulations of imagery and symbol, such a refusal of the openly discursive, that the experience of reading her work can be baffling though also intriguing. What her mesmeric music achieves, as Tom Clyde noted in *Krino*, is the direct expression of her world; unlike many of her male contemporaries, her work does not identify 'the gap between appearance and actuality, or the magnification of the everyday by comparison with the extraordinary. McGuckian dissolves her being into that of her object, which thereby becomes subject.'[54]

Her collection *Captain Lavender* brings those attentions to bear more explicitly than in her earlier work upon the violence in the North in poems which set personal relationships as ontological metaphors for the political and historical situation of Ireland. Throughout, issues of language and communication are to the fore as awkward conveyors of that loss and separation which exists in both areas of experience. In the collection's final poem 'Dividing the Political Temperature', as elsewhere, it is the title which gives the clue to a possible reading in terms of public issues. The cruelties and violence within relationships form the poem's central idea, and lead, as they do throughout the collection, to images of death, but also to a subtle sense of fragile unity where 'we intersect/without meeting', where 'nothing will now disturb our night.'[55] The suggestion and hope (often unfulfilled) throughout McGuckian's work, even in this most 'public' of her collections, is that the shades of personal feeling express something shared but as yet not fully articulated; poems represent for her an absolutely free space in which that intense feeling is put into process. There is, then, little for her in the negotiations which I describe between the lyric space and the historical moment in poets' responses to 'the Troubles' or in their modernist concerns. The 'public' is continuous with the private for her, the difference between the two not an issue, and this is the political claim of her work; the formal means of achieving that continuity receive little emphasis as a result. Rather, McGuckian's work places its emphasis upon the suggestive extensions of its symbolism; the work assumes its immediate relevance through its subtle ontology.

Such different concerns enable McGuckian implicitly, and Eavan Boland explicitly, to argue in ways that few of the male poets would seek to do that modernism itself is finished as a historical phenomenon. In her prose collection *Object Lessons*, Boland pursues a related feeling of freedom to McGuckian's – a freedom which she often describes as 'clarity'. It is a freedom which she feels allows her to claim, based on what she calls 'a historical reading', that woman's poetry is in fact absolutely central to contemporary writing, 'that the woman poet is now an emblematic figure in poetry, much as the modernist or romantic figures were in their time.' For her, the disjunctive, distancing modernist concerns of male contemporaries are themselves seen as dated alongside the more relevant project which recognizes 'the democratization of our communities, of which [woman's] emergence is one aspect.' Women have recently gone from being 'mute objects' of male poets' eloquence to expressing lives and points of view that had previously been unwritten. So *Object Lessons* begins with Boland's moving attempt to retrace the last hours of her grandmother's life, a grandmother who died in childbirth in 1909. It is an act of historical retrieval – the grandmother has no place in 'history' until Boland writes her into it – which marks a counter-move to what Boland sees as the cause of the woman writer's disadvantage but also of her clarity and newness, her debarral from the 'inner sanctum of a tradition'.

Object Lessons circles autobiographically, seeking to resolve the split between the woman writing now and the fact that there were few prior woman poets writing in Ireland, that the tradition as well as the poetic world of her contemporaries remains male:

> As the author of poems I was an equal partner in Irish poetry. As a woman – about to set out on the life which was the passive object of...poems – I had no voice.[56]

While Boland does not disregard Ireland's history of defeats and violations, that history is often of importance for her in its complex relation to the exclusion of women from 'official' history, as she explains in that section of the book she calls 'Outside History'.

While feeling that the simplified figures of woman which stand as nationalist symbols in the male tradition – Cathleen Ni Houlihan, the Old Woman of the Roads, Dark Rosaleen – force ostracization for women readers and also present an underlying fault in Irish poetry itself, Boland yet sees a risky but strong association between such historical traumas inflicted on the Irish as the Great Hunger, and the marginal, silenced role of women in history. Boland has earlier in *Object Lessons* written powerfully of the painful experiences she underwent as a young girl living out of her country in England and America; but now she describes a sudden, liminal understanding which clearly authorizes her later writing and which exemplifies its quality of subversive vigilance:

> I was excited by the idea that if there really was an emblematic relation between the defeats of womanhood and the suffering of a nation, I need only prove the first in order to reveal the second. If so, then Irishness and womanhood, those tormenting fragments of my youth, could at last stand in for each other. Out of a painful apprenticeship and an ethical dusk, the laws of metaphor beckoned me.[57]

One virtue of the clarity which Boland constantly insists is gained by those, particularly women, who are 'marginalized' within history and tradition is, then, that the experience described in their lyrics is both more intensely personal and therefore (paradoxically) more assuredly and dangerously (a word Boland uses a lot) metaphorical than that of the male poets. What Heaney sees when writing on Friel as the 'overwhelming question' of modern writing – the relation between personal experience and historical process – is rendered irrelevant for her. Rather, the personal is riskily and dangerously the historical – such are the painful freedoms that women's experience gives the writing. Boland's 'outside history' is a two-edged phrase, both registering the historical lack of women's voices and also seeing those voices as history, as history made present in poetry.

When, in *Object Lessons*, Boland describes the writing of her 'first political poem', 'War Horse', she shows her attentive awareness of the facile definitions which might ensue from correlations between the personal and the political if they exclude the for her far more difficult task of making 'myself the political subject' of poetry. 'War Horse' was written, she says, in a time of violence in the early 1970s, when news of deaths in the North were coming in all the time. When a horse surprisingly wandered into her garden, the damage which it did seemed to have relevance:

> ...That rose he smashed frays
> Ribboned across our hedge, recalling
>
> ...A cause ruined before, a world betrayed.[58]

In her prose description of the same experience, though, Boland finds the immediate communal reference which personally witnessed experiences take on 'against a background of communal suffering' dangerous, because it instantly looks beyond the 'difficult "I" of perception' to the 'easier "we" of subtle claim'.[59] It is only, she implies, when, in the light of the historical repression of women, the true authority of the speaker is established – to her the more difficult task – that the metaphorical possibilities of personal experience can be freely explored.

The process and politics of Boland's own career have moved, therefore, from centring her own experience as a modern woman as the subject of poetry, as in poems like 'Suburban Woman' and 'Ode to Suburbia',[60] to seeing that experience as 'emblematic'. What is striking about the title sequences of her two collections *Outside History* and *In a Time of Violence*, and what sets them apart from the poets who form the object of this study, is their unerring metaphorical directness and concurrent lack of emphasis upon or attention to Adorno's 'constructive methods'. The sense that the female 'I' of the poem is the container of histories liberates the writing from (sometimes un-) constructive restrictions – many of the incidents in 'Outside History' are indeed close poetic versions of those prose renditions of them in the section of the same name in *Object Lessons*. In 'The Making of An Irish Goddess', the persona compares her own timeboundedness to that of the timeless goddess Ceres, but discovers in that a continuity with historical deprivations in her country:

> in my gestures –
> the way I pin my hair to hide
> the stitched, healed blemish of a scar –

must be

an accurate inscription
of that agony:

the failed harvests,
the fields rotting to the horizon....[61]

The establishment of such continuity ensures that myth itself becomes part of time and of the 'wound' which the individual life leaves in it; the poem ends by returning us to Boland's own time, the suburb in the foothills of the Dublin mountains where she looks for her daughter playing in the twilight.

In these later sequences, Boland's sense of the relation between her personal present and the nation's past resists any of the simplified, ornamental treatment of its subject matter to be found in male emblematizing. Her constant allusions to the Great Hunger in both the prose and in these poems make the Hunger into an archetype for all suffering, but one which particularly exposes *real* women's historical plight. So the letter 'March 1 1847. By the First Post' from 'Writing in a Time of Violence' recounts an incident in which a woman is seen lying

> *across the Kells road with her baby –*
> *in full view. We had to go*
> *out of our way*
> *to get home & were late*
> *& poor Mama was not herself all day.*[62]

While the tone and the final line reveal the terrible division in the luxury and indulgence of sentiment available to those of the landed class as opposed to the anonymous population who were victims of the famine, our attention is here drawn once again to the silent plight of women throughout history. 'History' serves to confirm the poet's newly liberated reading of it from the perspective of the present; such 'impersonal' poems as this in Boland's later work only serve to confirm the terrible and often silenced voices of real suffering which also form part of these sequences.

For Boland, then, as for all the poets from North and South I have discussed, history presses intensely upon the present moment – even when it is a history which is rather differently inflected.

Another poem in this sequence, 'The Dolls Museum in Dublin', imagines the horror of the timeless state of the cracked and damaged dolls who are stranded out of their time: 'To be the present of the past. To infer the difference/with a terrible stare. But not to feel it. And not to know it.'[63] That 'feeling' of history, however defeated and oppressed, remains ultimately the space of Boland's dangerous freedom as a poet. The poem 'Outside History' itself reconfirms Boland's involvement with the dark 'ordeal' of history and her hopelessness within it; coming upon some of history's victims, she says that 'We are always too late.' But that move into history has already been seen within a larger rhythm at the beginning of the poem: the stars are 'outsiders'

> whose light happened
> thousands of years before
> our pain did: they are, they have always been
> outside history.[64]

Such a continuing sense of a space beyond the historical, which is also a debilitating space of woman's experience that has not been articulated, liberates Boland's poetic into history and establishes its clear metaphorical and political power. Paradoxically it is this sense of historical debilitation which frees her writing, as similar recognitions free the writing of Ní Chuilleanáin and McGuckian also, of the modernist dilemmas about constructive methods and form in those male poets seeking to write about the history of their land after Yeats's sonorous retrenchment in Thoor Ballylee. Boland's own response to Yeats is equivocal, but ultimately embraces his work as a model in ways that none of the male poets are able to.

When, in *Object Lessons*, Boland describes herself as a 16-year-old reading Yeats, she says 'I took in, with some kind of recognition, and through the gestures of language, exciting and powerful statements.' But, as she grew older, she became troubled by his work, doubt set in, because 'Before he even lifted his pen, his life awaited him in poetry. He was Irish. A man.'[65] Yet that troubling, later in the book, resolves itself into a wonderful and surprising recognition that Yeats had already done what Boland wanted to do in her political poems. Writing about 'Meditations in Time of Civil War', Boland celebrates the way in which Yeats does not let the public events of that time dictate to him; rather, at the end of the fifth section of the poem, Yeats re-establishes himself as a pastoral poet, one authoritative and resolute in his private world as he 'turn[s] towards my chamber, caught/In the cold snows of a dream.' It is the recognition that it is not the public event but 'the vivid and divided world of the subject', the proposal of 'a private world in a political poem' which is vital that inspires Boland. This example cheers and encourages the woman poet wanting to 'see the effect of an unrecorded life – a woman in a suburban twilight...on pre-scribed themes of public importance', as it does not as unreservedly any of the male poets caught in filial emulation of, and scepticism about, the intransigent formal demands which Yeats's poetic makes in its refusal to negotiate with history. Their sense that their poetic must falter before extreme and violent events is finally and perhaps diminishingly at odds with hers, that 'an inner world' can 'suffer the outer world so powerfully that history itself faltered before its gaze.'[66]

2

John Hewitt: An Honest Ulsterman's 'Poemosaics'

John Hewitt is in many ways the most concertedly traditional of the writers who published poems in response to events in the North of Ireland from the late 1960s onwards. His long writing career, extending from the mid-1920s to his death in 1987, was marked by what Seamus Heaney has called 'an emphasis on the poet as maker, a concern for professional standards in the handling of form, a distrust of freedom and extravagance that has not been earned by toil within the traditional modes.'[1] In his essay 'Irish Poets, Learn Your Trade' Hewitt himself outlines the virtues of tight form:

> The couplet and the sonnet in particular, although they may admit resounding rhetoric, nevertheless are strict, limiting to the natural sprawl of words and ideas, involving compression, order, balance, the decorum of a stable tradition.[2]

Hewitt's huge poetic output gathered in the excellent edition of his *Collected Poems* contains great numbers of poems in couplets handled with an Augustan ease, well-turned sonnets and carefully measured blank verse which exemplify these craftsmanlike qualities.

Yet, while accepting the widely held view of Hewitt the traditionalist, I want in this chapter to push to the fore another side of Hewitt's work, one that is uncertain and unsettled, one that recognizes the contingency of his poetic resolutions, particularly in response to the North of Ireland's traditional divisions. It is an uncertainty and contingency which makes Hewitt's belated emergence in the late 1960s of immediate and defining significance in the context of the breakdown into civil strife there. I want to reconsider the importance of the poems Hewitt wrote in direct response to those events from the perspective of his perennial concerns, poems which even the editor of the *Collected Poems*, Frank Ormsby, has dismissed as forming an 'unenduring', 'instant, unmediated response'.[3] From a perspective which discovers a deep strain of unease about its traditional poetic resolutions, however, these late poems reveal that Hewitt's response to the historical moment is considerably more complex and dynamic than the view of him as a steady formalist allows, and that the moment even forces him to reconsider some of his earlier poetic 'certainties'.

Despite the traditional crafting, which it shares with writers like Robert Frost and Edward Thomas, Hewitt's work also shows much of the discontinuity and failure of coherence signalled in the poetics of the modernists Pound and Eliot and their successors like Auden.[4] Further, Hewitt's negotiations with the poetic of Yeats, as I will show, led him to adopt a rough and ready poetic himself which could admit of decay, transience and the abrupt changes wrought by historical events. There is a tantalizing suggestion in 'In Recollection of Drumcliffe, September 1948' that the influence of Yeats might have had a positive side for Hewitt, as we are told of 'what I shall never lose,/his chanted cadence, and the right to change/the masks with which I face my fellow men.'[5] If it is the case that the positions adopted in his poems are equal to different and chosen masks worn at different times, then this positive inheritance might underlie the scepticism and contingency towards Hewitt's subjects and his forms which I will explore in this chapter.

Yet is that ready consonance between on the one hand the unsettledness and discontinuity of this poetic as exemplified in the poems of the late 1960s and early 1970s, and on the other the outbreak of violence in the North, which established the importance of Hewitt's thinking about the relations between poetry, politics and history for the debates in magazines like *The Honest Ulsterman* which emerged at that time. That thinking also directly affected the ideas of poets of the 1960s generation, like Michael Longley and Heaney himself, about those relations.[6]

Born in 1907, Hewitt had only had one commercial publication, and that from an obscure publisher, before his *Collected Poems 1932–67* appeared in 1968, to considerable acclaim for its exemplary tolerance and honesty. Following this belated 'popularity', he rapidly garnered awards. He is the only poet who has received the Freedom of the City of Belfast, which he did in 1983, along with honorary doctorates from both Queen's University and the New

University of Ulster. Further, his poem 'The Colony' entered public political currency when it was quoted by the Taoiseach Jack Lynch at a speech in Philadelphia in 1971.

The relations between poetry and politics, which gained an urgency in the light of events in the late 1960s, had formed a crucial and vital element of Hewitt's concerns as a writer across his career. He was a lifelong socialist, a practically committed one through his attendance at Peace Groups and summer schools. Hewitt followed a utopian socialism on the model of William Morris, whose 1891 novel *News from Nowhere* imagines an ideal society in which absolute equality and compassion coexist. Yet, when that utopian note enters into Hewitt's poetry, it does so in a very abstract and generalized way, a way which is dislocated from the complexities of the poetry's experiential substance. Such dislocation is, further, integral to the gap between his pastoral celebrations – particularly of his beloved country around the Glens of Antrim – and his portrayal of the scarred, variously war-torn city of Belfast where he lived, barring a period living in England, for most of his life. There are, then, throughout Hewitt's work discontinuities between the political ambition of the poetry and its actual content, between the pastoral idealism and the violent urban actuality, which hold also for the generations of poets seeking to negotiate the divisions in the North who came after. Indeed, in some cases, Hewitt's inspiration for later poets, his providing, as Tom Clyde as argued, 'foundations and inspiration for more recent generations by simply being there, proving that that thing (modern poetry) could be done in this place (modern Ireland)',[7] tended to mask the irresolvable difficulties about politics and history which the poetry was actually involved in.

The reviews which appeared of *Collected Poems 1932–67* show some of these tensions between a perception of Hewitt as an exemplary figure in his tolerant and thoughtful response to history and the actuality of the poetry itself. Tony Bareham's review in the recently founded *The Honest Ulsterman* (begun in 1968) recognizes the vulnerability in Hewitt's response to his inheritance, but also elides some of the difficulties which the poetry fails to resolve:

Hewitt's dilemma is Ulster's own. To be honest is to be denounced, derided or disinherited, and spiritual atrophy may set in. This circumstance is turned to use in 'An Irishman in Coventry'... where he manages with a finely tuned control to

speak both personally and generally of the predicament of the
honest among his 'creed-haunted, God-forsaken race'.[8]

It is clear that here Hewitt is being made to represent those
virtues which give the magazine in which Bareham's piece appears
its title. John Hewitt *is* the Honest Ulsterman, and that is his
dilemma as well as his strength as a writer. The 'finely tuned
control' of the poetry is what allows Hewitt to perform this exemplary function, to speak of the 'predicament' of those among the
Ulster people who share his personal qualities, qualities readily
mirrored in the ordering power of his poetry. Bareham sees Hewitt
as having magisterially situated his poetry in such a way that it can
take up the strains of denunciation, derision or disinheritance
which his honesty brings upon him, and then turn them against the
denouncers, deriders and disinheritors.

Yet Bareham's attempt to establish the exemplary status of
Hewitt's poem 'An Irishman in Coventry' is itself a strained one,
involving him in special pleading. In the poem itself, Hewitt does
not claim a particular 'honesty' for his representation, nor is the
poem about his disinheritance or those who have denounced him.
In its second stanza the poem momentarily registers the poet's distance from his people, as he sits at an Irish social gathering in
Coventry – 'in enclave of my nation, but apart' – before diagnosing
the 'fate' of that nation, 'the dream's distortion and the land's division,/the midnight raiders and the prison cells.'[9] But such distance
does not lend the poetic voice the easy authoritative status which
Bareham claims for it.

In the poem – which Hewitt completed in 1958 but did not
publish in book form until Collected Poems 1932–67 – the beginning is somewhat different from the later description of the 'god-
forsaken race'. Instead, it establishes the reconstructed Coventry
after the Second World War as an urban utopia:

> A full year since, I took this eager city,
> the tolerance that laced its blatant roar,
> its famous steeples and its web of girders,
> as image of the state hope argued for....[10]

He is immediately concerned to establish the effect of this 'eager
city's' tolerance upon his own 'rhetoric', which has 'swung
round...to the precision of the well-gauged tool', a 'rhetoric' which

is in tune with the 'logic' of the huge glass landscapes of Coventry itself. The pull which the distorted, disasterous, suffering 'fate' of 'my nation' exerts is against, then, the ideal, 'tolerant' 'state' which Coventry represents, a vision of order to set against both personal 'rage', 'pity' and 'our own weakness'.[11] Yet the poem offers no resolution to its own blatant juxtapositions between the socialist, comprehensive-schooled utopia in its first stanza and the unravelling of Ireland's crazy, tangled woes in the second. The drift of the diagnosis of the 'fate' of the nation in that stanza is, in its turn, brought up against an abrupt mythic simile in the poem's last two lines. Those lines relate his country's plight to that of Lir's children, set adrift on the sea, but craving the sound of bells on the land – lines which perhaps establish the poet's own nostalgia for his home territory from exile, rather than the general plight of his race.

The poem offers us, then, an uncertainly related range of rhetorics from the utopian to the troubled-nostalgic to the mythic; about the latter, as I show later, Hewitt himself has difficulties. It is, indeed, in danger of merely repeating a clichéd but brutally repressive historical polarization in which England is seen as a dream of tolerant civilization and Ireland a traumatized place in which 'our weakness' and the wrongs inflicted from outside seem inextricably and disastrously meshed.[12] Hewitt's socialist utopianism only serves here to further remind him of his people's irreconcilable distance from such tolerance.

Despite Bareham's claims for the poem's representative status, then, 'An Irishman in Coventry' is a poem which is rather more all at sea in its elisions and unnegotiated divisions than one revealing 'a finely tuned control'. Hewitt himself later put the division between the two places, Coventry and Ireland, rather differently but in a way that again repeats a Unionist, Britain-oriented view of events: Coventry is a 'progressive community...which has attracted people from all quarters of these islands, giving the city a cosmopolitan flavour', as he put it in an interview of 1959. 'This is in vivid contrast to the ingrown parochialism of the Irishman.'[13] The poem does little more, then, than establish that 'vivid contrast'. The inclusive word 'Irishman' in both the poem's title and in the interview ends up as being exclusive, since the poem repeats without criticizing or alleviating the traditional English-held polarization between Ireland and England. Rather than 'speaking of' the 'predicament', as Bareham's review would have it do, then, 'An Irishman in Coventry' seems both trapped within it and determined by it. The poem's self-conscious reference to 'rhetoric' is symptomatic of its own despair and failure. Its relation to history seems irresolvably fraught; we are left wondering whether it is a poem *about* the dilemma, or whether it is a poem whose utopian rhetoric is *part of* its dilemma when weighed against intractable conditions. The poem's disjunctions might either signal the breaking off which it achieves with history – a breaking off into a new, idealized space – or they might simply reveal the fractured and irreconcilable nature of that history which cannot be escaped.

Hewitt's poetry throughout his career was a poetry of 'vivid contrasts', one constantly denying the magisterial overview which Bareham's 'speaking of' suggests. When he collected his earlier poems together in a notebook in about 1930, he gave them the collective title 'The Red Hand: a poemosaic'.[14] It is the implications of that coinage 'poemosaic' which, in the light of such unnegotiated juxtapositions as those in 'An Irishman in Coventry', I want to examine in order to question the line usually taken by critics who accept Hewitt's own internal Augustan rhetoric of precision and order – the calmness of what he called in *Conacre* (1943) 'one who needs the comfortable pace/of safe tradition'.[15] Hewitt himself acknowledged something of an awareness of the potential discontinuity working against any overview when he called a pamphlet of 1967 *Tesserae* (after the small pieces of marble or tile which, when assembled into a pattern, make up a mosaic pavement) and gave his 1981 collection the title *Mosaic*.

In the title poem of *Mosaic*, Hewitt argues the socialist historian's case that those 'bystanders accidentally involved' in historical events should be recognized along with those who seem to be the main players, the 'soldier, functionary, rebel':

> History is selective. Give us instead
> the whole mosaic, the tesserae,
> that we may judge if a period indeed
> has a pattern and is not merely
> a handful of coloured stones in the dust.[16]

History itself is made up of different pieces, and the relation of the parts to the whole, as well as the actual coherence of the whole, remains finally unclear. In the potential disjunction which he seeks to syntactically slide over here, the disjunction between 'the whole mosaic' and its constituent 'tesserae', lies much of Hewitt's dilemma, both politically through his dialectical model and in the 'vivid contrasts' which cannot be resolved poetically. The whole mosaic both is and is not its tesserae. A historical period, like a poem, might have a pattern, but it might just be beautiful, incoherent detritus.

Indeed it is this dilemma which fruitfully opens up and simultaneously renders uneasy the relation between the politics and the poetry and which resonates in the attempts to attain coherence in the work of the later poets confronting the violence in the North. Is there a solving pattern to be offered, or is there mere anarchy which the poetry repeats? Hewitt's is a model which recognizes the history of the individual, but how does the individual 'piece' fit into the whole 'mosaic' which is society? These questions affect the relation between the personal, the general and the social, between the poet and his 'race', between the poem and its audience.

It is clear, however, that Hewitt sees the individual poem as a small piece in the whole mosaic which makes up the life's work, and this is how he tended to approach the laying down of his collections from the late 1960s on, by setting poems from various stages of his life against each other. His last collection, *Freehold and Other Poems* of 1986, for instance, includes the first publication of the play 'The Bloody Brae' of 1936 alongside the title poem completed in 1946 and poems from the 1970s and 1980s. With the curious process of publication his work underwent, poems across the history of his whole career became pieces to arrange and rearrange into final patterns. Hewitt's practice of collection-making is curiously consonant with that of the self-declaredly modernist John Montague which I discuss in Chapter 4, a practice which Montague calls 'collage'.

That scattering of pieces which might or might not add up to coherence is, further, integral to the question of literary influence upon Hewitt's work. As he noted in 1978 when explaining why his collection *The Rain Dance* contained such a mixture of poems written at various times of his life, at the age of 70 he had been reading poetry for over 50 years, following 'the fluctuations of fashion' in moving from 'Shelley, Whitman, Rossetti and Morris' to 'Eliot, Pound...Day-Lewis, Auden' to Yeats, Edward Thomas, Robert Frost, R.S. Thomas and thence to Larkin, Heaney, Mahon, Longley, *inter alia*.[17] In other words, his reading across his life ranged from the socialist, democratic poets of the nineteenth century who had a formative influence on his politics, through the years of modernist experimentalism and its aftermath, to the poetic 'renaissance' on his own soil in the 1960s. The 'nourishment', as he called it, which he might obtain from this diverse gathering in his own writing is far more diffuse and stylistically contradictory than the authorities usually ascribed to a single tradition might allow for, one in which the question of style becomes more openly functional, a matter of finding suitable forms for each occasion: 'The good craftsman is truly a functionalist; if one may still use that unfashionable word.'[18]

In vulnerable, tentative moments, Hewitt's poetry itself openly admits the Frostian temporary stay it has to offer against the change of the seasons or of human history and experience. In 'The Return', the diffuse and sprawling Part xxv of the unpublished 'poemosaic' 'The Red Hand', Hewitt asserts the endurance of a civil art against hostile reality, 'For it is not wars we remember/but the chiselled face...the temple, the sonnet: these are Man'. But some 30 lines later, at the end of the poem, such assertion of the value of the aesthetic is partly retracted, in a typically premonitary 1930s sense of impending doom and slide towards a second world war:

> I wrote these words out, ever recognising
> the shifting lights I missed in definition,
> yet sure the fumbling pattern was not worthless,
> that I or you in dark days coming after
> might not despair because of the uncharted....[19]

The 'black wing' of 'imminent' international war leads Hewitt to revalue the sureties which he held about the timelessness of art. The pattern itself seems 'fumbling' in response to that crisis. But the 'crisis' in the poem is also local: the poem was written in 1935, at a time when the hard quest for scarce jobs in the North led to the first breakout of sectarian violence since 1922. On 12 July, at the height of the marching season, a trivial incident led the Orangemen to feel that their parade in Belfast was being attacked; nights of sectarian violence and rioting followed: 'In the streets/crowds brandished the blunt slogans of their hate,/drove from their midst the strangers of a creed,/and set the lithe flame licking up the curtain', as Hewitt's poem has it. 'The Return' is an early poem which typically sets pastoral images, firstly from a holiday on Rathlin island, then on a visit to England and the Mendip hills where 'life was eternal, involving every instant', against the divisions which threaten all kinds of peace – something I will take up in relation to Hewitt's poems of the 'Troubles' below. But the end of the poem is vital for his later work in recognizing that in 'dark days' poetry itself is a crude imposition upon experience, not a worthless one but a clumsy and inexact one. Such recognitions punctuate all of Hewitt's poetry that broods upon timelessness. 'Substance and Shadow', of six years later, reveals the poet attempting to 'temper time...in my mind's defence', but failing in his Horatian ambition as 'the substance and shadow break adrift/that needed bronze to lock them, bronze or stone.'[20]

Yet Hewitt famously sought to contradict his sense of disruptive forces in an idea which he held, often bravely in contrast to other trends, across his career. During the 'dark days' of the 1940s, Hewitt struggled to counter the paralysed, unmanageable nature of the modern world with a simpler, more human and local unity. As he explained in the 1972 article 'No Rootless Colonist', 'with the Second World War, we were cut off from the larger island to the east and from...Europe':

> During this period my thought...found itself directed towards, and settled upon, the concept of regionalism. This proposed that since the world about us is so vast and complex, strangled by bu-reaucratic centralisation – 'apoplexy at the centre, paralysis at the extremities' – we must seek for some grouping smaller than the nation, larger than the family, with which we could come to terms of sympathetic comprehension, within which our faculties and human potentialities could find due nurture and proper fulfilment.[21]

Such local rooting is at odds with the cosmopolitan/local split Hewitt was later to make in the 1950s. Yet, as a response to the turning inward in the North which resulted from the Republic of Ireland's neutrality during the war, 'regionalism' had a powerful appeal for Hewitt, not least because also within this 'concept might be found a meeting place for the two separated communities'. More importantly, as is revealed by an article written in 1947, closer to the date of these preoccupations, the concept of 'regionalism' seemed to reconcile the dilemma inherent in his 'mosaic' metaphor, the dilemma of the individual's relation to the community. In 'Regionalism: The Last Chance' he had argued that 'although [re-gionalism] too begins in the individual, [it] must immediately pass beyond the individual and react upon the community.'[22] Despite his recognition that the interest in this concept faded in about 1951, it is this seamless interweaving which remains the political and poetic ambition of Hewitt's work early and late, and which exerted a considerable influence over the next generation of writers from the North.

Hewitt's poetics and politics of transcendence centred upon the individual became a vital strain in the thinking of those who became more optimistic at the shifts in opinion which led to the founding of the Civil Rights movements in the late 1960s. Hewitt's own move to the centre of such debates coincided, as I have said, with the founding of *The Honest Ulsterman*, in the review columns of which his poetry was accorded an exemplary status (he had been associated in the regionalist years with the anti-sectarian magazine *Lagan*). Over the first seven years of its publication, *The Honest Ulsterman* printed many poems of Hewitt's and chapters from his autobiography 'A North Light', alongside early work by Seamus Heaney, Derek Mahon and Michael Longley. What seems to bind Hewitt's thinking on regionalism to that of this generation of poets starting out in Belfast in the mid to late 1960s is the sense of the exemplary importance of the individual poet's experience in relation to the history of the 'nation', and of the seamless continuity between the two.

When *The Honest Ulsterman* was begun in 1968, its founder, the poet James Simmons, proclaimed it as 'a magazine of revolution'. The first issue arrived at a time which was being seen as a watershed in the history of the North. In March 1968, the Derry Housing Action Committee invaded the Guildhall there and read out a declaration demanding a crash housing programme to alleviate cramped conditions for the minority population, and the pace of the campaign for civil rights accelerated from there. Simmons's response to this watershed in his first editorial of May resounds with Hewitt-like regionalist terms:

> Political progress from now on will not depend on our allegiance to leaders, ideas and systems, but in the individual's allegiance to himself, his courage and wit to use all the wisdom and experience literature puts at his disposal, to get off his knees and stop praying to be set free, to realise that he is already free. ...Just as it is necessary for each individual to claim his own freedom and make his own decisions, so it is important for the regions, small,

manageable social units, to establish their independence... I look to a new flowering when not only men and women but towns and counties will assume their real, unique personalities.[23]

Integral to the 'revolution', then, – and not surprisingly given the nature of Simmons's own writing – is the change which literature might bring to the 'individual consciousness' (a similar centrality is accorded it, as my first chapter argued, and again unsurprisingly given the nature of its board, by the Field Day Theatre Company's interventions into the situation). In an article which he also wrote for this first issue of his magazine called (in a play on a title of Nietzsche's) 'The Use of History', Simmons attacks those 'historians and teachers' who rely on 'economic affairs' to draw their conclusions and who 'pretend that History is a science':

> I don't know what it is in the past we have to know to shake Ulster from the present paralysed conditions, but this is what our historians should be telling us. It points once again to history as an aspect of literature, for it is this sort of information that our serious poets and novelists are giving us.

Simmons then quotes Yeats's 'Easter 1916' and 'The Stare's Nest At My Window' to back up his attack, arguing that 'these insights echo in the present. They make me wonder if History has any special value at all, for they seem more the product of Yeats's mind than the study of history.'[24]

This sense of the absolute importance of literature to the historical process is a more tentatively put concern of John Hewitt's 'regionalism' also, and involved him in complex negotiations with his most immediate poetic forebear, Yeats. At the end of 'The Bitter Gourd: Some Problems of the Ulster Writer' of 1945, Hewitt argued that poets 'are endeavouring to recreate [Ulster's] story, that art, that enhancement...playing our parts in helping to make her what...we realise she should and can become.'[25] And in telling this story, Hewitt is certain of the importance of the region and of genealogy in forming the type of artist a writer might be:

> [The Ulster writer] must be a *rooted* man, must carry the native tang of his idiom like the native dust on his sleeve... a writer...ought to feel that he belongs to a recognisable focus in place and time. How he assures himself of that feeling is his own

affair. But I believe he must have it. And with it he must have *ancestors*. Not just of the blood, but of the emotions, of the quality and slant of mind.[26]

Hewitt's rhetoric here is strikingly Yeatsian, both in nativizing Yeats's 'dust on an old man's sleeve' and in recalling the invocation of John Synge as 'that rooted man' in Yeats's 'The Municipal Gallery Revisited' with the 'thought' that Synge shared with Lady Gregory and Yeats himself: 'All that we did, all that we said or sang/Must come from contact with the soil, from that/Contact everything Antaeus-like grew strong.'[27]

Hewitt's reworking of the 'Antaeus-like' side of Yeats's ideas, however, serves both to establish the border between the North and South of Ireland and to aid in the definition of his own poetic.[28] He has written his own version of this poem, calling it 'The Municipal Gallery Revisited, October 1954', which tellingly captures and distances himself from the apathy which crept into life in the Republic in the years succeeding the War; an apathy which contrasts absolutely with the brazen grandeur of Yeats's earlier vision of what the independent state might be:

> I moved among these images
> ...still emblems of the power
> that wrought a nation out of bitterness, and...
> ...wondered which of these
> may hold a meaning that will long endure,
> see, before me, threatening, immense,
> the creeping haircracks of indifference.[29]

Yeats's mythic 'contact' is here undermined by the actual bitterness of the Civil War and the stagnation which later came upon the Republic with the international isolation it suffered as a result of its wartime neutrality. When, during that war, Hewitt wrote his Northern, Planter version of this Antaeus idea he did not dismiss it outright, indeed he expressed a desire to strike that note, but registers something of this scepticism as he recognizes a personal and circumstantial inadequacy which prevents his doing so.

In his most famous poem, 'Once Alien Here' of 1942, Hewitt invokes 'my fathers' before setting his own, and his poetry's, claim within the tradition. Because of all his ancestors buried in Ulster, and the way in which the region's landscape and weather are 'native' to him, Hewitt feels a need to discover a consonant 'native' mode through which to articulate his people's 'individual wisdom'. Yet:

> ...lacking skill in either scale or song,
> the graver English, lyric Irish tongue,
> must let this rich earth so enhance the blood
> with steady pulse where now is plunging mood
> till thought and image may, identified,
> find easy voice to utter each aright.[30]

This is a very assertive claim of the Planter's rights through inheritance to the land (the 'plantation of Ulster' from the early seventeenth century colonized the best land with English or, very often, with Scots settlers). Yet it also recognizes a continuing poetic and historical alienation from a mode through which to articulate that experience, a mode correlative to Yeats's Anglo-Irish grandeur. 'Once Alien Here' stakes a claim for a poetry which will rise from that land and be distinctive from both the English and the Gaelic traditions.[31] As so often in Hewitt's work, the urge is beyond a perceived personal wildness ('plunging mood') and poetic inadequacy ('lacking skill') towards an 'easy' *mot juste* which will utter the Planter's rhythms of thought. But as with his other attempts to link a poetic rhetoric to a political ambition, the desire is abstractly expressed rather than enacted, a hoped-for future mode rather than a presently realizable one. Hewitt's remains a poetry of liminality, able to describe what he seeks, but never fully able to write it out or to live it beyond a few mystical, hallucinatory moments such as that described in 'The Response', where 'being, like water, finds its shape/no longer bottled into selves...'.[32]

Hewitt's critical, failed reworking of Yeats's mythic vision of Irish history as a regional claim to the soil is crucial to his attempts to resolve the dilemmas in his own work. In the essay 'Irish Poets, Learn Your Trade', which derives its title from Yeats, he argues of the older poet that

> it is the fashion for the multitude of thesis-mongers to fix their attention on his symbols, his myths, his masks, for they have not been taught to realise that the nature of poetry exists in the pattern of words and sounds employed. Never tired of quoting Mallarmé's advice to Degas, that poetry consists of words and

not ideas, they never apply their dictums to their own thinking. In fact, Yeats was tremendously skilled and versatile, with an expert ear for the renewal of neglected and forgotten forms. In all this he was a practical writer, never a theorist of prosody... .[33]

This is very much an empiricist defence of 'words' not 'ideas' as being the poet's primary concern, and also a defence of the poet as formalist within the tradition, as renewer of neglected poetic forms.

All of these various elements of anti-myth and craft come together in the self-consciously Yeatsian 'Homestead', written in 1949. Here, the form of the poem mirrors the form of a dreamt house: 'It is time now for me to build a house/to be a shelter in the rough days', the poem begins. Naturally enough, though, given the role of Thoor Ballylee in standing against the anarchy of history for Yeats's later work, this architectural analogy for poetry leads Hewitt closer to the older poet's concerns. Hewitt initially seeks out his own symbolic vocabulary, rejecting the Christian ('The power of Christ' is rejected as 'seasonal only as nature'), before opting for the local man of action and poet 'Oisin, I said is my symbol', 'warrior and bard returning again and again...Oisin, who baffled Patrick, his older faith/tougher than the parchment or the string of beads'. Yet with this seeming access of poetic power and discovery of a potential mask for himself in the Yeatsian manner, Hewitt immediately recognizes that this invasion of Yeats's poetic territory cannot last. A typically autobiographical recognition intervenes, asserting that the myth has already been inhabited, and that the older poet's mythic and symbolic order is literally dead and buried, that he has left Thoor Ballylee for ever:

> Yeats was Oisin.
> The dinted symbols rust in the crumbling tower
> but Oisin is not there now. I saw Yeats carried
> to the wailing of bagpipes through the wind-washed town,
> and watched Oisin elbow back through the holiday crowd,
> going the opposite way as we followed the hearse.

Although he momentarily tries to claim that the spirit of Oisin lives on in the local 'flat foot, red-necked farmer', this is an idea soon dropped as the poem, like 'An Irishman in Coventry', abruptly breaks off before restarting itself – 'Yet those, familiar with business, suggest instead...'. Hewitt rehearses other architectural styles in which he might build his 'house' and 'listens' to detractors who try and persuade him of the pointlessness of building at all because 'the house will fall;/it is the nature of stone to fall and lie'. That sense of the transitory nature of everything leads Hewitt to revise his 'plans':

> No. There is nothing for it but to build right here
> in rough-cut stone and spread a roof of scraws.
> Maybe a coal tit will nest here or a houseleek flower...
> The stonework will be simple, honest and sturdy,
> not showy, not even neat, but built to last.
> I go today to the quarry to tryst the stones.[34]

The use of the rough and ready, improvisatory building material is confirmed in these sometimes plodding final lines by the inclusion of the dialect words 'scraws' (the turfs used to roof a hovel) and 'tryst' (to arrange for) which strike the final blow for the modest and the colloquial against Yeats's universalizing mythic and symbolic ordering of history (and the use of these words anticipates Tom Paulin's interest in Ulster dialects for similar reasons). Hewitt's encounter with the earlier poet in 'Homestead' anticipates directly that imagined by Seamus Heaney in his poem 'The Master', in which (presumably) Yeats dwells behind his ramparts and unclasps his 'book of withholding', with 'Each character blocked on the parchment secure/in its volume and measure.' Against such intransigence, the persona in the poem feels 'flimsy', and the improvisatory language of the poem, as in describing the 'book', mirrors that uncertainty.[35]

From his own negotiations with the master, Hewitt's regionalism emerges as a much more modest and unsettled contingent poetic. His poetic architecture is wedded to the everyday, sceptical of the universalizing uplift of the mythic and the symbolic. He is rooted in the definition of poetry as being simply a specialized form of communication: '...the function of words is to communicate, not merely to remain as words...'.[36] For him, there is not the ideal audience which the solitary, wise fisherman represents for Yeats; rather, his socialism leads him to envisage communication itself as the medium of an ideal equal community.

An earlier poem of architectual transitoriness, 'The Ruins Answer' (from just before the Second World War, but not collected into book form until *Mosaic*), moves from an opening vision of the

bleakness of the contemporary town ('Our towns spill out, yet at
the heart decay,/where, waking, many greet a workless day')
towards a 'coda' in which utopianism is expressed in these terms:

> ...that we find
> a lexicon and syntax so aligned
> to purge our feelings, clarify our thought,
> the sound and sense enwrought,
> that in communion we communicate;
> for nowhere but in that society
> can we, at last, be free,
> necessity and nature of our human state.[37]

Once more, this implicitly aligns the poetic impulse with the development of an ideal state, claiming that the Rousseauist vision of
freedom is contingent upon the discovery of a suitable vocabulary
and syntax which is implicitly that of poetry's, 'the sound and
sense enwrought'. Hewitt's use of the Miltonic past participle here,
meaning 'worked into the fabric', distances the poetry's ambition
from easy presence and acceptance. Yet the appeal of the 'lexicon
and syntax' to both thought and feelings envisages a reconciliation
– albeit again at an abstract level – of what had been divided
between the two stanzas of 'An Irishman in Coventry', while 'in
communion we communicate' suggests a union beyond religious
differences which has an aura of religious intensity about it.

There is a striking continuity between the emphasis on communication in the poetic practice and political thinking explored
by Hewitt in these poems, and the socialist tradition traced by
Raymond Williams in his trio of early books *Culture and Society
1780–1950* (1958), *The Long Revolution* (1961) and *The Country and
the City* (1973). Particularly in his pages on 'The Creative Mind' at
the beginning of *The Long Revolution*, Williams strikes a tone which
is very reminiscent of the concept of the artist's ideal role in relation
to his or her community which Hewitt develops in the socialist
utopian moments towards which much of his poetry struggles.
Ideally and retrospectively, as I show below, Williams too sets
the communication of the artist alongside that of all other
communication:

> ...the purpose of the [artist's] skill is similar to the purpose of all
> general human communication: the transmission of valued

experience. Thus the artist's impulse, like every human impulse to communicate, is the felt importance of his experience. There can be no separation, in this view, between 'content' and 'form', because finding the form is literally finding the content....It is, in the first instance, to every man, a matter of urgent personal importance to 'describe' his experience, because this is literally a remaking of himself, a creative change in his personal organisation, to include and control experience.[38]

A similar notion to Hewitt's 'sound and sense enwrought' in 'The Ruins Answer' here governs that transcendence of the self which binds the artist's impulse to a common humanity. For Williams as for Hewitt, the grounding of art within a more general conception of the essential nature of the act of communication in both describing and forming perceptions means that 'the felt importance' of that experience is amenable to all:

We learn to see a thing by learning to describe it; this is the normal process of perception, which can only be seen as complete when we have interpreted the incoming sensory information either by a known configuration or rule, or by some new configuration which we can try to learn as a new rule. The process of interpretation is neither arbitrary or abstract; it is a central and necessary vital function, by which we seek to understand our environment that we can live more successfully in it....The painting, like other visual 'objects', has itself to be interpreted and described before, in any normal sense, it is seen. We realise, from this, the necessary social basis of any art, for nobody can see (not understand, but *see*) the artist's actual work unless he and the artist can come to share the complex details and means of a learned communication system.[39]

There is of course a deep anxiety within that parenthesis in the final sentence which shows the fragility of the system which Williams describes as operating in 'the creative mind' – and it is an anxiety which I am tracing in Hewitt's work as part of his unsettled, unsettling 'poemosaic' also.

The vision and insight which art offers for interpretation depends upon the development of that 'learned communication system' – but what happens if the system fails? Williams's socialism allows for the cultural and historical study of the mode of production and reception of works of art, the struggle either by the individual artist or in society at large to found that 'learned communication system' throughout the ages. Williams suggests that both the act of interpretation and the act of creation are equally vital and dynamic, furthering understanding and helping us to live 'more successfully' in our society. 'Communication', he argues in *Culture and Society*, 'is not only transmission; it is also reception and response', and so it forms a naturalizing, conventional basis for society itself and for interaction within it.[40] Yet, having established communication as the basis of democratic communities, he recognizes that that ideal, in this century particularly, is under threat from social processes which undermine the shared, customary bases of community itself.

This dilemma is, in Williams's thinking, the dilemma of modernity, where the means of communication have proliferated so fast that the vital processes of interpretation and creation are in danger of becoming redundant and solipsistic:

> In our time, clearly, we have change of such complexity, due not only to the rapidity of change in common experience but to the great extension and diversification of communities, that for a time at least discontinuity seems central, and we are primarily aware of art as the series of individual offers, the making of common meanings being almost lost.[41]

It is this discontinuity in the movement from individual to community which Hewitt himself sought to resolve through his call for regionalism to counter the 'vast and complex' modern world in the isolated years of the war. But that discontinuity is extreme in the historically founded religious sectarianism of his own place and, in Williams's terms, raises crucial questions about the poetry's efficacy with regard to playing its part in helping Ulster become what she 'could and should'. 'Ars Poetica', a poem from 1949, again recycles Hewitt's sense of poetry as simply one among many crafts ('With what I made I have been satisfied/as country joiner with a country cart/made for a like use') before baldly questioning the purpose of such gestures:

> What word of yours can...
> Give life and purpose to a workless lad?
> The hearthless house? Restore the strength they had

> to the smashed fingers? For the prisoners
> break down the bars? For mercy pray, and peace,
> for that unravished kingdom rightly theirs?[42]

Hewitt's socialist concern to set the problems of the unemployed alongside the civil decay brought about by inter-communal strife in the North in this poem (like that in 'The Return', 'The Ruin's Answer' and many other poems of the 1930s and 1940s), reflects the causes of that strife. Unemployment had stood at a level way beyond that of the mainland in the Depression years of the 1930s and had increased during the war despite a drop by half on the mainland.[43] Against such overwhelming modern social and sectarian problems, it is clear that poetry's 'function' is severely in doubt, that the dynamic and vital interpretative and communicatory purpose which it contains might be facile and futile. Hewitt's 'solution' at the end of this section of the poem – 'If you can frame the questions, it is well' – reads like false piety, an overly comfortable acceptance of the poet's 'apartness' which validates his role as raiser of doubts. Yet in this very validation is a refusal to confront the fact that those doubts, like Auden's in his work of this time, go to the very root of poetry's effectiveness, asking whether, as Auden did in his elegy 'In Memory of W.B. Yeats', poetry makes anything 'happen'.

In the second section of 'Ars Poetica' Hewitt makes a characteristic and abrupt shift of perspective and imagery, symptomatic of his response to such social and political dilemmas. He uses the example of the farmer in order to create a breach between the mode of production and modes of reception, the farmer who 'does not ask, before he casts his seed, that it be pencilled in who'll use each grain/...that it be decreed/the finished web serve such or such a one':

> So be the poet. Let him till his years
> follow the laws of language, feeling, thought,
> that out of his close labour there be wrought
> good sustenance for other hearts than his.[44]

There is within this profligate organicism a significant breach between the poet and his audience. Poems are simply broadcast on the soil, to fructify wherever they may happen to fall. At the end of the War, in 'The Bitter Gourd', Hewitt had complained of the 'careful rejection of the rhetorical and flamboyant' by the Planters, of the 'very inarticulateness of the Protestant block' and had shown what its effects on the Ulster poet must be: 'The Ulster ideology...offered the writer no inspiration. The Ulster public offered him no livelihood. Nor has the latter problem yet been solved.'[45] Hewitt, of course, earned his living in museum work. But his use of the farmer here as a simile for the disconnection from one's inheritance which simply being a writer forces on the Ulster poet is daringly naïve and idealized in itself.

Edna Longley has argued that that central polarity in English writing between pastoral and urban, the history of which Williams traced in *The Country and the City*, is 'only true up to a point' of Ulster poetry, because of 'Belfast's proximity to rural Ulster, the persistence of "old ways" after their transplantation to the city...[and] the ambiguity attached to "progress" in Ulster.'[46] Although this is undoubtedly true, it is also true that the *division* in Hewitt's poetry between the country – exemplified by the Glens of Antrim where Hewitt went every summer from 1940 to 1965 – and the city, predominantly a nameless place in his work but recognizably Belfast, remains one of the strongest 'vivid contrasts' and strongest sources of utopian projection. That division itself looks forward to the intent but vulnerable pastoralism in later poets I shall be discussing like Montague and Heaney.

It is just such a contrast which fuels the opening of Hewitt's first, privately published work, *Conacre* in 1943. The poem opens with a bewildered, phantasmagoric vision of walking through the city which recalls Wordsworth and also the fragmented vision of London in Eliot's *The Waste Land*: 'The lonely person looking for a nod/along the street; the old man dazed with God/howling his gospel, hoarse with prophecy;/the laden soldier laden with his family...'. Unsurprisingly, we are told that 'these close images...leave the quiet depths unmeasured still;/whereas the heathered shoulder of a hill...stab[s] the heart', and the poem switches between images of industrial decay in the city and pictures of the country as a Golden Age.[47]

This sense of the plenitude of the pastoral, its metaphorical possibilites within a fertile, widely broadcast poetic, reflects the new riches which he found in the Glens on first going there in 1940. In the early 1930s, Ulster agriculture had suffered first under the Depression and then under the economic war which arose when de Valera removed the oath of fidelity to the Crown from the Irish

Constitution and withheld the payment of land annuities to Britain. Yet, by the time the Hewitts first visited the Glens, Ulster agriculture was again booming as Britain started to suffer food shortages and Westminster ordered a 40 per cent increase in production from pre-war levels. With the expansion came an increase in the technology used to increase yields from the land; labour-saving tractors, for instance, numbered only 850 in the North in 1939 but 16 000 by 1950.[48] There is even a mini-eulogy to the progressive ideas of the farmer at the end of *Conacre*: '[he] turns no back on progress, dreaming still/of the broad tractors sweeping up the hill,/and the great binder worked by equal men,/lifting its swathes of fat collective grain.'[49]

Hewitt is always quick to celebrate the values of such pastoral images as a resource to set against the various wars and violence which he has lived through. 'Poem in May', from 1944, recounts a retreat 'close to terror at the sick world's plight/to this clean kingdom vehement with life'.[50] Yet, true to the contingency which runs through his poetic, Hewitt has remained sceptical both early and late about the worth of pastoral poetry in relation to the 'vast and complex' modern world, particularly when that world, as in his Ulster, is one in which a universal transitoriness is precipitated by violence. 'Because I Paced My Thought', a poem reflecting on the Second World War but much anthologized in collections of Irish poetry published post-1969, makes it clear that Hewitt recognizes that his principle dilemma inheres essentially in the genre of poetry which he is writing, that it is a problem of communication:

> Because I paced my thought by the natural world...
> rather than the city falling ruinous, slowly
> by weather and use, swiftly by bomb and argument
>
> I found myself alone who had hoped for attention.[51]

Against the violence of his times, the continuation of a traditional poetic formalism consonant with country crafts is seen as the plight of the unpublished. What is important for my discussion about the flexibility of Hewitt's response to the historical moment, however, is the fact that, from the late 1960s onwards, the perennially rich poetic resource provided by the pastoral is more radically questioned than ever in his work, and this questioning in its turn opens up a new possibility for the abstract rhetoric of his earlier utopianism. In 'Below the Mournes in May' of 1975, this kind of rhetoric allows for a brutal, self-mockingly ironic revision of Hewitt's whole poetic ambition. Having considered the 'little images waiting/for the nature poet', Hewitt turns harshly back upon himself and upon his own poetic past:

> Then I remembered that the nature-poet
> has no easy prosody for
> class or property relationships,
> for the social dialectic...
> So I was anxiously responsive
> to the fresh graffiti on the gables
> of roofless cottages at the next crossroads,
> for these reported something
> of more immediate significance
> than the stump of that round tower beside the church....[52]

There is an extreme awkwardness about the tone of this poem, one fraught with anxiety and uncertainty about the relation of poetry to the social situation, particularly once violence had flared again and the sectarian allegiances proclaimed on gable-ends seemed more relevant than the traditional virtues of nature poetry. Under these extreme conditions, the Augustan poise of Hewitt's poetic voice wavers uncertainly. The tone of the opening four lines here is – what? Self-mocking? Nervous? And what of that 'anxiously responsive'? Why the embarrassment over his instinctive responses? It is clear that the changed social conditions enhanced that severe, destabilizing effect within Hewitt's sense of the dilemmas he was writing under.

In the 'Postscript 1984' which he appended to the 1930s poem 'Ulster Names' that questioning is even more radical, as Hewitt laments the way the violence has impinged upon the comfortable store of rural images. The violence has enforced a destructive diremption upon the pastoral fastness evoked by the 'Names', where even Derry, with its 'crashing boom and the coiling smoke', gives way to the freedom and poetry of the oak grove which gives the place its name. But:

> Now with compulsive resonance they toll:
> Banbridge, Ballykelly, Darkley, Crossmaglen,
> summoning pity, anger and despair,

by grief of kin, by hate of murderous men
till the whole tarnished map is stained and torn,
not to be read as pastoral again.[53]

This is a much more absolute break with the pastoral than that dared by any of the 1960s generation. In Michael Longley (whose work Hewitt celebrates in 'Fontanel'), for instance, there is a parallel between his descriptions of his place of poetic resource, Carrigskeewaun, and the violence in his home city: 'This is ravens' territory, skulls, bones,/The marrow of these boulders supervised/From the upper air...'.[54] But the pastoral itself continues to be read and reread, written and rewritten in Longley's work.

Similar radical discontinuities characterize Hewitt's actual interventions into the 'tragic events', as he called them, in the North, interventions which show both the virtues and the uncertainties of his perennial preoccupations. In 1970, Hewitt undertook a reading tour to various towns of the North of Ireland with John Montague, and an accompanying booklet was published by the Arts Council called *The Planter and the Gael*. There was a clear notion behind the tour that the conditions might somehow be somewhat alleviated by reading poems which 'explained' something of the two traditions in the country. Hewitt's selection in the booklet is, however, thoroughly eclectic, blending allegories on colonization ('The Colony' and 'The Search') with poems celebrating the persistence of folk song and storytelling ('The Man from Malabar', 'The Long Bridge'), a piece of Clare-like nature observation ('The Watchers') and two poems about his nurse in childhood ('Betrayal' and an embarrassing redoing of Yeats, 'No Second Troy'). In 'The Green Shoot', a recognition of the bigotry which he himself displayed in childhood is rather clumsily modulated towards its organic closing image.

The more aggressively territorial 'Once Alien Here' appeared in the booklet, as did 'The Glens', a poem which shows a much more troubled relation to the land and its Catholic farmers: 'I fear their creed as we have always feared/the lifted hand against unfettered thought'. That odd pronoun slippage from 'I' to 'we' shows again Hewitt's deep unease about his place in the Planter tradition, and the involuntary responses it imbues him with, before the shift at the end of the poem back to aesthetics, away from the momentary dilemma, as the landscape appears to be the sole resource for his poetry ('And yet no other corner in this land/offers in shape and colour all I need'). It is the same shifting, uneasy tone from stanza to stanza which I have noted in 'An Irishman in Coventry', a poem which also appears in the booklet, and many other times in Hewitt's work.

The other poem in *The Planter and the Gael*, 'Conversations in Hungary, August, 1969', which attempts to set the Ulster conflict against the context of East European history,[55] also appears in Hewitt's other intervention into debates at the time. *An Ulster Reckoning* was privately published in Belfast in 1971. Hewitt was still in England at the time (he did not return to live in Belfast until his retirement from the museum service in 1972), and the book is a response to 'heartbreaking' events which immediately destroyed his hope – held from the 1950s on but presumably accelerated by the Civil Rights movement – that, as he put it in the Foreword, there had been 'an apparent softening of the hard lines and a growing tolerance between the two historical communities'. This 'heartbreak' induces the most exposedly unsure collection of poems from Hewitt, one in which all his concerns are nakedly to the fore in inconclusive, self-questioning array.[56]

What *An Ulster Reckoning* presents is a poetry which is alert to delusion. The sequence presents a series of portraits, often written 'in character' or Yeatsian masks, which expose the follies, particularly the follies on the Unionist side, exposed by the conflict. The shift in tone from poem to poem carries the doubts and uncertainties, the sense of anguished disruption of all that had held before. Within the poems themselves there is a racily, almost journalistic, idiom which deftly controls its ironies:

> We've seen that worried face upon the box…
> …pedigree supplies the flinty core
> to his opinions; they were always right…
> ('Prime Minister')[57]

Typically, however, this idiom of the moment and tonal disruption do not extend to the poetic form itself – the bulk of the collection is made up of tightly rhymed sonnets. This retention in itself carries moral and political resonance in Hewitt's poetic thinking as a resistance to that 'deluge and welter of words' which he had always found in Ulster and which was particularly raging at the time his was writing these poems. Whatever the virtues of the craftsman-like adherence to the tradition within the individual poems, however, in *An Ulster Reckoning* Hewitt uses form to the most varied and dramatic effect.

The book opens with a couple of sonnets in which Hewitt again reviews what he first calls 'the inflexions of my origin'. The second, 'The Dilemma', aggressively attacks the South of Ireland ('though they assert their love of liberty,/which craft has narrowed to a fear of Rome') in the name – an echo from 'The Glens' – of that 'stubborn habit of unfettered thought' which he had learnt from his father: 'I dreamed, like him, all people should be free'.[58]

It is more often the case, though, that in the pamphlet's later poems, Hewitt rounds upon his own, Protestant, people and their traditions. In the brutal dramatic portrait of 'An Ulster Landowner's Song' there is a generalized picture of the Orangeman, 'I'm Major This or Captain That...and keep the Fenians in their bogs,/the peasants at the gate.'[59] In 'The Coasters' he attacks the cosy, 'liberal' (in their own eyes), complacent Unionist middle classes, who had gained higher living standards during the boom years of the late 1950s and the 1960s (when there was an influx of foreign investment into the then strife-free country bringing a manufacturing growth rate of 5.7 per cent[60]), but who were blind to the divisions which the subsequent wider gap between the more affluent majority and the continuingly deprived minority would bring upon their own heads:

> You coasted along
> to larger houses, gadgets, more machines,
> to golf and weekend bungalows,
> caravans when the children were small,
> the Mediterranean later, with the wife....
>
> You even had a friend of the other sort...
>   [were] introduced, even, to
> one of their clergy....
>
> The cloud of infection hangs over the city,
> a quick change of wind and it
> might spill over the leafy suburbs.
> You have coasted too long.[61]

This shows a more direct engagement with social realities in the modern city of Belfast, a particularity of observation about seemingly unpromising material, which had sometimes been lacking in Hewitt's earlier work. But besides such attention to contemporary social developments in the city, the poem is a brave piece of *self-*questioning. Hewitt had, after all, himself coasted in some of the complacencies of that tradition (and, as 'The Dilemma' shows, sometimes continued to do so). Now, as the satiric touch of other of the poems shows, such complacency had been shattered, 'with no end in sight', as the last sonnet in the book has it. The violence has a correlative effect on his poetry to that of the metropolitan modernism described by Raymond Williams in a late talk – one in which language itself loses its defining and naturalizing basis in community and becomes 'in many ways arbitrary and conventional...more evident as a medium – a medium that could be shaped and reshaped'.[62] With the events in his home city, Hewitt's own communal and conventional poetic languages are exposed as such, and the bases for his earlier style are undermined.

The sonnet 'Memorandum for the Moderates' even viciously mocks what would seem to be an image of Hewitt himself at earlier stages in his career: 'Speak peace and toleration. Moderate/your tone of voice....Few will recall the names of any dead'. Other sonnets contain portraits of the 'Prime Minister' James Dawson Chichester-Clark, 'Demagogue' Ian Paisley (whose being 'loud of voice' typically rouses Hewitt's attention and doubt), 'Minister' Brian Faulkner, and 'Agitator' Bernadette Devlin, the only figure in the book to emerge with any praise because she showed many of the virtues which Hewitt himself continued to hold to:

> she spoke for 'people of no property'.
> Thus Tone addressed them once; now it is hers,
> that phrase, the warrant of her ancestry.[63]

By comparing Devlin to the leader of the United Irishmen, Wolfe Tone, Hewitt presumably hoped that her socialist principles would have the force of uniting the two communities. This inordinate praise shows that some of the early utopianist ambition survives even through Hewitt's heartbreak.

Elsewhere in the book he is much more sceptical towards his own rhetorical and poetic procedures, as well as towards the attempted parallels his poetry makes. 'The Tribunes' and 'The Well-Intentioned Consul', two poems which adopt the allegorical method more famously deployed in 'The Colony', where the classical world is made to stand in for the colonization of Ulster, are followed by the dismissive 'Parallels Never Meet': 'To find focus for my taut feelings/I thrust all back into a remote setting/...allegorising the action and the actors.../But they trip and flounder in their togas;/the classical names are inappropriate'.[64]

With its opening of his traditional forms to divisive modern subjects, what *An Ulster Reckoning* as a whole shows is that Hewitt's despairing but immediate response to history and a consequent poetic unease constantly sets him to doubt and review his own earlier procedures. Even that imagined community which the concluding gestures of the earlier poems had urged, aligning poetic order with some future order in the state, is here silenced outside 'Agitator'. The outbreak of violence in 1969 obviously acted on Hewitt, even in this pamphlet which is seemingly his most dramatically explicit address to public issues, in the same way that Williams felt modernity continues to act, through alienation, diversity and discontinuity. Hewitt cannot any longer presume that 'learned communication system' with his self-destructive people, and in 'A Belfastman Abroad Argues With Himself' can only lament his failure to speak out when 'that evil man [presumably Paisley] first raised his raucous shout', or to join the civil rights movement.

It is this severe unease about the function of poetry which punctuates and unsettles the tone of others of Hewitt's late poems dealing with incidents from the 'Troubles' – in 'At the Newsagent's', for instance, the bullet hole left in the door after a police reservist has been killed 'I suppose, might be considered/"an objective correlative"'.[65] But it is in the remarkable poem 'Neither An Elegy Nor a Manifesto: *for the people of my province and the rest of Ireland*' which was written a few days after Bloody Sunday, 30 January 1972, that all of Hewitt's concerns with rhetoric, with the determination displayed in 'Mosaic' to resist the selectivity of history and his ambition for a better society, combine in a magnificent, moving lament:

> Bear in mind these dead:
> I can find no plainer words....
>
> The careful words of my injunction
> are unrhetorical, as neutral
> and unaligned as any I know....

> So I say only: bear in mind
> those men and lads killed in the streets;
> but do not differentiate between
> those deliberately gunned down
> and those caught by unaddressed bullets:
> such distinctions are not relevant.
>
> Bear in mind the skipping child hit
> by the anonymous ricochet;
> the man shot at his own fireside
> with his staring family around him....[66]

The poem shows Hewitt assuming the bardic role as memorialist in speaking to his nation as 'this moment' demands. He is attentive to his own 'plain' language and to the histories which that language makes him attend to in its turn – the histories of those accidentally caught up in the crossfire, as well as those who have deliberately taken up arms for their cause. Later in the poem he does not deny the potential for mythologizing the dead as martyrs, indeed sees it as a necessary part of the history, but, in the demands of the moment, thinks that it is better to 'bear in mind these dead.' The poem dares all levels of rhetoric, from the detailing of the individual deaths to an abstract rhetorical consideration of patriotism. But the whole is contained by the repeated injunction to 'Bear in mind these dead'. Out of even this moment, Hewitt seems to be saying, there might come some greater understanding if the event is interpreted properly, if no part of its history is denied and if the rhetoric remains unaligned.

Hewitt emerges from these poems on the 'Troubles', as from the earlier work, as a much more tentative poet, a poet more attentive to the moment and to discontinuity, than some of his critics who accept only the rhetoric of 'the comfortable pace/of safe tradition' which the poems themselves offer at face value can allow. In this he is a *modern* poet, one who has learnt both from the more immediate example of Yeats and from the eclectic reading he conducted in poetry across the century. Certainly in the coinage 'poemosaic', and in the continuation of the 'tesserae' as a metaphor throughout his career, Hewitt emerges as a poet less at ease either in a single racial or poetic tradition than he at first seems. In the frequent divergences and abrupt diremptions between his poetic theory and his poetic practice, as in the strained attempt in his work to reconcile a tolerant, balanced politics with a divisive subject matter, resides many of the dilemmas faced by the next generations of poets responding to the violent history of their times.

3

Thomas Kinsella's Poetic of Unease

Contrary to John Hewitt's eclectic and hesitant Ulster negotiations with poetry and history, the Dublin poet Thomas Kinsella has for some decades been a purposeful explorer of two seemingly contradictory poetic impulses in the modern world. One impulse demands fidelity to the native yet, because of the nation's colonization, dual Irish tradition, which includes English and Gaelic writing. The other impulse is concerned to further the aesthetic and technical experiments of international modernist writers like Ezra Pound and William Carlos Williams.

Indeed, Kinsella has made the dislocation between these two impulses the basis of his own fractured and demanding poetic. Yet out of this division of impulse emerges a poetic that has proved fluent and adaptable to the historical and experiential moment; Kinsella has been able to translate it into some strikingly forceful and persuasive poems which respond to both public and openly political concerns. *Nightwalker* of 1968 reviewed the political and economic state of the Republic in the 1960s. *Fifteen Dead*, which appeared in 1979, was a gathering of four occasional poems which had appeared in Dublin in the early 1970s, and opened with *Butcher's Dozen*, an angry response to the report of the Widgery Tribunal of Enquiry into the Bloody Sunday killings. The high modernist demands within Kinsella's poetic, therefore, are crossed with a literary and political concern with events in the whole island, and offer a response to traumatic moments in its recent history which are both focused and immediate.

It is my purpose in this chapter to explore Kinsella's various dialectical, poetic mediations between those contradictory and contrasting local and international impulses which generate this adaptability, mediations grounded in his particular exploitation and appropriation of modernist theory and practice. These mediations in their turn parallel and illuminate wider aesthetic and philo-

74

sophical debates about the nature and function of poetry in relation to modernity. As my opening chapter showed, such debates
about the status and relevance of works of art in the modern world
have received urgent theoretical attention by Theodor Adorno as
he furthered the insights of his collaborator Walter Benjamin, particularly those of Benjamin's essay 'The Work of Art in the Age of
Mechanical Reproduction'. Both thinkers share with Kinsella a
sense of history as oppression and discontinuity, and in their
reading of these characteristics into the moment of modernity they
in their turn illuminate the uneasy mediations in Kinsella's work.

Thomas Kinsella was born in Dublin in 1928, was raised in a
village near the city, studied economics at University College, and
worked as a Civil Servant in the Department of Finance until 1965,
when he became first a poet in residence and then a Professor of
English in the United States. Even during his time as Professor in
Philadelphia, however, he managed to spend eight months of each
year in his natal city; 'I believe I might have festered and gone
sterile if I hadn't managed to come back to Dublin,' he said in an interview with John Haffenden.[1]

This attention to his home city has always extended to the fact
that he has actively been involved in making possible the publication of new work by Irish poets there. He finds the 'authoritative
publication of Irish writers by English publishing houses, and authoritative comment in English papers and journals validating the
work for the home audience' a scandalous after-effect of the colonization of the country, and has sought to counter that outrage in
several ways.[2] He was involved in founding, with Liam Miller, the
Dolmen Press in Dublin in 1951, and, since the 1972 *Butcher's Dozen*,
has issued his own sequences in pamphlets from his own Peppercanister Press. He has never himself primarily sought publication in
Britain, and the pamphlets were only later collected together and
published there through arrangement with Oxford University
Press.

Such deep personal and poetic rejection of the colonizer, operating
as it does in Kinsella alongside an allegiance to American modernist
poetic practice ('I'm certainly grateful to the work of Ezra Pound and
William Carlos Williams for having opened up particular lines of
style,' he also told Haffenden[3]), reflects the postwar condition of the
Republic which greeted his coming into maturity. The South's neutrality during the Second World War had served to isolate it from
the international community, and most particularly from Britain. But

Terence Brown has claimed that this inwardness paradoxically 'had mobilized Irish public opinion for the first time to consider the twenty-six-county-state as the primary unit of national loyalty':

> ...that it was possible for the twenty-six counties of Ireland to be a nation state without the distinguishing marks of language and a hermetically sealed national culture.[4]

There was an initial period of strong economic growth in the postwar years but this was soon followed by a slump which lasted for most of the rest of the 1950s, until radical plans were adopted by Sean Lemass to bring the Republic's economy into line with the others of modern capitalist Europe when he became Taoiseach in 1959. But despite this period of stagnation and uncertainty, there were signs that the way was being prepared for the future.

The new assurance that the Republic was an independent nation fit to take its place among other modern nations, and particularly as a nation independent of Britain, was confirmed by the External Relations Act of 1948, which finally broke the the country's links with the Commonwealth. In the immediate postwar years the Republic received money from the European Recovery Fund to improve housing and transport conditions; in 1946 President de Valera had stated his agreement with the UN's founding Charter, and in 1956 (after a decade of objection by USSR, aggrieved at the country's neutrality during the war) it became a full member of the organization.

Most crucially for the historical perspectives which I describe Kinsella's poetry taking up, the period of new international relations and finance brought a crucial shift in the country's population from the country to the city. In 1951 almost a third of Dublin's inhabitants had been born outside the city, and across the decade this expansion caused by people moving in from the country to find the new opportunities of employment there was to accelerate rapidly. This break with the rural values which had dominated Irish life and the nation's economy had a significant effect, among other things, on the numbers of Gaelic speakers in the country, which drastically reduced during these years. No longer was it as possible for the Irish nation to establish its identity on the basis of an insular, nostalgic, rural, Gaelic-speaking past.

But, as a result of even these tentative signs of change, there was a range of new cultural possibilities opening up in these years, with the founding of new literary magazines by a younger generation of writers, magazines like *Irish Writing*, *Poetry Ireland* or *Envoy*, which gave that generation greater opportunities of publication. For the first time since the 1930s when Denis Devlin and Brian Coffey (who both lived abroad) had sought to open Irish poetry to modernist experiment, the South seemed part of a broader international literary context. As a crucial part of this new openness, the activities of the Censorship Board were relaxed across these years, bringing a greater freedom to publish works which did not toe the line of the predominant ideology on religious and sexual matters dictated by the Catholic church. Further, for the first time it was possible to hear international symphonic music in Ireland; it was also possible to see the works of Irish painters and artists influenced by international modernist ideas in the art galleries alongside the continental originals.

Kinsella's thinking in response to this new internationalism produced in him a strong awareness of the disadvantages with which the writer from his own country was struggling. In 1966 Kinsella spoke of the dilemmas of 'The Irish Writer' who recognizes that to write in the Irish language would be to write in a language which 'is doomed, rejected by its people'. He claims that the meagreness of the poetry produced in the nineteenth century in English by Irish poets means the modern Irish writer is doubly bereft of a tradition upon which he or she can draw; they must therefore look with envy on those writing in England:

> ...[I] look for the past in myself. An English poet would have an easier time of it....No matter what his preoccupations might be, he will find his forebears in English poetry; as inheritor of the parent language he is free to 'repatriate' a great American poet or a great Irish poet. As he looks backward, the line might begin with Yeats and T.S. Eliot and continue with Matthew Arnold and Wordsworth and Keats and Pope – and so on through the mainstream of a tradition. An Irish poet will only have the first point in common with this. Or so I found in my own case, when I try to identify my forebears.[5]

The greatness of the loss involved in the dying out of Irish-language literature is re-emphasized by the fact that that literature 'has an air of continuity and shared history' which Kinsella keenly feels the lack of in modern writing by Irish writers using English.

This is reinforced further for him by the fact that the literature that Irish schoolchildren are brought up with is English, which does not include material familiar in everyday Irish life.[6] The Irish poet is, therefore, a solitary, totally isolated figure, having to make his writing from his personal resources.[7] Each modern Irish writer is, in effect, making a fresh start, developing his or her own means of conveying their experience on their own terms.

At the end of 'The Irish Writer', however, Kinsella makes a characteristic return upon himself. He reaffirms this sense of solitude and isolation for the modern writer, while extending his terms beyond the immediate national situation. Rather, he raises questions about the value of *all* tradition, wherever it is derived from. Does tradition, he asks, give a writer a deeper feeling for the experience which is gathered up in it, or lead to a better understanding of that experience?

> I doubt it. It is not as though literature, or national life, were a corporate, national investigation of a corporate, national experience – as though a nation were a single animal, with one complex artistic feeler. This maybe true for brief great periods that have 'unity of being', like those that produced Greek and Shakespearean tragedy....But for the present – especially in this present – it seems that every writer has to make the imaginative grasp at identity for himself....

Once again, Kinsella's aesthetic is closely interwoven with the opening of the South to the economics of modern international capitialism, with its concurrent cultural effects. Kinsella's version of Yeats's 'unity of being' is clearly derived from that sense of the greatness of the loss which the modern Irish writer suffers by being at a remove from the inheritance provided by poetry in the Irish language.[8] And yet the shift between this penultimate paragraph of the essay and the last one famously establishes such preoccupations within a world vision:

> To look at it more remotely still: pending the achievement of some total human unity of being, every writer in the modern world – since he can't be in all the literary traditions at once – is the inheritor of a gapped, discontinuous, polyglot tradition.
>
> Nevertheless, if the function of tradition is to link us living with the significant past, this is done as well by a broken

tradition as by a whole one – however painful it maybe humanly speaking. I am certain that a great part of the significance of my own past, as I try to write my poetry, is that that past *is* mutilated.[9]

This in effect links the modern experience of the world in its discontinuity with Ireland's history, which has been actively 'mutilated' through its colonization by the British.[10] The international seems to Thomas Kinsella both a projection of the local world and the provider of suitable literary models, in the figures of Pound and Williams, by which that world might be ordered.

It is on these grounds that Kinsella had, earlier in this essay, finally dismissed as a suitable influence on his work the one *poetic* forebear he felt the modern Irish poet writing in English might have: W.B. Yeats. As a poet, he argued, Yeats is 'preoccupied with the leading work of the imagination which renders demagoguery – and all the doings of history that are not embodied in his imagining self – of no account. The continuity or the mutilation of traditions becomes, in itself, irrelevant as the artist steps back from his entire world'. In Kinsella's view, then, Yeats's striving for a 'unity of being' to set against the debilitating drift of the 'filthy modern tide' makes him unable to accept into his writing the true conditions of modern Ireland. In the quest for a forebear, Kinsella turns to the one Irish writer who he thinks has harnessed that reality to his own art:

Joyce's...relationship with the modern world is direct and intimate. He knows the filthy modern tide and immerses himself in it to do his work. ...The filthy modern tide does not run only in Ireland, of course, and Joyce's act of continuity is done with a difference: he simultaneously revives the Irish tradition and admits the modern world....Joyce is the true father.[11]

Joyce's Catholic inheritance and his centring of his work on Dublin makes him of course more immediately relevant for Kinsella than the Anglo-Irish Yeats. It is Joyce's ability to go with the flow, to key into the deepest national tradition and myth while sustaining a picture of the modern world as a disjunctive, polyphonic place, which establishes him for Kinsella as offering redemptive hope for the tradition: 'Joyce stands for [tradition] as continuous, or healed – or healing – from its mutilation', he is 'the first major Irish writer to speak for Irish reality since the death of the Irish language.'[12] Joyce's sheer inclusiveness, as compared to Yeats's isolating selectivity, manages to contain those divisions which are inherent within the history of Ireland, while simultaneously setting that history within the wider context of similar divisions experienced by everyone in the modern world.

Kinsella's own poetry, however, reveals the difficulty in attaining that inclusiveness and integration – indeed the near impossibility of doing so within the ever-changing modernity of Ireland, a modernization which has accelerated greatly since Joyce's day. Therefore lines of the struggle between his possible native forebears continue to be complexly traced through Kinsella's poetry. The two literary forebears involved in his dialectic, Yeats and Joyce, are not always as clearly divisible as the resolved terms of his argument in 'The Irish Writer' might suggest. Joyce's 'stream of consciousness' technique lies behind the nightmarish, hallucinatory dreamworlds of Kinsella's sequences from the 1968 *Nightwalker and Other Poems* onward, but Yeats still figures both as important interlocutor and as influencer of the method of the poetry itself.[13]

Indeed, this negotiation with the influence of Yeats figures in the *Nightwalker* collection itself, in a poem which complicates and questions the architectural metaphors in Yeats's work in ways that Hewitt had done and Montague and Heaney were to do. In 'Magnanimity', Kinsella describes himself responding to a suggestion of Austin Clarke's that 'Coole might be built again as a place for poets':

> I am sure that there are no places for poets,
> Only changing habitations for verse to outlast.
> Your own house, isolated by a stream, exists
> For your use while you live – like your body and your world.[14]

This confirms the argument posited in 'The Irish Writer' that the modern poet must be self-sufficient while not seeking to step outside of the flow of history. The artist is conceived of as being in a permanent state of exile, with no fixed place or tradition to inhabit. 'Helpless commonness encroaches', we are told, in what seems an ambiguous, perhaps even regretful, reproach to Yeats's assertion of the nobility of art. 'Houses shall pass away, and all give place to signposts and chicken wire.' Kinsella rejects the Yeatsian quest, as exemplified in the Byzantium poems, to establish art's timelessness. He rejects the founding of places of writing, of a transcendent bulwark against history, and the demagogic separation of the writer from the world. For him, change offers a challenge to all platonic endurance, a challenge which poetry must continually struggle to overcome. Kinsella in this poem wants art to recognize the flow of history, history as loss and passing away in accord with Irish experience. He recognizes the need to pay tribute to the fugitive and elusive nature of that history.

Yet, in the title sequence of *Nightwalker*, Kinsella seems to offer a contradictory view to this one, a view which steps outside and sets itself against the grain of history in ways exactly anticipated by Yeats. Kinsella produces an attack on the Ireland of the 1960s which is the equal to anything in Yeats's dismissal of the Paudeens, the rising Catholic middle classes, of his own day. After Sean Lemass became Taoiseach in 1959, he instituted a plan which led to massive economic expansion and increase in foreign investment in the Republic. But this was not the kind of import that Kinsella as a poet cared for. He had, of course, directly witnessed the beginning of Lemass's changes as a civil servant in the Department of Finance, and 'Nightwalker' contains some details of his daily life in the office when putting the plans into effect. He launches a withering attack on the 'fixed ideas' which he had to operate within, in a string of sarcastic rhetorical questions:

> ...[Is it not] acceptable
> That during a transitional period
> Development should express itself in forms
> Without principle, based on fixed ideas –
> Robed in spattered iron
> At the harbour mouth she stands, Productive Investment,
> And beckons the nations through our gold half-door...
> While native businessmen and managers
> Drift with them, chatting, over to the window
> To show them our growing city, give them a feeling
> Of what is possible; our labour pool,
> The tax concessions to foreign capital....[15]

True to his resistance to such fixed ideas, the persona of the poem immediately rejects this as 'Morose condemnation.../It is a weakness, and turns on itself'. Contrary to the terms of Lemassian open market economics, Kinsella's is a poetry of process, one in which seeming fixities of position and of tone are immediately undercut. But the splenetic, Yeats-like moment of denunciation here still stands out, its critical force in relation to contemporary history seemingly at odds with his ethos of a Joycean immersion in 'the filthy modern tide'.

Such contradiction continues into the poetry of the later part of Kinsella's career. The tone of wilful cantankerousness in his 1994 *From Centre City*, the splenetic denunciations of the Dublin City Corporation for its inner city development policy, and the scorn for his contemporaries again conjure the spirit of Yeats. Indeed, Yeats's 'own sour duel with the middle classes' is meditated upon in the admiring poem 'At the Western Ocean's Edge', where, despite the 'mental strife' the duel involves, Yeats is seen as having won through to mastery, to personal, even religious insight, 'renewal in reverse,/emotional response, the revelation'.[16] Once again it is the challenge offered by contemporary circumstance in its debility which is directly a spur to poetic achievement for Kinsella, an attention to the quotidian which serves to define the *personal* vision. We see Kinsella reconfirmed as an isolated, Yeatsian poet, railing against the capitalist ethos into which modern Ireland has lapsed. This raises questions, unresoved here or elsewhere in his work, about the critical role which poetry might play in relation to society and its politics. A total immersion in the modern tide might involve a total complicity with its terms, a destruction of aesthetic distance and corruption of the poetry by the terms of consumerist expansion. Kinsella's poetic economy bears a shifting, uneasy relation to modern political economies, one which counters their 'fixed ideas' with its own critical attitude which is then immediately reviewed as part of the poem's structural momentum.

This has crucial effects upon the formal dilemmas integral to his poetry. Kinsella builds long sequences out of self-contained poetic paragraphs or episodes, which he then at once questions, as in the attack on the new economics in 'Nightwalker' quoted above. His career is rare among contemporary Irish poets in that it contains an epic ambition on the lines of Pound's 50-year labour in *The Cantos*. But, as with Pound, the relation between the individual poetic or lyric image and the musical or hegemonic structure of the whole remains radically uncertain, even potentially incoherent, as I will illustrate. What I would want to question is way in which some of Kinsella's reviewers perceive easy and finally mystical continuities in his work. Brian John has claimed that:

The poet shapes chaotic, disparate experiences into an ordered unity, throwing light on the nature and evolution of the self and the world. He establishes correspondences, linking present and past, family with national histories, and tracing a dialectical process at the very heart of existence itself.[17]

But the immediacy with which this shaping and establishment of correspondence is envisaged here is at odds both with the tentative tone, the ennui and the frequent self-referential images of labour in the work – as in 'Worker in Mirror, at his Bench':

> It is tedious, yes.
> The process is elaborate, and wasteful
> – a dangerous litter of lacerating pieces
> collects. Let my rubbish stand witness…
> Smile, stirring it idly with a shoe.
> Take, for example, this work in hand:
> out of its waste matter
> it should emerge light and solid.[18]

This is a poetic which very much accepts the modern world as a waste land and sees the process of making as involved in that, casting off dangerous materials in order to attain what form it can. The rubbish then stands as evidence of that process, something to be picked over and played with by its viewer/reader.

This process is one which Kinsella takes up when describing the relation between the form and the content of poetry, as in the interview with Haffenden. Kinsella makes much of what he calls the writer's necessary 'responsibility toward actuality', in which, in the Joycean manner, experience is simply described as it happened in the poetry rather than altered to fit a pattern. The references in the poem must 'be exact': 'I would settle for the "random pursuit" of a poem rather than labour to produce something coherent and recognizable and traditional.'[19]

Further to this rejection of the coherent and the traditional if the content does not demand it, Kinsella has several times insisted in interview that he no longer believes even in the unity or coherence of a single poem. He told Dennis O'Driscoll that:

One of the things that has disappeared, by comparison with the early work, is the notion of a 'complete' poem, the idea that a poem can have a beginning, middle and end and be a satisfactory work of art thereby. The unity is a much bigger one than that. And it isn't a sequence or a set of connected long poems. It's a totality that is happening, with the individual poem a contribution to something accumulating.[20]

The totalizing ambition of this is obviously equivalent to Pound's in *The Cantos* as well as to what Kinsella calls 'a kind of creative relaxation in the face of complex reality', which he told Haffenden he learnt from William Carlos Williams – 'It's a matter of staying agile so that one's poetic organism can respond fully. The response becomes one's life-work, rather than a sequence of individual poems.'[21] Kinsella's adoption of a poetry of anti-narrative, one paradoxically governed by an organic metaphor, is concurrent with his vision of history and literary tradition as gapped, discontinuous and, in Ireland's case, 'mutilated'. Further, it might be claimed as a basis of this style of argument (and this is of extreme importance for Kinsella's response to Bloody Sunday) that all poems are by definition *occasional* poems, representing a phase in the growth of the accumulating 'poetic organism'. The individual poem is a moment's experience in the life-work.

What we constantly find in Kinsella's writing, then, is an awkward integration between, on the one hand, the Yeatsian lyric, aesthetically and politically standing against the flow of experience, and, on the other hand, a more expansive, cumulative modernist poetic of process. The larger sequences continue to offer this Yeatsian critical and self-critical view, as when in the poetry Kinsella contradicts the seamless vision given in the O'Driscoll interview by questioning its founding organic metaphor (Eavan Boland has described this 'search of a dislocated intelligence determined to find some order and suspicious of what he finds as soon as he finds it' a sign of Kinsella's resolute modernism[22]). Images of growth often associated with love are often modulated into, or set directly, against images of decay. The 'credo' which blazes forth from the third section of 'Nightwalker' – 'I believe now that love is half persistence,/A medium in which, from change to change,/Understanding may be gathered'[23] – is immediately modified by the next verse paragraph, in which an address to the moon serves to confirm the poet's own unhappiness in the drained world of the contemporary city – 'Virgin most pure, bright/In the dregs of the harbour: moon of my dismay...'. The end of the sequence then accepts this as the true note – 'I think this is the Sea of Disappointment'.

The understanding which might have been gathered through love (in which some resonances of religious experience remain) leads inevitably to failure. At the poetic level, of course, this might be read as the self-acknowledged failure of the poem to give adequate expression to its experience. Yet the 'Disappointment' here might also be one which anticipates the audience's response, one which recognizes Kinsella's inability to offer any of the traditional consolations of poetry. Kinsella's resolute and extreme modernist poetic does not seek to offer the kinds of hope or lyric resolution contemplated, say, by Seamus Heaney's albeit tentative dalliance with the notion that 'the end of art is peace'.[24] Kinsella recognizes that his is an isolated stance, but within his dogged refusal to console lies his persistence with, and adherence to, the modern world, a world correlative to Ireland's historical experience. His remains a deterministic history and poetic, which wins its moments of hope from a background of mutilation and failure.

'Hen Woman', one of the most achieved and anthologized of Kinsella's poems, is marvellously suspended in this contradictory dilemma between organicism and fragmented failure. Time and process are slowed as the poet and reader fascinatedly watch an egg emerge from a chicken held in the woman's arms then fall towards a drain. The poem seems caught in a continuous round from potential to waste:

> Through what seemed a whole year it fell
> – as it still falls, for me,
> solid and light, the red gold beating
> in its silvery womb,
> alive as the yolk and white
> of my eye; as it will continue
> to fall, probably, until I die,
> through the vast indifferent spaces
> with which I am empty.

The tentative ('seemed', 'for me', 'probably') historical mediation between past ('it fell'), present ('it still falls') and future ('it will continue/to fall') offers an explicit paradigm of Kinsella's poetic. A proferred promise or hope in the egg symbol is determined and withheld by a repetitive, entropic movement towards dissipation, waste and failure. The Hen Woman's cheery assertion that '"It's all one./There's plenty more where that came from"' wryly promises both more poems of this kind and a deep difficulty in adopting a critical distance from them – to what end such waste? will it ever end? This difficulty is captured in the poem's last two lines 'Hen to pan!/It was a simple world', where the tone is deliberately all awry. Is there triumph in the exclamation, triumph at the poem's masterly enactment of the 'fall' of the 'egg of being', or simply shock at the brutal intransigence of that process? Is it the case that the world is no longer simple, that the past's seeming innocence can no longer be countenanced, and that modern processes are more thwarting than previously? Is the Hen Woman's hope naïve, is the last line ironic, or savagely sarcastic?

The poem is inscrutable, refusing finally to read its own processes while seemingly demanding that such a reading must take place, that the tone be judged correctly. Yet the poetic voice refuses to establish a tonality which governs process, making the potential for growth towards artistic plenitude itself questionable and uncertain. The process continually spirals down from an experience in which even the perceiving eye is implicated (the egg is 'alive as the yolk and white/of my eye') towards the future 'drained down'. This paradoxically serves merely to confirm the poet's indifference and emptiness: 'there is no end to that which,/not understood, may yet be noted/and hoarded in the imagination/...there to undergo its...growth'. Kinsella toys with a Romantic paradigm in which play of the imagination on experience might lead to growth and understanding, but recognizes also that the process is endless, a continual 'searching in its own tissue/for the structure/in which it may wake.'[25] The poetry is, then, locked in a present which cannot guarantee fulfilment even as it proffers it. The poem's perpetual transitional phase underscores its modernism, but it is a modernism that is also deeply historical, continually searching for a structure and pattern which continually eludes it. In this sense the poem might provide an allegory for the fate of the Republic itself; an original hopeful unity which runs to waste in diffuse Lemassian economics.

Often elsewhere in Kinsella's poetry, the 'actuality' and elusive presence behind the 'historically changing constellation of moments' has been provided by the history of his own family, by memories of and stories from and about his grandparents and parents. There is a telling recycling of some of the passages from

'The Irish Writer' essay which I quoted above in a 1973 essay called 'The Divided Mind'. In this later piece, sentences describing the 'greatness of the loss' which the death of literature in Irish had brought about for the Irish writer are swung dramatically towards a different conclusion, one closer to home than the literary considerations which so governed the earlier essay:

> I recognize that I stand on one side of a great rift, and can feel the discontinuity in myself. It is a matter of people and places as well as writing – of coming from a broken and uprooted family, of being drawn to those who share my origins and finding that we cannot share our lives.[26]

The national and literary discontinuities which exert so great a pressure on Kinsella's work are continually present, therefore, in the poetry about personal and family experience. As with a reading of Eliot's *The Waste Land*, it is difficult to extricate the status of the poetry as cultural/historical diagnosis from its status as personal testament; but it is the experience of brokenness which is made to form, paradoxically, a continuity between the two.

This has the important effect of making history in Kinsella a matter of report, something carried down through the family into the poetic voice rather than through remote sources. History, like Kinsella's experience of the discontinuities of the modern world, is conflated into 'my past'. In 'Ritual of Departure', Kinsella makes a metaphor of uprooting literal. The poem includes history – the past of the city of Dublin after the Act of Union ('a century and a half ago...stripped of Parliament,/Lying powerless in sweet-breathing death-ease') – alongside the migration of the Kinsella family from the country into the city. There is, however, no compensatory pastoral nostalgia derived from that migration, anachronistically in line, perhaps, with the growing concentration of the population of the South in Dublin across the years of Kinsella's maturity. The country lies outside of his, and the people's, modern experience. The 'names/Settling and intermixing' on the country soil show 'The seed in slow retreat, through time and blood', while the city is equated with suffocating enervation as the family 'light' comes to 'creep across grey floorboards,/Sink in plush in the staleness of an inner room.' In the final lines of the poem the rooting in the earth for continuities uncovers blight. The history of Ireland, and the history of the Kinsella family, are cast as continuing Great Hungers (after the period of famine caused by potato blight in the 1840s, a famine in which, it has been claimed, Britain did little to aid the Irish and even made things worse):

> I scoop at the earth, and sense famine, a first
> Sourness in the clay. The roots tear softly.[27]

The move of the family from the country to the city does not provide, then, any opportunity for the poetry to attach itself to the resources of an earlier, transcendent tradition of the earth. There is a sense of familial and national historical blight here which runs counter to poetry's organic potential, one which, indeed, stalls any enactment of that potential. Rather, it confirms Kinsella's vision of history as a continuous falling away from a source that was already receding in the countryside and which can never be recovered. The history of the oppression of the Irish nation, caught here at the moment of 'forced Union', where the Georgian facades of Dublin simply provide a theatrical backdrop for the impoverished native population – 'A portico, beggars moving on the steps' – is consonant with the history of the family. But Kinsella inserts another turn which once more confirms the loss of a shared history, this time because of his anxieties surrounding the forcing of an aesthetic 'reading' on that history. He acknowledges his own distance from the family history by self-consciously casting it as a 'Landscape with ancestral figures'.[28] All settings seem hollow and false as the history itself spirals down sickly through them.[29]

'Ritual of Departure' sets family history baldly alongside national history by breaking up the poem into sections separated clearly on the page. To a certain extent the reading of continuity between the two strains, although implied in the process of reading sequentially through the book, is a critical act. Elsewhere in Kinsella, history appears as part of the series of vignettes which set autobiographical poems against poems describing historical prints of the city of Dublin in 'St. Catherine's Clock' from *Blood and Family*; as a part of the family inheritance in the handing down of stories related to the 1798 United Irishmen rising from one generation to the next in the earlier 'His Father's Hands' from *One and Other Poems* ('Your family, Thomas, met with and helped/many of the Croppies'); or as part of the perambulations of 'A Country Walk' from *Downstream* ('There the first Normans massacred my fathers'). However, such explicit and potentially nationalistic description of the history of colonization which Ireland has suffered is, as the title of this last example shows, always moved away from. Kinsella's modernist poetic of process indeed makes him the ideal perambu-latory poet, a poet reminiscent of Benjamin's *flaneur*,[30] casting his eye on one detail and recounting one thought before passing on to something else. In these ways his poetic also follows Joyce's mod-ernism, founded as it is upon similar movements of his novels' characters around the same city. 'A Country Walk' has been fol-lowed by later poetic strolls between past and present in 'Nightwalker', in 'The High Road' from *New Poems 1973*, which again includes a passage of 'straight' history, this time literally in-serted into the walk by being placed between brackets, and in later works such as 'The Back Lane' in *From Centre City*.

The trajectory of the early 'A Country Walk' remains typical, however. After the passage recounting the Norman and Cromwellian conquests of Ireland, Kinsella arrives at a cross comem-morating someone who died in the Easter 1916 rebellion, then:

> Around the corner, in an open square,
> I come upon the sombre monuments
> That bear their names: MacDonagh & McBride
> Merchants; Connolly's Commercial Arms....[31]

The names of the leaders of the Rising at Easter 1916, names chanted in Yeats's heroic lament for them as 'A terrible beauty is born', are here seen to have been stripped in modern Ireland of that mythic status. In a recognition once again recalling Yeats's and Kinsella's view that commercial values had predominated over symbolic ones, the leaders' names appear on commercial and pub signs. As the resonance of that history is lost or forgotten, the poet is once again returned upon himself as:

> Their windows gave back my stolid self
> In attitudes of staring as I paced
> Their otherworldly gloom, reflected light
> Playing on lens and raincoat stonily.

'Too long a sacrifice/Can make a stone of the heart', Yeats's poem acknowledges; Kinsella recognizes that, with the prolonged history of suffering in Ireland, history has indeed become petrified within the living stream, and that he can only strike attitudes within its 'reflected light'. At the end of 'A Country Walk' the River Liffey eternally carries the detritus of such waste history, 'An endless debris through the failing dusk'. There is some stirring of 'the inert', some loosening of 'heart and tongue' for Kinsella at the end of the walk, as the evening star rises, but the hurtling waters of the river continue to bear their reduced, troubled aftermath.

Kinsella's vision of history adamantly resists, therefore, a sense of it as progress, but rather, as in the writer's career, one of accumulation, and accumulation of cast-off detritus. To string such punctuating moments of 'real' history together into a coherent redeeming narrative would be to betray those who have made sacrifices. It would also betray the sense that even heroism is of the moment, and that heroism, like poetry, is partial and liable to fragment, that it will be read differently as time flows on. As such, the episodic nature of Kinsella's poetic sequences, their refusal of the resonant architectonics of Yeatsian formal unity while containing self-sufficient moments within their progress, is a warrant of their openness to history. The episodes in the poetry are part of the larger flow onwards, but are self-contained and self-contradictory verse paragraphs in themselves, their relation to the rest of the poem often abstract and seemingly random. In this, Kinsella's poetic mirrors the modernist, materialist historiography put forward by Theodor Adorno and by Walter Benjamin. Benjamin, who equated progressivist, universalizing versions of history with the reactionary oppression of the Nazis, argued against it by writing that 'Its method is additive; it musters a mass of data to fill the homogeneous, empty time. Materialistic historiography, on the other hand, is based on a constructive principle. Thinking involves not only the flow of thoughts, but their arrest as well.'[32] Such arrested thoughts he gave the Leibnitzian title of 'monads'.[33]

Because of its frequent need to recognize arresting moments within the 'tide' and to revise its episodes from within, Kinsella's totalizing modernist poetic of process shares none of the inevitable flirtation with totalitarian politics in his poetic master, Pound. His concern to acknowledge the 'actuality' of the individual moment and the specific 'mutilations' within the overall flow of history directly counters Pound's self-misconceiving audacity in claiming on behalf of poets that 'All values ultimately come from our judicial sentences.'[34] Rather, Kinsella's poetic inverts that dictatorialism and accepts a consonance between the historical and the aesthetic such as that suggested by Benjamin's collaborator, Adorno:

All works of art...belong to a complex of problems. As such they participate in history, transcending their uniqueness. The specific problem-context of each and every one of them is the place where the external empirical world impinges on the constitution of the aesthetic monads. It is here that the aesthetic particular interacts with its concept. History is thus an integral part of aesthetic theory, whose categories are radically historical, so much so that the development of aesthetics seems to have a deterministic quality to it.[35]

This passage from Adorno's *Aesthetic Theory* carries the full burden of the paradoxical nature of all such thought, whereby the potential contradiction between works of the moment is held in tension with a movement beyond in which they become part of a historical 'complex of problems'. This is consonant with the contradictions and paradoxes in Kinsella's own practice and theory of poetry.

The organic metaphor to which he constantly returns presents the work as an accumulation of such 'aesthetic monads' both within the separate verse paragraphs of the sequences and between the sequences and books as a whole. He has made the complex of problems surrounding loss and discontinuity along with an anguished sense of temporality integral to his modernist poetic. It is a poetic which simultaneously reflects and captures and is part of the dissolution of the history out of which he is writing, a history which infects every aspect of his subject matter and form. It also mediates that awkward clash of influences which I have been describing in his work, between a Yeatsian, critical, isolationist stance and a Joycean immersion in the flow of the 'filthy modern tide'. Each verse paragraph might be taken as an arrest, a fix upon history (in Benjamin's terms 'a constellation pregnant with tensions'), but only until the poem moves on again. In the awkward integration and setting of one such paragraph against the next, there is an opening for a critical act to enter, and for Kinsella's audience to take their own possible, if never final, 'fix' upon the poetry. It is through the gaps between the lyric moment of history and its correlative failed epic that an audience, and specifically an Irish audience which shares a historical mutilation with these aesthetic ones, might begin their reading.

As a further element within the contradictory strains in his poetry, Kinsella's collections also contain many abstract, mythical pieces, often carrying his theme of Irish poet as originator into concerns of nationhood and racial origin. These poems stem from, repeat and extend his familiar fraught recognition of loss and distance. They re-emphasize loss at either the personal-familial and the literary-national levels, and establish those continuities claimed in 'The Divided Mind' passage between the two (Pound's own epic including history, *The Cantos*, also seeks out rhymes between historical and mythic experiences).

To take the earliest example of this, the poem 'Tear', from *New Poems 1973*, recalls the visit of Kinsella as a boy to the deathbed of his grandmother, and his failure to give her a parting kiss. He cries a solitary tear at his failure:

> Yet I had to kiss.
> I knelt by the bulk of the death bed
> and sank my face in the chill
> and smell of her black aprons.
>
> Snuff and musk, the folds against my eyelids,
> carried me into a derelict place....
>
> I found myself disturbing
> dead ashes for any trace
> of warmth, when far off
> in the vaults a single drop
> splashed.[36]

The loss commemorated in this poem is then to resonate through the poems in the second section of the book, which is divided from the first by a blank page, and then a page carrying only the phrase 'a single drop'. This section is made up of mythic/allegorical poems on origins and loss, with the drama of meeting and contact between its characters fleeting, brief and literally divisive. 'Nuchal (a fragment)' recalls the 'monstrous' dream of a woman who is the divider of a rivulet into 'Four rivers reaching toward th'encircling sea,/that bitter river'. 'A single drop echoed in the depths', we are told, after the momentary blaze of light brought about by the meeting of the moon figure with Endymion in the poem of that title.

'Survivor' continues the theme of a self-divided, isolated individual into a myth of colonization and origin ('our first home') which does not lead to reconciliation. 'Far back, a lost echoing/single drop' is heard, which is both the source of the poem and of the inability of the poet to recover fully the original narrative behind it. The poem exists as a sequence of hallucinatory fragments, in which we gather that the hope engendered by the discovery of a new land has brought a recognition that this is 'a land of the dead' bringing sickness, starvation and disease. Yet even the hopeful discovery of the new land is in turn a source of uncertainty as to true origin:

> Long ago, abuse and terror...
>
> O fair beginning...
>
> landfall – an entire new world
> floating on the ocean like a cloud
> with a forest covering and clean empty shores.
> We were coming from... Distilled from sunlight?
> or the crests of foam?
> From Paradise...
> In the southern coasts of the East... In terror...[37]

Even this dubious hope and excitement is soon betrayed for the 'Survivor', however, as the images of terror and paucity recalling those used elsewhere in connection with the Irish Famine take over; 'There is nothing here for sustenance', we are told, 'Naked. Wretch. Wither.'

Consonant with Kinsella's argument that there is a larger organization to his work, that we must look not only beyond single poems but beyond each book for the accumulation which makes up the 'poetic organism', the themes of 'Survivor' are taken up in 'Finistere' in the next book, *One and Other Poems*. This book explicitly addresses the theme of artistic solitude derived from Yeats; the artist's situation becomes a paradigm of Irish historical disconnection, whatever its adaptation of wider modernist practices. In 'Finistere', the isolation of the survivor-persona is fed into the numerical organization of the book as a whole in the poem's opening: 'I/One...'. This poem on foundations is, however, generally more positive in tone than 'Survivor', although again it uses the description of historical/mythical discovery to address questions of ultimate origin. After a hellish journey across the sea ('We drew close together, as one,/and turned inward, salt chaos/rolling in silence all around us'), the 'bad dream ends' as the travellers land and we hear the first poem of the poet/narrator on landing:

My tongue stumbled

Who
is a breath
that makes the wind
that makes the wave
that makes this voice?[38]

The celebratory instinct at landfall is somewhat qualified here by the larger uncertainty as to whether this voyage echoes a cosmic patterning, whether the words of the poem are truly inspired and so whether they can be anything other than tentative 'stumbling'.[39]

In Kinsella's projection of experiential, autobiographical recognitions onto a mythic scale, then, there remains that open-endedness and doubt in which one seeming arrival at 'home', a settled origin, only serves to open up further questions and uncertainties. At no stage in Kinsella's career, least of all at the end of the individual poem or sequence, does it seem that a point of stasis or coherence has been arrived at, and at no point is it therefore possible to take perspective on the fragmentary, obscure 'narratives' we have been given. The 'actuality' to which the poet must be responsible rapidly dissolves into abstraction, and this corollary of history's failure is increasingly foregrounded in Kinsella's work. In 'The Messenger', a sequence commemorating his father, scenes from John Kinsella's life are punctuated by italicized passages again asserting some 'mythic' (compensatory? consolatory?) coming-into-being:

An eye, pale with strain, forms in the dark.
The oddity nestles in the slime

functionless, in all its rarity,
purifying nothing. But nothing can befoul it
– which ought probably to console.

He rolled on rubber tyres
out of the chapel door. The oak box
paused gleaming in the May morning air....[40]

As 'C.G. Jung's Years'' in *One and Other Poems* and many examples elsewhere demonstrate, Kinsella's interest in national origins includes the sources of the self – there is for him a continuity between the disturbing roots of individual consciousness and the collective unconscious, something which Heaney also tunes into when relating the individual writer's experience to Irish history. And yet, in this passage from 'The Messenger', the relation between the section in italics and the simple recounting of the events of his father's funeral remains irrefutably personal, uncertain and obscure, its hope questionable again.

But the founding of such relations, however vague, remains true to Kinsella's assertion in 'The Irish Writer', that if the poet 'can find no means in his inheritance to suit him, he will have to start from scratch'. And it is a 'start from scratch' in the widest sense of the phrase, since all of Kinsella's 'myths' are of emergence, of coming-into-being, of foundation and of beginning. Yet they remain intractably obscure, the 'continuity' between myths and the more traditional, autobiographical moments of lyric poetry in the sequences an awkward one which always makes the tone of Kinsella's poetry difficult to catch when it is not bellowing with Yeatsian scorn or Baudelairean ennui. As an inevitable yet potentially debilitating result of the sublimation of self into history and process, we continue to hear in the poetry, as Heaney has said of Kinsella's translations, 'something genetic at the roots of Kinsella's own Dublin speech', a gene pool he shares with the rhythm and assonances of Joyce's prose (witness the play on 'o' sounds in 'He rolled on rubber tyres/out of the chapel door. The oak box...').[41] Yet that speech mediated through the poetry is one lacking in emphases, one refusing to distinguish between registers and to be modulated by its content.

However, such abstraction remains part of the necessary condition of modernity itself as Adorno sees it:

> ...in modern works of art the irritating abstractness, which always leaves in doubt what they are and what they are for, becomes a cipher of the essence of the works themselves....

Adorno ascribes such abstractness to the condition of late capitalism, in which 'what is being consumed is no longer the use-value of things but their exchange value', so that 'the new in art is the aesthetic counterpart to the expanding reproduction of capital in society.'[42] Capitalism drains both the religious mystery and the symbolic power from every artifact, setting it within an open and endless paradigm of exchange in which everything could potentially be anything else. As I have argued above, Kinsella's daily experience of expanding capitalist reproduction from his desk at the Department of Finance inspired the Yeatsian passages which have constantly punctuated his work. Yet to counter this draining of value, in the early sequences published by his own Peppercanister Press, a (also Yeatsian) potentially visionary power of numbers is deployed as a structuring principle. The 'egg of being' in 'Hen Woman' had featured earlier in 'Notes from the Land of the Dead' as a zero; the next sequence was called 'One'. 'A Technical Supplement', Kinsella's work after 'One', plays upon the notion of division which feeds into his modernist questioning of the concept of identity and origin:

> Two faces now returned my stare
> each whole yet neither quite 'itself'.
> (But then the original could not
> have been called 'itself' either.
> What but some uneasiness made it divide?)[43]

While this numerological system again questions the unitary power of origin and suggests that slip between various polarities through-out Kinsella's work, these lines also show the quibbling which the system can lead his poetry into. In the later sequences, the 'mysti-cal' power of number has been dropped, presumably because it remains as rigidly damaging to the organic process as Lemass's economics were, in Kinsella's view, for the Republic.

Yet Kinsella's use of this accumulating yet abstract structuring principle is exactly consonant with his increasing adoption of a more radically experimental modernist practice in the sequences from the early 1960s on. The increasing rejection of his earlier Audenesque use of rhyme and stanza in *Downstream* (1962), *Wormwood* (1966) and *Nightwalker and Other Poems*,[44] almost exactly mirrors the move through Lemass's implementation of an eco-nomic plan which brought about the arrival of Ireland as a modern capitalist nation. So, Kinsella's Joycean adoption of such imagery and of a circling, open-ended, fragmentary poetic can be sympto-matic of the modernization taking place in Irish cultural, social and political life at the time. But in its inscrutable furtherance of such self-regarding structuring abstraction as numbers, and obscurity in relating the mythic and historical to the personal, it is also a Yeatsian comment upon those present conditions. It is just this paradoxical, fraught adaptation to circumstance which Adorno sees (later in the passage from which I have just quoted) as that necessary mimesis which paradoxically governs the distancing critical role which modern art retains for itself in relation to the valuelessness of the modern world: 'The only way in which art can henceforth transcend the heteronomy of capitalist society is by suffusing its own autonomy with the imagery of that society.'

By insisting upon the current 'commodity character of art', Adorno embraces Walter Benjamin's conception of modernity, in which an increasing technologization and commercialism have brought about the destruction of what he called the 'aura' of a work of art, that often religious specialness and uniqueness which it had before debasing technologies took over. Benjamin puts this point most clearly in the essay 'The Work of Art in the Age of Mechanical Reproduction':

> Even the most perfect reproduction of a work of art is lacking in one element: its presence in time and space, its unique existence at the place where it happens to be. This unique existence of the work of art determined the history to which it was subject throughout the time of its existence…that which withers in the age of mechanical reproduction is the aura of the work of art.[45]

In Adorno's later extension of, and variation upon, these ideas, it is the loss of different kinds of 'aura' which underpins the newness, experimentalism, but also the abstraction of the modern work of art. 'Modernism', he claims, 'negates tradition itself…The modernity of art lies in its mimetic relation to a petrified and alienated reality.'[46]

Kinsella's use of 'structuring' (but ultimately failed) numerical and 'mythic' systems suggests that he might not have totally given up on (Yeatsian?) 'magic', at least as a potential means to coherence – before boredom or exhaustion sets in – within the poem itself. But the literal abstraction of these elements from the autobiographical material makes the positing of such ordering deeply uncertain. The poet-persona's 'stumbling tongue' in 'Finistere' recalls the way in which Kinsella had pulled himself up short near the start of 'Notes from the Land of the Dead' with 'perhaps/you won't believe a word of this'. This in its turn can be projected forward to the sceptical (mocking?) tentative apparent question near the end of that sequence, '…Would you agree, then, we won't/find truths, or any certainties…?'[47] The poetic of loss which everywhere punctuates

Kinsella's statements on tradition (and which underwrites his reading of history as a Joycean *via negativa* from which his nation and the modern world might, perhaps, awake), renders each moment of his poetry abstract and dubious, punctuated by violence and ruin.

But it is in this that Kinsella's poetic draws closest to the history out of which it is written, that it moves from simply being a matter of his own experience of personal and literary loss towards understanding that loss within history – and that it becomes most modernist. As I showed in my first chapter, Adorno has convincingly linked the violence and discontinuity in modern art to the fact that the artist has no secure form or content with which to work, and that this throws emphasis upon form itself. Each modern artist, as in Kinsella's sense of the Irish writer's plight, must strive to develop their own solutions to the radical disjunctions with which the breakdown of tradition presents them.

Adorno's argument is suggestive of the way in which the autobiographical or other apparently self-contained 'actualities' in Kinsella's output search for accommodation within larger ordering sequences. His use of constructive, patterning abstractions such as myth and number is essentially an awkwardly attempted sublimation- and it is an awkwardness advertised from within the poetry – of the narratives offered both by his own or by received notions of history. Indeed, when history appears explicitly in the poetry, it does so in abruptly disjunctive and awkward ways, interrupting and distorting the flow of personal, lyrical reminiscence.

It is at this point that Kinsella's work moves back into the sphere of influence exerted by Yeats. He has argued that Yeats in effect became a modern poet only when, after Easter 1916, he admitted the violence of the historical moment into his poetry.

> [This] new verbal violence intensified with the experiences of the Civil War, which added bitterness, cries of vengence, and an indulgence in senseless tumult. There is an outbreak of understanding in the poetry, of the place of violence and the random at the heart of vital processes.[48]

Such a moment, the equivalent for him of Easter 1916, arrived for Kinsella on Bloody Sunday, leading him to instigate his Peppercanister series with his angry response, *Butcher's Dozen*. On 30 January 1972, paratroopers fired on a Civil Rights march in

Derry injuring 13 and killing 13 men. The Tribunal of Enquiry set up to look into the killings was chaired by Lord Widgery, who in his report acknowledged that some of the shooting had 'bordered on the reckless' but, despite overwhelming evidence that the victims were innocent of any attempt to fire on the troops themselves (many of them had indeed been shot in the back), exonerated the action by the troops. The protests and violence which followed the shootings led to the British government establishing direct rule over the North of Ireland.

Butcher's Dozen is interesting in that again it is an abstract work, remote from the actual events of 30 January. It is not a direct response to Bloody Sunday itself: 'There are too many dead, on all sides, and it is no use pitting them hideously against each other', Kinsella said in his commentary when the pamphlet was collected in *Fifteen Dead* in 1979.[49] The poem is, rather, a response to the report of the Widgery Tribunal, which was an attempt to give an official version or history of the event which denied the 'actualities' to which the poet holds himself firmly responsible.[50] That abstraction is mirrored in the nature of the poem, which adopts the form of a Dantean series of encounters with the 13 dead in a purgatorial Bogside in Derry, a form consonant with the procedures of those modernist forebears invoked in interview by Kinsella – Pound and Eliot. It is a procedure which he had himself used successfully in one of his early experiments with modernist hallucinatory poetry, in the title poem of *Downstream*. Yet, paradoxically, Kinsella acknowledges the one-off, autonomous nature of the poem's response to a single historical event, as well as adding Swiftian bite to its satire, by returning to a tight form which he had abandoned in his modernist experiments.[51]

By giving the ghosts of those killed on Bloody Sunday voices in this way, Kinsella is able to dramatize the range of reactions which the troubled history of Ireland provokes. The initial 'encounter' gives the lie to the Widgery version of events, in which one of the victims, Gerald Donaghy, was alleged to have been found with a nail bomb on his body. By recreating the event through a sarcastic 'speech' by Donaghy's ghost, Kinsella ridicules the official story:

> A bomber I. I travelled light
> – Four pounds of nails and gelignite
> About my person, hid so well
> They seemed to vanish where I fell.

> When the bullet stopped my breath
> A doctor sought the cause of death.
> He upped my shirt, undid my fly,
> Twice he moved my limbs awry,
> And noticed nothing....[52]

What is at issue in the poem is the way the Tribunal 'Report' reveals what Kinsella sees in the 'Commentary' as 'the operations of the real evil causes' of the Troubles, the evasion of 'awkward, deep-seated causes in Ireland' in the name of 'passing expediencies'. Kinsella's Adornoan, modernist poetic of expediency makes him especially and ironically alert to its deployment by the colonizers, as that doubling viewed in 'A Technical Supplement' is turned to use in unmasking the falseness of British rhetoric. The third ghost makes the point against British 'justice' explicitly: 'The shame is theirs, in word and deed,/Who prate of Justice, practise greed,/And act in ignorant fury'. Another ghost then chants a witches-in-*Macbeth*-style recipe to explain the confused, conflicting genealogies brought about by Britain within Ireland ('make a mess./A most imperial success!'); another puts the case for the armed struggle against oppression in terms which again attack languages of officialdom:

> ...The milder forms of violence
> Earn nothing but polite neglect.
> England, the way to your respect
> Is via murderous force, it seems;
> You push us to your own extremes.[53]

The next ghost voices the Troops Out argument, another gives a scathing view of a caricature Unionist. This ghost ends with '"Who could love them? God above..."', before the thirteenth ghost raises the tone of the poem by arguing for the integration and mutual understanding between all views and creeds in the country:

> Yet pity is akin to love...
> They, even they, with other nations
> Have a place...
> Doomed from birth, a cursed heir,
> Theirs is the hardest lot to bear,
> Yet not impossible, I swear,

> If England would but clear the air
> And brood at home on her disgrace
> – Everything to its own place....[54]

The argument is essentially Joyce's, as voiced by Leopold Bloom in his debate with the Citizen in *Ulysses* – that everyone born in Ireland, whatever their national or religious origin, is Irish, that all blood is mixed, 'mongrel'.[55] Yet within the context of the North itself such integrationist doctrine is itself suspect; the Bloomian rhetoric of that last 'speaker' is perhaps why *Butcher's Dozen* continues to be highly valued by the nationalist community there.[56]

But this is, in its turn, to accept too fully notions of arrest over process in reading such poetry. In continuation of the contradictory nature of Kinsella's modernist poetic, its ironic and tonal uncertainties, this integrationist hope is not allowed to stand unchallenged as the culmination of the poem. In what seems like a lyric, pastoral, 'panning back' of perspective in order to include recognition of Derry's foundation by St Colmcille, there is only a confirmation of the harshness of the loss in the deaths:

> The gentle rainfall drifting down
> Over Colmcille's town
> Could not refresh, only distil
> In silent grief from hill to hill.[57]

There is, then, no relief from the history, only reminders of it, as pastoral vision declines to pathetic fallacy, and the reference to Derry's origins only reminds us of the perpetuity of such suffering, the determination of it by history.

In *Butcher's Dozen*, then, we see Kinsella exploiting his modernist 'monadic' techniques to dramatic effect. He adapts the Yeatsian mask, allowing the ghosts' 'speeches' to give the lie to the official English version of history, and to *all* official languages of history, while also voicing a possible (Joycean) future in the light of these events. It is the very roughness of the drama, its clumsiness and the violent modernist discontinuities between the speeches, which pays witness to the trauma of Bloody Sunday and to the anger at the injustice of the Widgery Tribunal's verdict.

It is, however, this necessary unevenness which has caused a wide variety of responses to the poem in Ireland. Dennis O'Driscoll felt that the poem showed too great a closeness to events, too little aesthetic distance: 'It remains the stuff of politics, of letters to the newspaper, and is neither revelatory, healing, nor very well-written.' Gerald Dawe, on the other hand, remembers his excitement on reading the Peppercanister pamphlet version of the poem as a student at the New University of Ulster: 'The ballad cauterized the wound.'[58]

Yet a review by the poet James Simmons best illustrates the immediate difficulties posed for reading such fragmented texts by the backdrop of the conflict in the North. Kinsella produced the poem as a pamphlet in April 1972; on 11 May *Fortnight* magazine in Belfast reprinted the poem in full with a review-commentary on the facing page by Simmons. Despite the fact that he was writing in the magazine which was giving the poem currency in the North, Simmons saw it as a failure. He attacked the passage from one of the 'ghosts' arguing for the armed struggle, as though the poem's message was that all should join the IRA. In arguing against that 'message' Simmons put the case again for the Civil Rights movement. He then compared the poem with Joyce's satirical 'Gas from a Burner', but argued that Kinsella's failure is in not instructing his reader how to read the poem: 'Joyce too is vicious, prejudiced and over-simplified, but the diction warns you that here is a reckless angry man letting himself go.' What ultimately marks Kinsella's as an 'artistic failure', as well as a political one for Simmons, though, is the awkward mixture of styles and attitudes adopted: 'Kinsella mixes uneasily, attempts to be rough and satirical, with implications of more subtlety and solemnity and even allows himself to drift off on the lyric touch' (he then quotes the end of the poem).[59]

Simmons's immediate response and despair at *Butcher's Dozen* is both symptomatic of, and a witness to, the daring and risk-taking in Kinsella's inveterate modernism. Yet it also reveals the dangers of deploying such techniques in a situation where more is demanded of poets in terms of taking an attitude towards events. Kinsella's poetics of failure refuses, unlike Heaney and Field Day's directors, who were immediately close to the Civil Rights ideal, the redemptive note, and refuses also critically to favour one perspective over another. The poem diagnoses the situation in the North, despite its wrath at the Tribunal, as simply one of different perspectives in conflict, mutilating one another in the way that the voices of the poem contradict each other.

In common with the negative critical responses attracted also by Hewitt's 'Troubles' poems, Simmons looks for a traditional poem which says something about the awful event, whereas Kinsella's adoption of a dramatic perspective, continually moving-on and self-undercutting, resists such easy accommodation, as it pays its dues to the history of loss and failure which it is written about and out of. 'Nothing is more detrimental to a theoretical understanding of modern art than attempts to reduce it to similarities with what went before,' Adorno argues. 'Under the aegis of this kind of methodological *déjà-vu*, modern art is assimilated into an undialectical continuum of tranquil developments while its explosive specificity is ignored.'[60] And yet Kinsella's poem might be seen also as a victim of its own abstraction from the event, its ghostly history. While 'explosively specific' in itself, it provides in its open-endedness and incompletion no grounded hope of answers to the history it reflects, but merely a continuation of the present situation. Its satiric commentary, and even its utopian Joycean vision of a mongrel integration, remain uncertain, lacking in resolution in all senses of the word.

Yet it is this which marks the poem as vital within the ongoing development of Kinsella's poetic, in the later work of the Peppercanister series. Derry's murdered citizens in 1972 turned the city's streets into that 'land of the dead' from which Kinsella began to send back autobiographical and mythic 'notes' in *New Poems 1973*. But in those later sequences, as in *Butcher's Dozen* itself, modernist perplexities about the relations between process and commentary, between flow and fixity, between the moment and history, and between the poet and his or her audience, continue unabated.

4

A Failure to Return: John Montague's *The Rough Field*

Like Thomas Kinsella, John Montague has remained consistent in his espousal of a poetic which is open to the influences of international writing – as is most explicitly clear in his essay of 1973, 'The Impact of International Modern Poetry on Irish Writing':

> Like a composer or a painter, an Irish poet should be familiar with the finest work of his contemporaries, not just the increasingly narrow English version of modern poetry, or the more extensive American one, but in other languages as well....I would say that my contemporaries are not just the Irish poets I admire, but those with whom I feel an affinity elsewhere, Ponge in France, Octavio Paz in Mexico, Gary Synder and Robert Duncan in San Francisco. I seem to be advocating a deliberate programme of denationalization, but all true experiments and exchanges only serve to illuminate the self, a rediscovery of the oldest laws of the psyche.[1]

As with the historical and mythic matter of Kinsella's poetry, the return upon the self in the last few clauses here suggests that it is a lyric, Jungian exploration which Montague expects to emerge from this modern poetic of denationalization, experiment and exchange. The self is seen to be absolutely contiguous with a wider poetic derived from experiences and experiments alien to its own. The modern international poetic is directly consonant with the most primitive elements within the Irish poet.

It is the formal consequences of this presumed contiguity and emergence – of the processes of translation between the international, the Irish and the personal – which I wish to trace in relation to Montague's most direct and political response to the history of his island and the renewed outbreak of violence in the North in 1969, *The Rough Field* of 1972. It is the very modernity of this book-long meditation on the history of his country and the history of his own family which makes the continuities which Montague describes in 'The Impact of International Modern Poetry on Irish Writing' unsettled, contingent and even obscure and uncertain.

The Rough Field is, as Montague says in introducing it, a collection which was put together at intervals across the 1960s in response to a vision he had while returning to the place in Tyrone where he had been raised, a vision 'of my home area, the unhappiness of its historical destiny.' While he resists the idea that the sequence was a response to any particular set of events, he acknowledges that, when the 'Ulster Crisis' broke, 'I felt as if I had been stirring a witch's cauldron.' The internationalizing impetus of his thought emerges as he links the agitation on his home ground to that he had witnessed by students in Paris and America; but, in a final return on himself, Montague acknowledges that 'one must start from home – so the poem begins where I began myself, with a Catholic family in the townland of Garvaghey...'[2] ('Garvaghey' being the anglicization of the Gaelic placename which means 'a rough field').

The Rough Field is a poem in ten sections with an Epilogue. The sections cover concerns including his own upbringing in the house of his aunt and her simple religious piety. There is a section on the history of the Irish people ('A Severed Head'), on his republican father, on the nationalist dreams of his country ('Patriotic Suite'), on the destruction of the countryside by modernizing engineering work ('Hymn to the New Omagh Road') and on the outbreak of violence in contemporary Derry ('The New Siege'). Each section is made up by combining several lyrics on similar themes together; alone of all responses to the violence post-1969 in the North the whole book reveals an epic ambition to treat all aspects, historical and present, of its subject. In its exploration of the historical and traditional roots of that violence, *The Rough Field* anticipates some of the themes and methods of Seamus Heaney's most public collection, *North*, published three years later. But Montague's book reveals, unlike Heaney's, a desire for inclusiveness and formal expansiveness which goes beyond its basic poetic unit, the lyric. 'Sooner or later', he has said in discussing the work of Hugh MacDiarmid in 1967, 'the desire grows to write a long poem or sequence, something more expansive than the lyric to which anthologies have reduced English poetry, something which is co-terminous

with at least one whole aspect of one's experience.' It is to the nov-
elists, and particularly to the Joyce of *Ulysses*, that we go to see the
details of twentieth-century life in their fullness; poets have constrained themselves into producing only 'complex, asocial tones'.[3]

An epic ambition is, therefore, for Montague both an ambition to
write a 'social' poetry and one that includes 'one whole aspect' of
an individual poet's experience; the two are co-terminous with each
other. It is an outlook which makes for an interesting and
significant reservation when it comes to reading the next generation of Irish writers on from his own, the generation which
emerged in the 1960s 'from that forgotten and history-burdened
area, the North' of Ireland:

> There has been some criticism in the Republic of the way Ulster
> writers tend to look to London as their literary capital, and it is
> true that the poems of Longley, Mahon, Heaney and Simmons
> share an epigrammatic neatness which shows the influence of a
> limiting British mode.... What is striking in all the northern
> writers is how well they write, though I would hope for a more
> experimental approach, if they are to confront the changes in
> their society.[4]

This view of the older poet upon his young contemporaries dates
from 1974, and so does not take into account that move away from
'neatness' which has followed later, particularly in the work of
Heaney as I show below. But it is the formal point which is interesting and striking here, the suggestion that a 'more experimental approach' might somehow enable the poets to 'confront' 'change',
whereas a more limited, 'neat' approach presumably traps the
poets in their own personal themes, sets them solipsistically at a
remove from the movements within their society. This is surely a
striking and curious definition of an Irish difference from England,
one proclaiming the Republic as a centre of modernist experiment
and England as trapped in a traditional lyric mode which, presumably because of the continued British colonization of the North, it is
hard for the young poets there to break free of.

Yet, despite the defiant proclamation of a modernity unavailable
to the limited metropolitan mode, Montague's own 'epic' sequences from *The Rough Field* through to the 1984 *The Dead Kingdom*
are built from an accumulation of such smaller lyric units. It is
the strained relation between those two forms, as between the

individual lyrics which go to make up the books, which I wish to describe in this chapter, strained relations which call into question the easy continuities between local and international, modernism and the 'psyche' maintained in the prose.

Montague never really theorizes more about the relation of form to content in his chiding of the new poets from the North than here, but – as will become clear later – he is tapping here as elsewhere into modernist ideas of poetry as process, poetry as metamorphosis. He is making a clear link between the breaking up of poetic formalism as it was contained in 'neat' units, and the disjunctive, eclectic and polyvocal nature of the modern world – particularly when that world is as riven as is the world in the North of Ireland. Much depends on his use of the word 'confront', though, which would almost seem to suggest that by the deployment of a more experimental poetic the poets in the North will be able to align themselves actively towards social movements. It is a call for poetry to be not merely reflective of the changes, but to take a stance toward them, as is similarly reflected in the Joyce/Yeats division of anxieties of influence which I described in Thomas Kinsella's work.

Montague's insistence on this stance to the circumstances of the poet's time can be seen to approximate to Frederic Jameson's description of 'dialectical criticism', in which the opening of art to its historical situation leads to a revaluation of the kinds of formal balances which are integral to the 'neatness' of British writing. Jameson seems to infer that, from a perspective within history, the traditional focuses of critical attention (imagery, formal resolution, for example) must be seen as continuous with, and dependent upon, all other (previously ignored) parts of the poem. 'Dialectical criticism'

> replaces the older absolutes of truth or beauty with a judgement in which the insistence on the preeminence of the historical situation underlies the inseparability of strengths and weaknesses within the work of art itself…and stands as a concrete object lesson in the way in which the very strengths themselves, in all their specificity, require the existence of determinate and correlative weaknesses in order to come into being at all.[5]

What this definition would seem to do is to open the various elements of a form to the process of history in which the inseparable 'strengths and weaknesses' are constantly in relation to processes of change, rather than being, as they are in a New Critical stance, an internalized part of the poem's balanced mechanism. What the argument amounts to in Jameson's discussion of the relation of artistic form to history is an attack on those who value *only* what they see as the 'strong' elements in a work, such as its use of symbol or paradox, elements which set the work seemingly apart from 'reality' or the processes of history. As part of the establishment of a dialectical criticism, Jameson wishes to see the form as a whole, but, as with Adorno's ideas discussed in earlier chapters, as a whole in which the elements are made again a part of the historical background against which they appeared or against which they must be viewed. So, the prioritization of the symbolic in art must be seen as a historical phenomenon, a phenomenon which is visible because of the clear disjunctions between various elements in the form, and because of the way other elements are suppressed there.

And, for Jameson, this critical stance makes a radical break from past ideas into the present of modernity; it is not to persist in the old systems of valuation ('strong' and 'weak', for example), but to open up the notion of valuation itself to scrutiny:

> History is indeed precisely this obligation to multiply the horizons on which the object is maintained, to multiply the perspectives from which it is seen, and I believe that to see differing judgements or evaluations in this fashion is not to speak out for some theoretical objectivity or neutrality, but rather to replace us at the very source of value itself and of such structural permutation, and to translate apparently literary disagreements back into the ultimate reality of conflicting groups in the historical world.[6]

Rather than accepting a single perspective upon a work of art, therefore, the acceptance of a plurality of possible readings enables the work to re-enter the 'ultimate reality' which is the world. History seems in this reading to both preside over works of art and to be the final destination of their disagreements, to form both the beginning and end of reading and of valuation. Art can make a conscious stance towards history, and establish its own system of 'strengths' and 'weaknesses', but that system will also always be rejudged by history itself, which will establish different relations between those elements.

It is this complex system of possible historical readings which I wish to explore in relation to the experimental poetic adopted by Montague. That poetic is one which, through its very adaptibility in its reading of his forebears, of his own earlier work and also, ultimately (to transpose the literary-critical basis of Jameson's terms to the poet's stance towards 'reality'), of historical 'change', seems to have to allow what Montague would define in his prose pieces as 'weaknesses' with relation to poetry to yet determine some of that poetry's essential terms and judgements. Of course, the 'conflicting groups' of Jameson's history have a reality in the North of Ireland which makes all questions of criticism and of the poet's relation to those conflicts more urgent. Gerald Dawe has argued that for all the obvious range of Montague's poetry

> a stock of favourite words and images create a stylisation of experience which is essentially literary. It is as if the poet were self-consciously setting out to prove something about the past and its potency as a poetic theme. This side to Montague's poetry is characteristic of much Irish poetry in English and it surely has a lot to do with the colonised basis of our English.[7]

The danger which Dawe is addressing here is that poetry in Ireland simply becomes trapped in postures of pleading for the relevance of its contents against the tradition of the colonizer, that it is the issue of what represents suitable poetic experience which subsumes all others in a colony. In countering such arguments about determined entrapment, the critical force of Jameson's stance proves useful in describing Montague's confrontational poetry. Because of its adoption of an open, polyvocal form, the poetry often performs a dialectic within itself, viewing history from a perspective which remains sceptically in dialogue with its own processes of valuation and also with its own various yearnings towards a single, self-contained version of history. From this there emerges an international modernist poetic which is also adaptive to locally and personally experienced 'changes' on his childhood ground, but it is a poetic which he paradoxically developed, in Joycean fashion, by leaving that ground in his teens.

Montague's opening to such poetic possibility has its roots in the way in which personal history made him susceptible to ideas and movements which initially seem alien to that sense of place conveyed in *The Rough Field*'s title. Born in Brooklyn, New York,

Montague had been reared by the aunt celebrated in his 'epic'. The break came in 1946 when Montague won the Tyrone County Scholarship to attend University College Dublin where he read English and History. Although, as the essay 'The Figure in the Cave' makes clear, he initially felt isolated from the 'Guinness-swilling' 'sons and daughters of the first middle class of the Irish Free State' among whom he found himself, he made rapid progress towards being recognized in literary circles, publishing poems in student magazines, winning a poetry competition organized by Austin Clarke, succeeding Patrick Kavanagh as, of all things, the film critic for the *Standard*, before in 1951 contributing a controversial article to the 'Young Writers' Symposium' in *The Bell* magazine. He was to contribute articles to *The Bell* on Anglo-Irish literature for the next few years; in the meantime he re-established his connection with America by attending an American Seminar in Salzburg in 1950 and winning a US government-sponsored scholarship to study in the States in 1952. He attended courses there until 1956, meeting Auden, Lowell, Blackmur, Ransom, Wilbur and William Carlos Williams among others.

Montague's experience of the postwar South was correlative to that of Kinsella which I described in the last chapter, one in which the isolation and stagnation brought on by the country's wartime neutrality was gradually giving way to an international and assuredly non-British cultural outlook. One of the most siginificant interventions into debates about Ireland's stance in the modern world was that provided by *The Bell* magazine, a rigorously secular periodical founded by Sean O'Faoláin in 1940 and edited by him until 1946 (it eventually closed in 1954). The magazine provided an important forum for Montague's developing alertness to the need for a critical, evaluative stance with regard to the relations between poetry and its political, historical and cultural circumstances.

O'Faoláin had recognized the fact that Ireland was feeling the cold blast of social change in full force, and set his magazine the task of being in the forefront of helping to bring that change about – the first issue, for instance, contained sustained attacks on the Censorship Board. He waged cultural warfare on those who still maintained that a separate and distinctive Irish state must be founded on its ancient language, Gaelic. Irish people should be 'honest and realistic', he argued, 'and admit that our object is not unilingualism, but that we should speak, according to our moods and needs, both Gaelic and English.'[8] What is most significant in this regard is the way in which this refusal to be trapped by a single vision of the past becomes a rejection of the nationalist 'myth-kitty'. In his first editorial, O'Faoláin made this polemically clear:

> That is why we chose the name of 'The Bell'....We could not use *any* of the old symbolic words. They are as dead as Brian Boru, Granuile, the Shan Van Vocht....These belong to the time when we growled in defeat and dreamed of the future. The future has arrived and, with its arrival, killed them. All our symbols have to be created afresh.[9]

This harnesses the new national self-confidence in the separate Southern state with a radical break into the modern, contemporary world from the symbol-ridden past. O'Faoláin set about his de-mythologizing task by using *The Bell* as a forum for a documentary and empirical exploration of Irish life. Among other things, there were articles on life in Irish prisons, in the slums of Dublin, on crime, horseracing and art galleries.

It is, however, this *sociological* version of the present which forms the substance of Montague's criticism of the magazine in 1951:

> ...by constantly keeping in mind the social angle or problem [the magazine] has tended to lead writing away from its real purpose at the present time, the imaginative and honest expression of the writer's own problems, not those of his sickening community, though the one will be indirectly reflected in the other....In this approach *The Bell* has approximated to the...older tradition of close natural description and poetic undertones....They miss the point of Ezra Pound's remark that there is only one artistic sin: doing something again which someone else has done better.[10]

In his selection of Pound as the particular authority to cite for his argument Montague's allegiances are clear, although his conflation of two different traditions is slightly odd: he sets a Romantic lyric dependence on the 'expression of the writer's own problems' alongside an innovative, anti-naturalistic, experimental international modernism.[11] He espouses what he calls at the end of the contribution 'honest-to-god writing' against concern for 'local authority in matters literary' and regrets the move by 'our best novelist' and short-story writer, O'Faoláin, into social polemic. In

Jameson's terms, then, the 'social angle' represents a 'weakness', one inimical to the 'real purpose' of contemporary writing.

The terms of this early disagreement and some sense of the possible literary dilemmas surrounding it – as involved in O'Faoláin's implied rejection of a Yeatsian symbolic world – are transposed into a poem by Montague which originally appeared as 'The Siege of Mullingar, 1963' in the collection *A Chosen Light* (1967), and which was to reappear as poem 9 in the 'Patriotic Suite' part of *The Rough Field*. Montague clearly feels that the inhibited, provincial world of O'Faoláin's short stories – economically prudent, subservient to church authority – failed to carry through the criticism of prevailing ideology as they seemed to be claiming to do. Rather, the stories simply reflected the stagnation and resignation to be found everywhere in the country. Montague clearly espouses the Poundian modernist notion that poetry must 'make it new', that it must alter the terms by which the prevailing conditions are recorded and therefore seen, even if simply by honestly recording the writer's own 'problems'.

The tone of 'The Siege of Mullingar, 1963', set at the Fleadh Cheoil music festival at the time Pope John was dying, is, despite this seemingly clear sense of allegiances, strangely elusive and indirect. The poem's refrain sets it as a belated, ironic echo of Yeats's great lament for an older generation of revolutionaries in 'September 1913': *'Puritan Ireland's dead and gone,/A myth of O'Connor and O'Faoláin'* (Frank O'Connor being a short story writer in the same vein as O'Faoláin) harks back to Yeats's 'Romantic Ireland's dead and gone/It's with O'Leary in the grave'. In 'September 1913', Yeats sets a clear castigation of the contemporary middle-class mercantile piety ('What need you, being come to sense,/But fumble in a greasy till/And add the halfpence to the pence...?') against a vision of that nobler 'delirium of the brave' which he felt had been demonstrated by Irish nationalist heroes.[12] Montague's refrain is clear about seeing O'Faoláin trapped in another version of the myth of Ireland despite his claims to be de-mythologizing the country in his polemical pieces in *The Bell*. The poem is determinedly set in the modern world where young lovers listen to the 'agony' of Pope John on their transistor radios, a world countering the vague, timeless pastoralism of O'Faoláin's stories. What is less certain is the link of this normalized modern piety with the succeeding and final stanza which begins 'Further on, breasting the wind.../We saw a pair, a cob and his pen,/Most nobly linked.'

This sighting brings about a revision of Montague's casual perspective, as 'Everything then/In our casual morning vision/Seemed to
flow in one direction'.[13] Montague's altering vision seems to allude
to the swans in Yeats's 'The Wild Swans at Coole':

> Unwearied still, lover by lover,
> They paddle in the cold
> Companiable streams or climb the air;
> There hearts have not grown old;
> Passion or conquest, wander where they will,
> Attend upon them still.[14]

Montague seems to want to set a more sonorous Yeatsian and
'noble' music against the inhibitions of nostalgia in 'Puritan
Ireland'; he seems to see this as a reversion to a more 'simple' but
also more *poetic* 'direction' than the disillusioned, submissive world
of the 1930s short story writers O'Connor and O'Faoláin. It is a
curious turn for the poem to take, and the slight tonal uncertainty is
perhaps captured in the strained line ending 'Everything then/In
our...', which forces the interpretation of the image, reading it for
Montague's own polemical purposes (what, in the absence of the
Yeats poem, has the vision to do with the swans?). By doing so, it
ends by registering the uncertainty and the precariousness of the
poem's critique of O'Faoláin – who Montague had, after all, in his
first contribution to *The Bell* called 'our best novelist'.

The poem, with its disjunction between casual modern detail and
'symbolic' ending, seems to register the difficulty of rendering the
contemporary world non-sociologically, of escaping an artistic
'weakness'. The religious intensity of the 'agony' of the Pope is rendered matter-of-fact and unimportant by its appearance on the
lovers' radios; the nobility and hinted countering passion in the allusion to Yeats seems anachronistic, its dismissal of O'Faoláin un-
stable given that writer's own rejection of national symbolism. The
final stanza of 'The Wild Swans at Coole' anticipates the flight of
the 'Mysterious, beautiful' swans, recognizing the inevitable
decline of the Anglo-Irish tradition which Yeats would later seek to
reinvent through poetry. Montague's belated echoing of the image
can carry nothing of that communal relevance, and so stands as uncertain critique or celebration of modernity.

That yearning for passionate Yeatsian sonorities to set against the
casual modern world, with its vision of the swans 'nobly linked', is

clearly a modulation of the concerns of the poem which appears two pages earlier in this section of *The Rough Field* as poem 7. It is a modulation or even a reversal:

> The visitor to Coole Park
> in search of a tradition
> finds
>   a tangled alley-way
> a hint of foundation wall...
>   and a lake
> bereft of swans.[15]

The 'tangled alley-way' contrasts significantly with the modern simplicity of everything flowing in one direction which appears two pages later. The suggestion in the earlier poem 7 is that the Yeatsian 'tradition' is difficult to find, merely hinted at by the remnants of the big house, protected and bereft of its passionate or conquesting emblems. In this poem from 'Patriotic Suite', though, the change has happened (and thence its critical or ironic patriotism?), the process is complete. This poem reads as a lament for the decline of the Republic from some of its symbolic high founding ideals into modern banality and ruin. Its heroic monuments, like the beech-tree upon which Yeats had inscribed his initials, are now ring-fenced to protect them from defacement by tourists.

The contrast between this vision of the Yeatsian 'tradition' in decline and that hinted at in the reprinted 'The Siege at Mullingar, 1963' is stark, then. Montague's Mullingar poem is a re-envisaging on his own terms of the tradition in order to write off 'Puritan Ireland' and its proponents. The attitudes taken in the two poems are not finally reconcilable; Montague's reprinting of the earlier poem here forms a dialogue and dialectic which dramatizes the unsettledness and uncertainties of his own relation to the tradition (poem 8 is a savagely ironic attack on the Lemassian economic reforms in the early 1960s along with one on the continuingly benighted Vatican). The fractured lines of the Coole Park poem 7 reflect the loss of sonorities which only two pages later he has recourse to in order to distance himself from the lesser, limiting world which intervened between Yeats and his own generation of more eclectic, international writers.

What remains clear throughout these shifts of poetic valuing, however, is Montague's sensitivity to the ways in which the social and the public can overwhelm what he at this time sees as the primary 'tangled' concern of poetry – its countering stance, either through the adoption of traditional (Yeatsian) form and symbolism or a modernist poetic of change, to the details of the times.[16] In the shifts between these two formal possibilities lies the dynamic of his poetic, its dialectical critical force. And of course, as has already emerged in my discussion of *The Rough Field*, part of that shift of value and attitude is a literal one; in writing of his childhood place and the unhappiness of its historical destiny, Montague is also crossing the border and chiding the failure of the revolutionary founding vision in the South of Ireland. His own history as a poet moving between the two parts of the island means that he adopts an All-Ireland position, in which the violence in Derry recounted in 'A New Siege' remains just the latest manifestation of a continuing colonization ('brisk with guns/British soldiers/patrol the walls/the gates between/Ulster Catholic/Ulster Protestant'[17]).

Working within this 'tangled alleyway' of influence and shifting focus upon reality, however, there remains an overall structuring principle for Montague's poetic sequences, one which finds common features between international and local musics:

> ...music means much to me; the structure of *The Rough Field* reflects years of debate with O'Riada....Old Irish music threads through the poem but there are also parlour songs, the silvery sound of the papal count which soothed our post-Treaty limbo-land, drifting through *The Dead Kingdom*. But the larger units there are a homage to the symphonic structures of late nineteenth-century music, Brahms and Mahler, Bruckner's Eighth where the mountains seem to dance.

Elsewhere he has described the music of Mahler and Bruckner as that of 'infinite variation'.[18] Sean O'Riada is the dedicatee of the 'Patriotic Suite' section of *The Rough Field*; the sequence 'O'Riada's Farewell' in *A Slow Dance* (1975) is Montague's elegy for him (Kinsella and Heaney have also written elegies paying tribute to his cultural importance). O'Riada was an early admirer and polemicist in Ireland on behalf of late nineteenth-century symphonic music. He had also, and almost singlehandedly, brought about the revival in traditional Irish music which occurred in the 1960s, going to the increasingly fewer areas in which it was played (that reduction being consonant with the reduction in the number of Gaelic speakers, even in the West of Ireland), meeting the musicians and recording the music. The recordings were often made by Claddagh Records, which Montague had helped to found in 1960 and for which he continued to work as literary director until 1975. The epigraph which Montague sets at the head of 'O'Riada's Farewell' tellingly encapsulates the significance of O'Riada's work for him – he cites Ezra Pound's phrase 'To have gathered from the air a live tradition'. This is of course what O'Riada did in his researches into Gaelic music – and he put that tradition back into the air by founding the group The Chieftains to play that music.

But it is also clear from the citation that Montague recognizes O'Riada's work to have been at that time more than simply a local act of recovery within the larger movement towards cultural openness. The gathering of neglected material under the threat of extinction is very much part of international modernist experimentalism. Pound described *The Cantos* as 'an epic including history', and that work includes passages throughout cited from historical documents and translations from Greek, Latin, Provençal and Chinese. Further, Montague would seem in his various prose statements to be acknowledging the importance of *music* to that experiment, music forming a crucial link between his own poetry and that of the modernists Pound and Eliot. It is the musical ordering of the chaotic modern world, as suggested in the titles of sequences like Eliot's *Four Quartets*, which governs the more local idiom of Montague's own sequences.

What is striking after this seemingly consistent argument, though, is the way in which the music of O'Riada summoned in 'Patriotic Suite' does *not* offer the redemptive and harmonizing sense of materials being brought together into an assured, live tradition which it might have been expected to do:

> The gloomy images of a provincial catholicism...
>
> wound in a native music
> curlew echoing tin whistle
> to eye-swimming melancholy
> is that our offering?[19]

This is the last section of 'Patriotic Suite', and beneath it is printed the crest of the United Irishmen, the movement founded by Wolfe Tone in 1791 which united both communities in a struggle to throw off the English oppressor. The crest would seem to offer a national vision of a reunited Ireland and a patriotism founded in that. But the crest stands in awkward and obscure relation to the poem that precedes it. The act of faith in printing the crest would seem to be asserted here rather than assuredly held; the culmination of 'Patriotic Suite' is in itself as disjunctive and dialectical at the end as it had earlier been. And the inclusion of yet another medium within the poem – the visual image making us alert to the design of the book, as music does to other possible structuring principles – furthers this sense of the vulnerability of any one of them in adequately containing this historical material.

The final line of this poem 10 suggests the way in which 'that note' has *not* led to a sense of possession or a sense of the poet moving confidently and masterfully (like Yeats) across his territory. In the latter part of the poem, Montague had offered a vision of a landscape in the West of Ireland suggesting the kinds of restoration afforded by the traditional recourse of Irish literature (as, for example, in Synge and Yeats's praise for Synge) to seek to tune in to the 'authentic', pristine Western landscape. For Montague, the vision raises again the 'note' of the tin-whistle. But the vision and the music it conjures are, the last line informs us, received in a hired car – Montague realizes that he is only a tourist in this territory, that he must return to a contemporary reality at the end of the day. The rediscovery of the ancient note of Irish music and the suggestion that it taps some real Irish identity themselves become contingent and temporary, open to passing habitation by a day-tripper and to sceptical attitudes forced by modernity on the poet.

Yet the poem also shows how Montague's poetry *continues* to be invaded by the kinds of 'weak' content which he had chided *The Bell* for in 1951. Sociological material appears intermittently throughout *The Rough Field*. Here it seems to represent an intransigent reality (that 'ultimate reality' appealed to by Jameson) which the kinds of cultural recovery achieved by O'Riada cannot deny. The slightly sentimental Gaelic music is seen as being of a piece with the 'gloomy...provincial catholicism' which provides the tenor of national life. That music is seen later in this poem as regressive both when set against the experimentation of modern European music (personified by Pierre Boulez), and also against the rapid expansion in the Gross National Product of Ireland during the time in which O'Riada was carrying out his researches. What this end of 'Patriotic Suite' establishes, then, is a curious disjunction between, on the one hand, a modernist urge to recoup a live tradition (and to celebrate the nationalist potential of that recouping) and, on the other the modern Irish world itself, in which both its innovatory artists and new capitalist drives are perceived as failing by the values set in the poetry. Native music, however much it shares some Poundian qualities, is ultimately provincial and unpossessable; capitalist economics destroys symbolic value in whatever form, religious or artistic.

Montague's is an intransigent modernity, then, a modernity which contains tonal and perspectival echoes of O'Faoláin's editorials in *The Bell* of the 1940s so that even while celebrating the work of his friend O'Riada he recognizes that that work – like a return to Gaelic as the basis for national definition – could be taken as a dangerous nostalgia for an Irish identity which is no longer possible (in this, he is even more intransigent than Thomas Kinsella, who shares some of that nostalgia almost despite himself). As for O'Faoláin, so for Montague, it is not a question of either Gaelic or English but of a blending of both; it is not a question of either Irish quarter tone music or Bruckner symphonies as structuring principles for the poetry, but of both.

Yet it remains to be shown how that modernity does in practice affect the structuring principles of the poetry, and also how it establishes its indirect link between its personal, public and historical engagements. What is it about the experimentation of Montague's poetry which enables him to claim that it is somehow more responsive to the 'changes in society' than what he sees as the more English-orientated, tighter formal structures deployed by the younger generation of poets from the North? Is it the poetry's openness, its unaligned polyvocalism, its dialectical criticism of its own valuations, which forms his notion of the 'public' in poetry?

With regard to this, it is important to note that Montague's poetic sequences derive their complexity of reference, their shifting between various polarities of content and address, from the setting of (lyric) *poems* in relation. This is where Montague's preference for the music of 'infinite variation', as practised in the symphonies of Mahler and Bruckner, crosses with his preference for a modernist, polyvocal, experimental poetic. A frequent method of his, as the example of 'The Siege of Mullingar, 1963' in *The Rough Field* discussed above shows, is to reuse his poems in different contexts.[20] This reuse is clearly aligned with the variations on a theme worked in the great Romantic symphonies, where themes from one movement frequently reappear in others, with new variations woven around them.

Like Kinsella, Montague complicates the Poundian sense of history as 'planes in relation' by remaining in dialogue with his own history, with the history of his own writing. And, from *Tides* down to *The Dead Kingdom*, each of his collections was carefully structured in other ways, being broken down into sections or 'movements' with common 'thematic' interests. So the reprinting of a poem in a new context in a new collection reflects Montague's sense that poems are not fixed, that they must be seen (as in Jameson's 'history') from different perspectives across time, that their effects are always contingent upon their relation to the poems around them. Montague literally multiplies the perspectives in which his work is seen, as Jameson urges that dialectical criticism must, by rearranging the poems again and again.

This has immediate impact upon the relation between the personal and the national political history in these collections, whereby a poem of reminiscence can, by its resetting, take on immediate historical impact. To take but one example – 'The Wild Dog Rose', which tells the terrible story of the rape by a drunken, old, lonely neighbour of a lonely 70-year-old woman 'who haunted [Montague's] childhood'. When it appears in the first part of *Tides*, the poem is set with others describing an emergency operation, a lover's argument, and a translation of the ninth-century Irish poem 'The Hag of Beare' to prove (in a metaphysical statement correlative with the rhythms which dominate the collection, the sea's rise and fall) that 'Where once was life's flow/All is ebb.'[21] Life is seen here as always linked to death, innocence to violation.

When the poem reappears a year later as part of *The Rough Field* itself, we are made to see it anew. It occurs between 'A New Siege' and the 'Epilogue', which mourns, while recognizing the dangers of sentimentality in doing so, 'Our finally lost dream of man at home/in a rural setting.' In this new context, the woman in 'The Wild Dog Rose' becomes a belated traditional figure for Ireland itself; the poem an horrific version of an *aisling* or vision-poem in which Ireland was traditionally represented as a maiden. Her rape seems a figure for the country seen in the light of the British troops' presence again on its streets in response to the sectarian violence which had broken out in the North. That figure, of the rape of the (female) land by the (male) invader, is a traditional Irish poetic trope, one which will reappear in Heaney's 'Ocean's Love to

Ireland' and 'Act of Union' in *North*. (Such tropes horrifyingly confirm Eavan Boland's view that the images of romantic national-ism in Ireland are founded upon simplification and violation, that they are an affront to 'real women of an actual past'.[22]) It is possible to see anew the poem's culminating image, which returns to the flower of the title, in at least two ways:

> Briefly
> the air is strong with the smell
> of that weak flower, offering
> its crumpled yellow cup
> and pale bleeding lips
> fading to white
> at the rim
> of each bruised and heart-
> shaped petal.[23]

From the perspective of the first part of *Tides*, this is an extraordi-narily delicate piece of writing in the 'pathetic fallacy' manner, the description of the rose reflecting the hurt suffered by the old woman and raising it to a religious intensity: the flower reminds the woman, she tells the poet who tells us, of the sufferings of the Virgin Mary. From the perspective of its placing in *The Rough Field*, the poem becomes historically representative of the sufferings of Catholic Ireland under colonization, one of the many confirmations in the private and intimate sphere of the poet's personal experience of the material reviewed in the poems which treat public issues directly.

The final image represents a brief correlative for the historical hurt suffered by Ireland, an image which is itself, as the 'Epilogue' confirms, in some ways a reversion to that rural world which has traditionally been recognized, not least in the native Gaelic tradi-tion, but which no longer holds:

> Our finally lost dream of man at home
> in a rural setting! A giant hand
> as we pass by, reaches down
> to grasp the fields we gazed upon.
>
> Harsh landscape that haunts me,
> well and stone, in the bleak moors of dream

with all my circling a failure to return
to what is already going
                      going
                        GONE[24]

And so *The Rough Field* ends in acknowledging its own failure: 'that
[rural] note' which Montague had sought to recover in his circling to
return home to Garvaghey has eluded him. Again, the point is historical as much as it is personal or poetic (and it is a history which
has been developed from the time of the articles in *The Bell* on). Yet
again the note is obscured by the modernity which has come upon
the island North and South despite its traditional woes. The end of
the book recognizes the movement right across Ireland of the population away from the farms into the cities, the building of roads (as
commemorated in 'Hymn to the New Omagh Road') and the introduction of mechanized farming practices within the countryside
itself: the replacement of horses by tractors in the fields and the use
of grain silos and milking machines which look the same from
Ulster to the Ukraine. Under this modernizing aegis, internationalism holds little value, since all of Europe seems bound into the same
mediocrity and uniformity which threatens once more poetry's
values. The traditional pastoral resource of poetry, 'man at home/in
a rural setting' is passing into a 'bleak economic future'.

The preceding line to those just quoted has described the
Garvaghey scene as 'remote but friendly' as is Auburn in
Goldsmith's poem 'The Deserted Village'. In this literary reference
placing the 'lost dream', there is something more complicated happening, something which signals the historical perspective of the
poem, a perspective which enables the sequence itself to re-enter
history at the end. The 'remote but friendly' echoes the divergent
forces working on the Irish writer which were described by Joyce
through Stephen Dedalus's reaction to the English Dean of Studies
in *A Portrait of the Artist as a Young Man*: 'His language, so familiar
and so foreign, will always be for me an acquired speech. I have not
made or accepted its words.'[25] Such tensions inhere crucially in
Montague's allusion here to Goldsmith, whose poem does indeed
seem to underlie many of Montague's own preoccupations in *The
Rough Field*, preoccupations centred upon the repeated descriptions
of an Edenic childhood village community which has been destroyed by expanding commercial interests which intervene from
outside. 'The Deserted Village' follows a movement which might

loosely be described as 'circling', with a verse paragraph describing the idealized vision of the past set against one describing failure and ruin as the older narrator returns to the village in the poem's 'present'. And the characteristic motion of the narrator of Goldsmith's poem is in itself a circling one: 'In all my wanderings round this world of care...I still had hopes, my long vexations past,/Here to return – and die at home at last.' (ll. 83, 95–6). Montague in *The Rough Field* seems to be self-consciously identifying himself with the narrator of Goldsmith's poem, then.

But he had already, in a 1962 essay, reviewed for himself the perplexities surrounding Goldsmith's Auburn and the arguments as to whether the village is in fact a true description of the Lissoy in which Goldsmith had been raised, or whether it is a purely idealized, fictional place which Goldsmith created to make his public, political and polemical point:

> A song of exile from Lissoy, a protest against the Enclosure Acts and/or the new commercial oligarchy, a vision of the ills of Ireland: the poem does indeed answer to each of these descriptions. But it is also something more, something which transcends all these things: seen in the context of Oliver Goldsmith's career, it has the force of a final statement, the culminating vision of that decay in his own time, which haunted him....[26]

This sense of culmination might also be taken to describe Montague's project with *The Rough Field*, not least in his inclusion of poems from his past career within it; and he offers that overarching vision of decay, decay related both to the specifics of historical detail and to the general drift of history, which he identifies in the Goldsmith. But the literary allusion finally serves to reinforce the notion that, by the end of the book, the Rough Field itself has become translated into the book of that title, existing *only* in that ambiguous space maintained already by Goldsmith's poem. The 'remote but friendly' polarization serves to underline the fact that Goldsmith's poem is a complex, non-teleological production, both its place in history and the precise nature of its historical intervention uncertain.

Indeed, the culmination of 'The Deserted Village' is already self-conscious about its own literariness, and it is a self-consciousness which Montague's 'Epilogue' firmly echoes. In its final apostrophe, Goldsmith's poem turns against its own nature:

And thou, sweet Poetry, thou loveliest maid,
Still first to fly where sensual joys invade;
Unfit in these degenerate times of shame,
To catch the heart, or strike for honest fame;
Dear charming nymph, neglected and decried,
My shame in crowds, my solitary pride.
Thou source of all my bliss, and all my woe,
That found'st me poor at first, and keep'st me so;
Thou guide by which the nobler arts excell,
Thou nurse of every virtue, fare thee well.

(ll. 407–16)

Apocalyptically, the destruction of the village means the destruction of poetry itself, of the means by which the destruction has been expressed. Montague's last three words ('going/going/GONE') seem to make a similar recognition. As the landscape around his childhood place is auctioned off, so the book which bears the same name is sent into the marketplace. Again, while registering as he has elsewhere in the sequence his scepticism about commercial progress, Montague shows that finally his book, like Garvaghey, is a commodity. It is this 'literary' relation to Goldsmith which paradoxically signals Montague's true modernity. Landscape and rural ritual can only be momentarily commemorated before historical change brings the failure of the means of expression as it brings the failure of the land to produce. Poetry must continually be said farewell to as it continually has to re-enter the history of exchange.

In Jameson's dialectical terms, the poem's strength, its focus upon the harsh haunting place of Garvaghey, becomes in history its weakness, as that place passes away at the end of the book. The process of valuation is therefore an extremely fraught one, particularly with the exacerbated structural permutations which Montague brings to the book by including past poems of his own. History seems pre-eminent in determining the fractured, fragmented nature of the poem, but Montague has consciously arranged his lyric material to recognize that uncertainty of valuation from poem to poem. And, at the end, he consciously signals the transitory worth of that enterprise within the contemporary 'ultimate reality', not only of conflict, but of modern capitalist exchange. It is as though, with the advent of economic modernity and the violence in the North viewed in 'A New Siege', the possibilities for poetry, its old resources, are failing it. The poor land which the native population had been left to farm by the Jacobean Plantation of the country, when the English dispossessed the Irish of their land and handed it over to mainly Scots colonists, has served throughout *The Rough Field* as a paradigm of Irish historical plight. But, at the end of the book, in the light of new violence and a local modernity, even that possible parallel is seen as inadequate.

Yet a constant, unsettling sense of loss has energized the book as a whole, and is ultimately the means by which Montague subsumes his personal perspectives within a more public, even universalizing, poetic. As Maurice Riordan has written, the effort here 'essentially is to make a valid translation of the local (Garvaghey) into the universal (The Rough Field), whereby the local gains a paradigmatic significance through regaining its full cultural and historical identity.'[27] Montague consistently crosses the rhythms of his poems of place with larger, more 'universalizing' moments. Ironically, this attempt to see contemporary history against the background of cosmic change is the closest that Montague comes to Yeats:

> the emerging order
> of the poem invaded
> by cries, protestations
> a people's pain
> the defiant face
> of a young girl
> campaigning against
> memory's mortmain
> a blue banner
> lifting over a
> broken province
> DRIVE YOUR PLOUGH
> a yellow bulldozer
> raising the rubble
> a humming factory
> a housing estate
> hatreds sealed into
> a hygenic honeycomb
>
> Lines of loss
> lines of energy

```
always changing
     always returning
A TIDE LIFTS
     THE RELIEF SHIP
OFF THE MUD
     OVER THE BOOM
the rough field
     of the universe
growing, changing
     a net of energies
crossing patterns
     weaving towards
a new order
     a new anarchy
always different
     always the same.[28]
```

'A New Siege', from which these lines come, interweaves memories of the city of Derry to which Montague came as a child from America with images of the original siege in 1689 and contemporary ones from the Battle of the Bogside and the attacks on Civil Rights marchers at Burntollet. These latter images are contextualized internationally, as in the Introduction to the poem, by reference to student uprisings in America and Paris. But in these lines from late in the section, the modernity of the new housing estates and factories in the city are seen simply to provide a sanitized setting for traditional hatreds, as all literary or social rages for order are invaded by pain. The seeming promise offered by the relief ship is never more fully articulated; again we are unsure what emphasis or value to place on the single elements in the sequence.

In this context, Garvaghey becomes a paradigm not only of the state of the North and of the poet's inability to recapture the past ('Lines of loss') but is translated into a paradigm of universal movement and change. At the end of the most 'public' section of the poem, 'A New Siege' which is dedicated to Bernadette Devlin – the 'young girl' here who played a prominent part in the Battle of the Bogside – the 'emerging order' of the poem is dispelled by the 'cries, protestations/of a people's pain' which are in turn set within cosmic patternings, the swaying rhythms of the poem capturing that universal 'net of energies'. Montague reintroduces the idea of 'infinite variation' in the final lines quoted here, the poem itself taking on the 'new order, new anarchy' which is at the same time derived from the place and symptomatic of growth and change in the universe as a whole.

This is an odd and sudden leap beyond the immediate concerns with 'a broken province' and its history contained in the previous parts of the section. Yet it is important that the 'infinite variation' does not lead to a poetry or a politics of reconciliation on the formalist lines of later poets from the North, a poetry which Heaney hoped at one time in his career might 'continue, hold, dispel, appease'.[29] In Yeatsian fashion, order is immediately followed by anarchy, or the two are synonymous within this infinite perspective. If there is a lingering fatalism in this, then in the poetic's allegiance to change and disorder there is at least an alertness to 'a people's pain'.

Montague's deployment of the oldest metric in English – a version of the Anglo-Saxon line – in this part of *The Rough Field* is of course entirely within that modernist tradition (witness Pound's experiments with it at the start of *The Cantos*). The cosmic energies which Montague sees poetry harnessing in fact align his metric more closely with the violence in his 'broken province'; the modernist poetic becomes in his hands a paradigm of roughness and harshness, its rhythms swaying to the blunter harmonies of a stress-based line rather than to the pentameters of the English tradition favoured by the next generation of poets from the North.

This modernist technical shift extends to the recognition of the place of the poetry within history and its alignment towards an audience. Although the poetry remains true to the perceived 'people's pain', the poet does not set himself up as the voice of his community. This is the recognition reached at the end of the part called 'A Good Night', where a drunken Montague comes upon an unfinished dancehall:

> No lyric memory softens the fact –
>   this stone idol
> could house more hopes than any
>   verse of mine.
> I eye its girdered skeleton
>   with brute respect.[30]

A brief passage of prose situated before this section confirms the popularity of the new dancehalls. What this amounts to, though, is not only a recognition by Montague of the limited powers of his poetry, but also of the consonance of its indirectly lyrical, modernist aesthetic with the consumerism, the 'vague dreams' behind the dancehall craze. It is an industry 'built on loneliness', feeding the young's hunger 'for novelty, for flashing/energy & change.' This part of the book is immediately followed by 'Hymn to the New Omagh Road', where the impact of technological modernity is seen on the landscape ('A brown stain/seeps away from where the machine/rocks'[31]); but the 'energy & change' which is castigated as enervating in 'The Dancehall' is, of course, seen as patterning 'the rough field/of the universe' later in the book.

In a recognition similar to that of 'The New Siege', Montague is forced to realize that, having espoused a modernist poetic, other versions of modern 'energy' might supersede poetry itself. This consonance perhaps ultimately serves to confirm the limited effectiveness of poetry within the community, its active displacement by newer modes of change. Once again, Montague shows the equivocal relation of the poetry to the social life that it is concerned to register. The poetry reveals a strong ethical and political need to espouse the change wrought by experiment, but also a strong contrary movement to this in its critical stance, its urge to confirm the reactionary nature of poetry itself. Montague's own language of 'change', both social and poetic, also carries the drag of empty, valueless modernity which desecrates the very landscape which poetry centres itself upon. Again, he consciously registers his own consonance with the processes of history, while also recognizing that history dictates the limitations of his poetry's efficacy. He can diagnose the historical situation, but cannot alter it, such is the complex of modern values which contradict his own. In this, his poetic is paradigmatic of the dilemmas of modernism itself, which depended, as Jameson has argued, on a distinction between high and mass culture 'for its specificity, its Utopian function consisting at least in part in the securing of a realm of authentic experience over against the surrounding environment of philistinism'. But 'it can be argued that the emergence of high modernism is itself contemporaneous with the first great expansion of recognizable mass culture.'[32] As with Kinsella, Montague as artist emerges as an isolated figure, a peripheral voice speaking from the edge of modern experience and cherishing a passing resource within it.

It is this complex, contradictory stance and attitude which underlies the modulation, the shift in the last two parts of *The Rough Field* towards a reviewing of the rural scene as suitable image-hoard for expressing the 'kind of vision...of my home area, the unhappiness of its historical destiny' which Montague describes as having motivated him to write the book. That shift is on the surface something of a displacement from those historical concerns. The brief correlative between the flower and the nation at the end of 'The Wild Dog Rose' seems almost too delicate to withstand the kinds of historical weight which its positioning in the book would seem to want it to sustain, and the 'Epilogue' is notably more preoccupied with the uncertainty around the pastoral as resource rather than the 'unhappiness' of the area's 'historical destiny'.[33]

Such indirection finds its correlative again in Montague's reading of Goldsmith's 'The Deserted Village'. At the end of the essay 'Oliver Goldsmith: The Sentimental Prophecy' of 1962, Montague made larger claims for 'The Deserted Village' which clearly set it as a precursor for his own project in *The Rough Field* of ten years later:

> 'The Deserted Village' is one of the first statements of a great modern theme, the erosion of traditional values and natural rhythms in a commercial society: the fall of Auburn is the fall of a whole social order. It looks forward to Wordsworth; even, to Lawrence and Pound....Our attitude towards the poem, therefore, partly depends on our attitude towards modern history: one cannot help feeling, for instance, that Eliot's admiration for 'The Deserted Village' may be partly due to the fact that it represents an anticipation of certain aspects of his own work: a sort of rural *Waste Land*.[34]

This shows how Montague's meditations on literature are always necessarily meditations on 'modern history'. What 'The Wild Dog Rose' and the 'Epilogue' together establish in this context is, in fact, a recognition – albeit at the level of personal history – of the fallacy of a return to origins, consonant here with the fallacy of a return to pastoralism and to timelessness (the latter an ideological and poetic goal of the later Eliot).

The 'Epilogue' reminds us of the contribution which both sides of the religious divide have made to the 'ritual' which was life in the countryside, a 'ritual' which is carried through either when a priest blesses the corn or when a Protestant carries the fruits of his or her harvest to the kirk for a thanksgiving service. But the ultimate movement of the poem is not towards reconciliation, or a unitary healing and wholeness at a poetic, political or historical level. On the contrary, the modernity of the poem emerges as Montague's awareness of the failure of a Romantic pastoralism which will align the self with nature. 'No Wordsworthian dream enchants me here/With glint of glacial corry, totemic mountain' he has asserted in the very first part of the sequence,[35] and the lack of such a dream is realized in the surreal image of the hand reaching down to grasp the fields at the end. The 'failure to return' at the end is this as much as anything; it exposes the fallacy of a unity with the external world and the memories of one's own past as being obtainable through poetry. The conclusion remains pointedly historical, re-marking the changes in farming methods which have destroyed the 'pastoral' rituals of that landscape; but at the same time the failure is that of a certain kind of poetry, the kind of reminiscence that Montague had hoped to write, but that the 'attitude towards modern history' which he holds prevents him from writing. The tone of this recognition does not seem nostalgic or sentimental, but rather consonant with the harshness of the landscape itself.

Again, some of Jameson's terms serve as apt description for the tensions within the 'Epilogue' itself:

Hence the final moment in the process of dialectical analysis, in which the model strains to return to that concrete element from which it initially came, to abolish itself as an illusion of auton-omy, and to redissolve into history, offering as it does some mo-mentary glimpse of reality as a concrete whole.[36]

The 'whole' glimpsed at the end of Montague's sequence is, of course, the 'remote but friendly' one of other works of art, and the movement is towards memorializing itself and setting itself within a tradition of 'commemorative' works. The Rough Field claims for itself a status alongside Palmer, Chagall and Goldsmith at the moment in which it 'dissolves' back into history ('going/going/GONE'). The unity which it discovers is an eclectic unity among different works of art and across genres and traditions, not that of a reconciliation in or through history. The sequence recog-nizes itself as a part of history, not as a site for transcending or sym-bolically balancing and unifying elements irreconcilable within historical process. Its 'strengths' and 'weaknesses' are openly dis-played as part of its determining plight.

The fragments of history do lead to recognition on the poet's part, albeit a recognition of the failures of this kind of poetry and of the world which sustained it. The movement of the poem through 'A New Siege' to 'The Wild Dog Rose' and the 'Epilogue' does transpose the public recognition of cries and pain back to the local territory, where the violence, the harshness and the failure of the old ways comes to the fore and has to stand in for that 'public' pain. It is a 'failure to return' because, as Montague increasingly realizes through the various repetitions and variations of the work, it is *impossible*, given the modernizing forces present in Ireland and the new state of siege in the North, to return. The book is in dialogue with its own practices and aspirations, the unhappiness of its own destiny, as much as with recording personal and national histories. It also unconsciously undoes itself with the inclusion of unsettling quotidian contemporaneity. In the context, the 'social angle', which a modernist poetic redisovering 'the oldest laws of the psyche' should exclude, constantly invades the writing, and threatens or contradicts that psyche's own sources of value.

The poem's modernist difficulty and complexity centres, then, on a Jameson-like proliferation of perspectives which includes problems identified about the writing of history and of the poet's achieving a stance within and towards history. The demands made on the reader of *The Rough Field* centre on his or her need to recover the history momentarily alluded to, which, because of the fragmentariness and interrupted nature of the citations and the poetry, becomes a demand to recognize the complexity and violence of history itself. The poem's modernity is therefore constantly in tension with its historical vision, as Nietzsche, in his essay 'On the Use and Misuse of History for Life', claimed would always be the case in modern times – and therein lies the ultimate force of Montague's intervention into history in *The Rough Field*:

> ...the impulse that stands behind our history-oriented education – in radical inner contradiction to the spirit of a 'new time' or a 'modern spirit' – must in turn be understood historically; history itself must resolve the problem of history, historical knowledge must turn its weapon against itself – this threefold 'must' is the imperative of the 'new times', if they are to achieve something truly new, powerful, life-giving and original.[37]

The Rough Field's poetic is always a modernist poetic of failure. The thought of community, and of the achievement of some kind of harmony with it which might become attainable through poetry, is more a part of the *history* which the poem seeks both to dramatize and to criticize rather than to rest in. 'With all my circling a failure to return' could be read as an echo of Pound's admission late in *The Cantos* that 'I cannot make it cohere' (CXVI). That failure is everywhere written into the poem and is the basis of its 'infinite variation' and circling, which could also in itself be read as a demythologized, demythologizing belated echo of Yeats's theory of the gyres. It is the fragmentariness without progression which marks the process of the poetry, which forms the subject of its conversation with itself, and thence implicitly with the history out of which it was written.

5

History Is Only Part of It: Brendan Kennelly's *Cromwell*

Published in 1983 by Beaver Row Press, Dublin, Brendan Kennelly's comic-grotesque historical 'epic' *Cromwell* immediately received both critical acclaim and popularity, spending several months on the bestseller lists in Ireland (the book has subsequently gained further currency through its appearance as a school set text in the country). *Cromwell* is a fragmented work, one which takes the form of a nightmare dreamt by its 'hero', Buffún. The nightmare which Buffún undergoes is multifarious. It contains encounters with the 'historical' figure of Cromwell himself; memories drawn from 'provincial newspapers and from the conversations of survivors, and of the survivors of survivors, of the Civil War in Ireland' (as the Note with which Kennelly precedes the poem tells us); accounts of contemporary killings in the North of Ireland; bizarre personifications of 'mythic' creatures, the Giant, the Hand, the Belly; some seemingly more 'personal' lyrics involving a character called Mum; and other more surreal poems where the actual subject matter is sometimes obscure. With its centripetal focus upon one of Irish history's hate-figures (Cromwell's colonizing campaign was particularly brutal and desecrative), Kennelly's book raises crucial questions about the nature of the determining role which history plays within contemporary Irish poetry.

As I show below, the importance of *Cromwell* was immediately recognized by critics from both the North and the South of Ireland. The book was seen not only as a new start in Kennelly's own writing career; it was also regarded as a new start in the ways that Irish history could be poetically contained and perceived. The Belfast critic Edna Longley's review 'Beyond the Incestuous Anger', for example, a review which appeared in the Belfast magazine *Fortnight*, heralded the book as a 'creative breakthrough', not only for the poet himself, but 'in that all kinds of cultural trauma – "The terrible incestuous angers of Ireland" – bubble to the surface' in ways that they had not before in Irish writing about the country's violent past.[1]

The success of *Cromwell* ensured Kennelly's status as a high-profile media figure in Ireland. That status had indeed been growing since the late 1970s, with frequent TV appearances on Gay Byrne's *Late Late Show*, many articles in newspapers, and with large audiences for his poetry readings. Another kind of currency followed in 1987, when the Newcastle-based Bloodaxe Books published *Cromwell*, the first appearance of his work in Britain, to be followed by two selections from his earlier work, a selection from his prose, a collection of critical essays about him and, in 1991, his *The Book of Judas*. This even more voluminous 'epic' centred upon another of history's hate-figures came with plaudits from the Taoiseach Charles Haughey and from the rock band U2's Bono on the back cover.[2] The book was again an immediate success in Ireland, and Kennelly was once more on the bestseller lists there for several months.

In treating the 'cultural traumas' of his country, though, Kennelly remains a rarity. Unlike the slightly older poets who were educated in Dublin in the late 1940s, Thomas Kinsella and John Montague, Kennelly's work has continued to resist the immediate influence of international modernist forebears like Ezra Pound and T.S. Eliot. As the selection from his prose, *Journey Into Joy* illustrates, Kennelly's literary-critical interests remain resolutely Irish and also resistant to the poetic obscurity and difficulty heralded by modernist experimentalism. Unlike Kinsella's and Montague's appropriation of technical innovations from international authorities, there is about Kennelly a feeling of being inward-looking, of an urge to speak directly to the Irish people.

This difference might be ascribed to the division of Ireland itself. John Montague's Garvaghey is a childhood place defined by, disturbed by, and apt symbol for, his country's historical traumas; Brendan Kennelly's childhood in Ballylongford, North Kerry was spent in a place of 'terrific life...[one] totally acritical'. There, Kennelly was part of a spontaneous and immediate tradition: 'now that I would consider myself reasonably trained as a critic, I would cite my native flaw as someone who transfers from an oral tradition into a written...my tradition is oral; it's ballad tradition.'[3] Because of this sense of 'life' and communication, he would seem to share the ideas of one of his clear forebears Patrick Kavanagh, who, he claims, 'recognised that, in most cases, obscurity is simply a failure of the poet's imagination, the sanctuary of the inadequate.'[4] As Katie Donovan wrote in her profile/interview with him at around the time of *The Book of Judas*, 'Kennelly makes it his business, to write "good readable poems for people to enjoy or get mad over" and has no time for the more conventional notion of poetic language and a small elite audience.'[5]

While the popular success in the Republic of *Cromwell*'s shocking and playful incarnation of the Joycean nightmare of history is not in doubt, however, the precise nature of the 'breakthrough' which the book marks with regard to the country's cultural traumas remains a contentious critical issue. The various responses to the book from Edna Longley have been both crucial and symptomatic in this, as in much else. She has sought in her essay 'Poetic Forms and Social Malformations' to link the public acceptability of *Cromwell*, its openness, popularity and ready accessibility, to the different conditions which prevailed in the Republic of Ireland during the 1980s from those in the North. The Republic's movement during that time 'towards "a much more open attitude to experience and expression"' finds its echo, she argues, in the expansiveness and extrovertedness of the book when compared with even the most exuberant and playful of the poets from the North, Paul Muldoon. The case of Kennelly, her polemic continues, disproves those 'Republicans and Marxists' who claim that 'theoretical buzz-words, e.g.: "crisis", "colonialism", "identity"' might have 'undifferentiated application to the whole of Ireland'. Such application is a manifestation of 'a premature homogenization, that actually devalues what poetry can tell us about Ireland.'[6]

The theme of this 1989 essay developed, and in many ways moderated, the terms of Longley's original *Fortnight* review of *Cromwell*. But it is when seeking to describe the nature of what she had called there the 'cultural trauma' which bubbles to the surface in Kennelly's poem that Longley displays some of the aggression behind one of her perennial arguments. In *Fortnight*, she uses Kennelly's 'breakthrough' to lambast poets from the North of Ireland who have associated themselves with the Field Day Theatre Company project. Instead of 'exploiting "history" politically', Longley asserts, 'Kennelly explores it psychologically. Even the excess of *Cromwell*...contributes to a therapeutic primal scream.' By means of this psychological emphasis Kennelly manages, in her view, to overcome many of the cultural traumas felt keenly by the writers from the North, not least the traumas involved in being an Irish poet writing in those traditional poetic forms most powerfully exploited by English poets who were part of the Elizabethan colonization of Ireland. In *Cromwell*:

> Spenser escapes the whipping he usually gets from the Field Day rearguard action against linguistic and literary colonialism.... Kennelly follows Montague, Heaney and Friel into the language question, but somehow without the Northern illness that usually attends it....As a public poem imagined from the Republic *Cromwell* marks a salutary shift from the narrow vision some Northern 'political' poetry exports South.... *Cromwell* genuinely tries to awaken from the nightmare of history, rather than indulge in the usual masochistic wallow, or 'whine about identity.'

For Longley, because of the greater freedom within which Kennelly lives in the South, he is able to exploit a greater aesthetic freedom, and therefore come closer to some kind of true transcendence, than those who originally come from the North. As the later essay puts it, he can 'half-masochistically' (rather than the wholesale 'wallow' in the North, presumably) 'relish the irony' of being an Irish poet who writes in the sonnet forms of Sidney, Spenser and Shakespeare.[7]

It is true that the humour of *Cromwell* is sometimes openly generated out of mimicking the noble attitudes behind the decorousness of those English forms, as when, in 'The Position of Praise', Kennelly has Spenser – who was active in the Elizabethan campaign to colonize Ireland – 'say'

> ...friends shoved me
> Over here because I loved green tables
> And round tables and gentle chivalry.

Yet this poem complicates matters considerably by raising questions, as to whether, as Longley claims, by refusing to make a 'political' reading of '"history"' Kennelly then offers the possibility that he might 'awake from' it. How far would Kennelly in fact *agree* with the view 'voiced' by Spenser in this sonnet, that all a poet can do today or any day is to acknowledge the 'ugliness' which is disfiguring the old ways?[8]

This debate goes to the heart of seeking to define what kind of poem *Cromwell* in fact is. What remains admittedly obscure within Longley's terms ('genuinely tries') is just how far they allow 'The terrible incestuous angers of Ireland' to have been passed beyond, superseded or transcended, and just how this is achieved in the book.[9] There is a similar obscurity in the claims made for the work by Terence Brown, who comes to a similar separation-cum-accommodation as Longley's, in which *Cromwell* plays central role:

> [*Cromwell*] assumes the determinism of Irish history, but to portray this is not [its] primary purpose. Rather it is to allow the nightmare so full and complete an expression in a poetic imagining that Cromwell's time can be transcended....[S]uch imaginative transcendence of an historical dilemma may be the preserve of the artist. The state of consciousness to which it bears salutary witness, however, must compel attention as paradigm of that true freedom in history which it is the business of a liberating polity to serve.[10]

The refusal by both these critics to develop the distinction they make between the political and the psychological, or the association of 'full expression' with transcendence, marks in some ways an end to critical thought about the relation between the poetic imagination and the historical moment out of which it arises. By continuing to presume that there is some way in which poetry might ultimately break free of history, by refusing to theorize the relations between the aesthetic and the political, such criticism is in danger not of revealing and exploring, but of obscuring the bases of its own distinctions.

And it is the case that, even at the level of relative formal transcendence or freedom envisaged by Longley – Kennelly's greater ease with classical English poetic forms than that available to some writers within the immediate context of the sectarian divide in the North – *Cromwell* is not as readily accommodating as her review suggests. At the level of the individual poem, many of the sonnets, unlike those of the 'tradition' Kennelly draws from, are in unrhymed free verse, and deploy an energetic demotic idiom closer to the orality of Kennelly's childhood culture than to the literary-critical circumstances of his adulthood (he is a Professor at Trinity College, Dublin). At the level of the organization of poems in the book, Kennelly has clearly built in a feeling of randomness by following the mode of loose thematic arrangement described in the Preface to a selection from his poems: '[The] closenesses and affinities feel like accidents; yet, in the artificial symmetry of any "arrangement", they must be allowed to happen.'[11]

Further, the whole thrust of *Cromwell* is, as Longley also acknowledges, against formal closure and the imposed fixity of a single perspective upon the work. This is signalled by the somewhat gnomic note which Kennelly attaches to *Cromwell* in the volume *A Time For Voices*:

> Because of history, an Irish poet, to realise himself, must turn the full attention of his imagination to the English tradition. An English poet committed to the same task need hardly give the same thought to things Irish. Every nightmare has its own logic. History, however, is only a part of this poem. Buffún's nightmare is his own. Hence the fact that he is not a voice; he is many voices.[12]

It is clear from this that the 'breakthrough' which *Cromwell* represents in treating its historical material is largely a 'breakthrough' into a polyvocalism which complicates the lyric, psychological approach taken to the book of critics like Longley. This poem does its 'history' in different voices as modernist poetic sequences do. Rather than being centred in a formal tradition and relishing the irony of it, *Cromwell* wears its ludic, parodic anarchy openly. As his name suggests, Buffún represents a spirit of buffoonery and fun, and his nightmare constitutes a scary, dishevelled 'logic' in its energetic, wild excursion amongst historical and imaginative events which is inevitably restless and unsettling. It is this which makes it difficult, contrary to what other critics have claimed, to know where best to stand in relation to the poem and to its treatment of history, difficult to know what polarities or relations are being set up ('self' and 'history'? 'psyche' and 'cultural trauma'?), or ultimately how seriously to take them.

In a note written to an earlier poem, Kennelly makes great play of the way in which writing history is itself an inconclusive parodic process:

> The best histories always partake of the legend-making or legend-debunking faculty, and both legend-making and legend-debunking are legend-making, because a debunked legend will

always establish itself in another form. In the world of legend, refutation is a form of re-birth....'[13]

This sense of history or legend-making as participation in an end-lessly metamorphic activity both licenses the parodic playfulness contained in the nightmare of history undergone by Buffún and also the relation which the poetry makes with the 'English tradi-tion' as it is averted to in Kennelly's Note. That 'tradition' is only personally present in the book through the figure of 'Ed Spenser'. Yet Spenser's own mastery of a chivalric idiom is continuously travestied in the sonnets of *Cromwell* and becomes in Buffún's nightmare a pose adopted for purely selfish ends. 'Dedication', for example, brutally undercuts its characteristic courteous language of patronage and decorum:

> 'I am happy to make known to you
> The humble affection I have always professed....'
> [then he sighs]
> 'Anything to escape from fucking Cork!'[14]

There hardly seems enough here to justify the literary-cultural point that Longley seems to want to make: 'In practice Kennelly's iconoclastic methods get "the English tradition" off his back, as he bounces off it to pursue parallel purposes.'[15] Longley's point seems overly specific in the light of the actual representation (or under-representation) of English 'tradition' on its own terms in the book. While it is true that Kennelly in 'Master' discovers a ready identification with Spenser as he watches his epic grow gargantu-anly ('"I'm worried, though, about the actual bulk/Of *The Fairie Queene*.../I'm up to my bollox in sonnets" Spenser said'[16]), this 'English tradition' speaks very much in the racily demotic voice of Buffún himself. Rather than 'bouncing off' the alien tradition, it is arguable that by so readily translating that tradition into Buffún's own idiom the tradition is actually never fully realized, recognized or articulated in *Cromwell*. The ready lampooning of Spenser's chivalric idiom might hardly be described as 'turning the full at-tention of...imagination upon it'. Instead, that lampooning delights in exploiting the detachment of literary style from its author's true motivations, something which wryly removes authorial presence from the text while suggesting that it is still operative at an unarticulated level. Once again, Kennelly is playing on notions of distance between the vocal surfaces of his poem and what might amount to interpretation of them, so that notions of providing a complete critical reading of the poem become next to untenable – particularly if that reading gives to the poem exemplary status in the divided contexts of Ireland North and South. Kennelly in turn exploits and relishes the comic liberations in establishing that distance.

As *Cromwell* is a book formed of Buffún's nightmare, it is entirely natural that all its characters and voices should be translated into his own demotic. But this merely exacerbates the difficulty of judging the stance which it adopts towards the historical and literary material which it integrates. This is a point which worried Robert Johnstone:

> William of Orange...appears only in a couple of...quips. A damaging selectivity of vision? – on the poet's or the [Irish] people's part? The invented characters can be equally shadowy. Kennelly says Buffún is 'many voices', but he could be almost any voice – a casualty of the post-modernist technique.[17]

In the interview Kennelly gave to discuss *The Book of Judas*, though, it was still the polyvocal qualities of his earlier book which he chose to emphasize. 'Kennelly feels', Katie Donovan writes, 'that, like *Cromwell*, the different voices add to the dramatic quality of *The Book of Judas*...."Genres such as poetry and drama are beginning to break down in the work of today's writers," adds Kennelly, who sees *The Book of Judas* as very much a "voice drama."'[18]

The question of the success or failure of the book's dramatic differentiations goes very much to the heart, then, of Kennelly's artistic purpose. The question of a particular voice's authenticity is something which Kennelly's work itself often raises, if only, somewhat shockingly, to deny the possibility of such authenticity. *The Book of Judas* even has a poem, 'The Authentic Voice of Judas', which reveals that when it comes to speaking out against contemporary violent events (presumably this poem refers to the news reports in 1988 of the killing of two 'off-duty' British soldiers in the North of Ireland) the problem of authenticity becomes crucial:

> Witnessing a young man with a black moustache
> Dragged from his car, beaten up and shot
> By a zestful mob...
> I wondered if I had an authentic voice

> To speak against the mediaful
> Murder.[19]

The fact that the events leading up to the murder were shown on TV further undermines the possibility of having something real to say about it. In surreal fashion, 'Judas' then follows a voice down a 'starved laneway', demanding if it could be his own 'authentic' one. But he is inevitably rebuffed, told that he has no recognizable voice 'Unless it be this laneway packed with shadows, hungers', and this ill-defined, undernourished voice is hardly one which could speak out against the situation.

The 'voice' as it is described here, its 'shadows, hungers', is resonant of the affliction caused in Ireland by the Great Hunger which figures among the cumulative historical plights of *Cromwell* also (e.g. in 'Nothin', 'Famine Fever', 'Hunger'[20]). There is a strong sense here that the sickness and suffering which Ireland has had inflicted on it is the very cause of its poets' inability to speak out authentically against the causes of that suffering; that everything, including the poetic 'voice', is inevitably divided (as is the case obviously in Kennelly's adoption of the Judas-mask here).

Questions surrounding the authenticity of voice clearly go to the heart, then, of the relation which Kennelly seeks to establish between his poetry and the historical trauma in his country North and South, past and present, and also between his poetry and its audience. Again, in Spenser's 'terms', can the poet only witness 'ugliness' and so alert his audience to it, or can he discover ways to step beyond an intransigent, determining fate? The Preface which he wrote to the recent selection from his prose signals that he thinks of these relations as being potentially full of inadequacy and failure:

> Why can I only grudgingly concede that what is considered by many of the most articulate members of our society to be 'moving', 'beautiful', 'skilled', 'profound', 'important', 'accomplished', 'ultimately affirmative' is, in fact, pretty impotent, useless, an elegant, feeble, straw in the wind? The sneer on the terrorist's face may be the answer....Violence works. Murder works. Terrorism works....[Literature] may chronicle them but it won't change them.

From this point of view, the role which literature might fulfil is, then, a very limited one: that of 'witnessing the accuracy and courage with which other people reveal their experiences of this world'.[21]

It is important to note in this light the way in which the voice's inauthenticity, as also the poetry's inefficacy, is affected by the sheer enormity of the efficacy of destructive violence in the world Kennelly chronicles. *Cromwell* would seem to arise from this collusion between the world's propensity for violence (and, as Robert Johnstone notes in his review, the world remains Ireland in Kennelly's work, 'the aspects are always of Irish life, not human nature') and the inability to achieve any definitive vocal authenticity, even through the use of persona.

Notably, in *Cromwell*, it is the colonizer, Cromwell himself, who makes a claim to truth in language:

> Why listen to others? False speech is most
> Accursed, so false that it cannot even know
> That it is false, as the poor commonplace liar does.[22]

Under this severe sense of the necessary truth of language, the only people who have the right to speak according to Cromwell are those 'whose deeds forever mark [their] time'. That exact correlation demanded between words and actions then serves to make Cromwell a kind of author of 'History'. Indeed, in the sonnet of that title, there is an attack on academic versions of history, as personified by an Oxford historian with his motto *'mens sana in sano corpore'* (a healthy mind in a healthy body). This 'official' history-making is at odds with that espoused by his 'friend', Oliver Cromwell, who says in reply to his question '"What *is* history, then?"' '"History is when I decide to act."'[23]

This emphasis from the colonizer suggests that the traditional civilization/barbarian dichotomy between Britain and Ireland might be rewritten as that between active 'truth' which is self-serving and brutally exploitative and the colonized people's 'lies'. But if this is the case within *Cromwell*'s allegorical referentiality, then literature itself is very much aligned for Kennelly with both the sufferings and the freedoms won through rejection of 'civilizing', self-righteous standards of 'truth'. 'The worst violence, perhaps, is lies,' he has written, 'Literature, so often accredited with being concerned with truth, is fascinated by lies and remains faithful to its compulsion to explore their workings, their universality, their necessity and their style.'[24]

Cromwell is in its turn fascinated with all kinds of violence. Cromwell's action was, of course, in relation to Ireland one of extreme violence in conquest. As Christopher Hill acknowledges in a book which Kennelly notes as a source for his own, Cromwell had a 'racial contempt for the Irish' and showed it in his swift and brutal suppression of them.[25] Cromwell, as Kennelly admits, is one of the 'two most damned figures in Irish life' – Judas, the subject of his next book, being the other – because of the brutality of his conquest and colonization. In the Introduction he wrote to a recent selection from his early poems, *Breathing Spaces*, it is clear that Kennelly views the adoption of such nationally hated personae as imaginatively and psychologically liberating:

> 'Entering into' such personalities, legends, forces, mythical monsters, is an effective way to stir that mobile, boggy swamp of egotism known as the self....Engagement with such figures provides a breathing space for the imagination forced to live in the selfswamp. I'm very grateful for my historical and religious monsters; they've given my imagination a certain amount of freedom which I sometimes find frightening and always thrilling.[26]

Again this unsettles and questions any lyric basis for *Cromwell* and suggests that its poetic might be a dramatic one. Yeats remains the most obvious Irish forebear for this kind of 'entering into' an anti-self in order to breathe life into poetry. As Kennelly has written in 'W.B. Yeats: An Experiment in Living', 'He could arouse himself into a dramatic awareness of others.' Yet, at the same time, Kennelly again defends the complex, dualistic efficacies of literary style: 'Yeats's masks are an elaborate mode of self-discipline and, paradoxically, self-revelation. This discipline is a personal exercise, not an external imposition.'[27]

It is at this point that the various problems of identification in *Cromwell* are raised again. The tone of the poetry seems unsure, the identity of the protagonist and the central focus of the poem remains a problem for the reader to the end. As day dawns for Buffún in *Cromwell*'s final poem, 'A Soft Amen', the unconcluded process of 'Begetting, forgetting' which has run throughout the book seems set to continue. Buffún does not 'wake' from the nightmare, but remains a disparate, dissipated, deeply uncertain figure:

I know how to laugh, I know how to weep
As morning explodes inside me here
And I'm scattered like, well, I hope
Like Mum and Oliver, Spenser, the giant, William
And all the others striding through me,
Prisoners on parole from history,
Striving to come alive as I think I am... .[28]

History here is determined and imprisoning, locked away from the present which only releases the characters temporarily (and is there a submerged pun on 'parole' as 'leave' but also 'words'?) for the duration of the text or nightmare. These contrary surges of emotion and continuous 'striving' to be born hardly suggests an assured sense of what has been learnt from this nightmare. 'Are the makers mad?' Buffún asks here, as all time becomes undifferentiated, monotonous, in the book's final line: 'In the light of day and the light of night.'

When connected with these specific problems of reading, the method of the poem emerges as one of historical crisis rather than one of historical transfiguration. A perpetual debunking of history and legend fascinates Kennelly here and is, for instance, manifested in the anachronistic shifts of the book, as, for instance, in the conversation between the Oxford history don and Oliver Cromwell cited above. 'The method of the poem is imagistic, not chronological. This seemed the most effective way to represent a "relationship" [i.e. that between Ireland and England] that has produced a singularly tragic mess.' So Kennelly describes his method in his Note at the front of the book. Yet this method is in his terms closer to Irish experience, an experience which again the book 'chronicles' but does not seek to 'change'. That experience both determines the fragmented nature of *Cromwell* and represents its impulsive, spontaneous 'liberty'.

This potentially anachronistic method also validates Kennelly's setting of images from Cromwell's conquest alongside those from the Irish Civil War, as it does also the more outrageous flights of fancy in the book as when Cromwell becomes manager of the local football team, Drogheda United. But such concatenations of time also have a curious effect analogous to that noted by Johnstone. Surely these various moments of history are of a different order, the one to the other? The colonization of Ireland by Cromwell is linked in this debunking poetic 'epic' to the struggle for power in the newly formed Free State and also to the current war in the North.

Those concatenations are exacerbated by the fact that it is violence which seems to give energy to the shifts of period and voice in the poem. Far from 'qualifying' the 'colonialist' issue, as Edna Longley claims *Cromwell* to have done, however, Kennelly might equally be accused of blurring or of failing to confront it. Certainly there are historical parallels being created throughout: 'Nails' (which describes a van bomb which kills a group of children) might be set, for instance, against the sarcastic 'Work and Play' in which we are told that 'Killing children is not pleasant, even at the worst of times./Oliver's boys/Approached the task with Herodean vigour...'.[29] Yet there remains the problem of what to do with such parallels, with the persistent reminders here that once again children are being killed on Irish ground. It is hard to say what light is being cast on either the relationship of colonizer and colonized or on the war in the North by such images which, in many cases, seem randomly assembled ('Work and Play' and 'Nails' are eighty pages apart in the book) rather than set in creative historical juxtaposition. As will become clear later, there are several groups of poems in *Cromwell* which do centre upon specific historical subjects, but the shift from one to the other is often obscure, and the patterning of the whole book is one of accumulation rather than development from one part to the next.

It is at this point that Kennelly's claim in the Note that 'History...is only part of this poem. Buffún's nightmare is his own' needs to be taken more seriously than it appears to have been in other commentaries. In 'Ghouls', Cromwell resents Buffún's assertion that he might be a humorist: '"I'll leave that to you, Buffún./Yet, looking at the ghouls of history,/I see how laughter might engulf a man."'[30] Buffún's nightmare conjures the ghouls of history and of the imagination, and treats them with earthily humorous disrespect. Ultimately, therefore, Kennelly's use of the mask in *Cromwell* is less Yeatsian than Bakhtinian. It is hardly revelatory about history, the colonizer or the self in the way that the Yeats mask was, since all these things seem confusedly scattered in Buffún's nightmare. 'The mask', Bakhtin wrote in *Rabelais and his World*

> is connected with the joy of change and reincarnation, with gay relativity...it rejects conformity to oneself. The mask is related to transition, metamorphosis, the violation of natural

boundaries....It contains the playful element in life...such manifestations as parodies, caricatures, grimaces, eccentric postures, and comic gestures are per se derived from the mask. It reveals the essence of the grotesque.[31]

The epic space of *Cromwell* allows for the free play of materials or voices drawn from a variety of sources, a play which leads to a continual splitting of identity consonant with, as 'The Crowd' has it, 'losing what I had come to regard as myself.'[32] The poem constantly shifts its perspective, but, through this process of perpetual splitting, gives the curious feeling that, although its 'subject matter' is predominantly historical, the tense of the poem is that of the continuous present. In an opaque poem, 'The Right to Happen', we are told that 'Nothing can stop what has a right to happen.... There is nothing that is not in the present tense/And forever and not at all.' As Kennelly told Katie Donovan, 'past and present are simultaneous' in the poem.[33] Again, Bakhtin's reading of similar parodic-travestying moments in history provides a useful clue to the temporal simultaneities achieved in *Cromwell*. Bakhtin defined medieval carnivals, times when the people were released from 'official, ecclesiastical, feudal and political cult forms and ceremonials' into celebration:

They offered a completely different, nonofficial, extraecclesiastical and extrapolitical aspect of the world, of man, and of human relations....Carnival is not a spectacle seen by the people; they live in it....While carnival lasts, there is no other life outside it.... This led to the creation of special forms of marketplace speech and gesture, frank and free....This experience, opposed to all that was ready-made and completed, to all pretence at immutability, sought a dynamic expression; it demanded ever-changing, playful, undefined forms.[34]

For Bakhtin, this temporary release from the formal habits and expressions of the everyday world into the festivity of carnival in the marketplace provides a revival and renewal of energies, a liberation from temporal demands which leads to a restoring of life, something which Kennelly's 'lying' poetry might also claim to do. By so readily embracing the traditional pose of the rude stage Irishman in creating Buffún and setting him in contrast to the 'civilizing' Englishman Cromwell Kennelly disarms and undermines all criticism of his poetry in 'standard' or 'official' terms, and so frees it into a different order of being. Yet the relation of that carnivalesque space to the historical and current violence of his island remains a perplexed one.

The Bakhtinian definition of the carnivalesque is curiously consonant with the effects which Kennelly, in a 1988 essay, claimed that poetry and violence can have: 'The imagination of a man or a woman can be *nourished* by the same violent feelings and forces which would most likely repel that same man or woman in his or her attempts to have an ordinary, decent life':

> It would appear that poetry tells us that violence is inevitable and universal, that it has to do with vital and consequential change ... Poetry tends to recognise and demonstrate what a conventional morality will tend to outlaw and condemn....[35]

It is the responsibility of Irish poetry, therefore, to take account of 'both violence and its consequences' since 'Irish history is so riddled with violence'. But for this to properly occur, Kennelly feels, Irish poetry must 'develop more of a sense of humour, of comic selfmockery, thereby admitting its own seriousness and limitations. Our beautiful world is a horror-pit; how can our poetry not be comic?'[36]

Such critical statements serve both as a prescription for Kennelly's own recent work and also to reinforce the sense that for him the nature of *Irish* poetry – as comic-grotesque – is historically determined. Poetry then provides a space within daily life through which fiercely energetic forces of feeling can be brought into focus and articulated. Kennelly would, from this perspective, be impatient with the typical qualities of traditional English poetic forms. Indeed, his deeply felt awareness of the violence which has marked Irish history leads him to echo Walter Benjamin's statement that 'There is no document of civilization which is not at the same time a document of barbarism': 'At the roots of good taste lies barbarism.'[37]

Cromwell revels in its anarchic bad taste, and its comedy relishes the opportunities for sarcastic flights provided by the enormity of violence across Irish history. In 'A Request', 'The Secretary of the Irish Blood Donors Society' writes to Cromwell asking for a contribution, only to receive the reply 'May I suggest you send somebody/To accompany me on my Irish Campaign...?' The juxtapositions in the book between one poem and the next can also work to force comedy and violence up against each other. In 'Cream', Cromwell tells the story of a soldier in camp who gets his head stuck in a tub of cream ('"I love an innocent jest" Oliver purred'); in the next poem, 'An Example', a soldier tells the story of the hanging of a young girl in front of her father and the Limerick townsfolk.[38] Much of this humour is Rabelaisian as Bakhtin understood it. The poem is replete with exaggeratedly grotesque bodily images ('When Cromwell vanished up Mother Ireland's cunt...') and with coarseness in the language of all the personae barring that of Cromwell himself.[39] What is unnerving is that the 'grotesque realism' (to use Bakhtin's phrase for these carnivalesque qualities) of this kind of humour is so readily consonant in Kennelly's poetry with the barbaric violence in Ireland's history past and present. The lineation of 'Some People' makes literal that sense of the barbarism which can feed off of more positive or aesthetic virtues:

> Elizabeth Birch had a white neck
> They roped it
> George Butterwick of the strong body
> Looked awkward naked....[40]

Cromwell often reads as a cataloguing or listing of the grotesque horrors enacted on the victims of violence; its quality of discrimination merely operates to delineate modes of death and suffering. The supreme danger here, of course, is that such listing makes violence merely banal, and that the burlesque humour disappears under the constancy of its repeated few effects. The sense of historical determinism throughout the book means that the multiple perspectives of the various 'personae' – if they can be called that – merely throw different lights on the same subject. At the end of 'Nails', after the van bomb, we are told that 'Some children are whole, others bits and pieces./These blasted crucifixions are commonplace.'[41] Both the forcing of literal truth against angrily weak swearing in response to the outrage in the word 'blasted', and the compacting of the religious into everyday violent destruction in 'crucifixions', mean that the possibilities of prioritizing one strain of language in the book over another become virtually nil. All traditional resonances and meanings are leaked away or turned into parodic inversions of themselves by the disjunctive, 'polyvocal' context which bears witness to Irish history. Another danger, which I will explore later, is that this brings about a levelling of standards, values and perspectives which is limiting, even deliberately detrimental, to the poetry itself.

What sustains the book throughout, and what also makes all means of distinguishing personae or the hermeneutics of the writing impossible, are the restless colloquial energies of its voices, the poet's delight in the oral tradition out of which he emerged. The vibrancy which Kennelly succeeds in giving to them is marked by the way he often travesties formal grammatical rules, even making nouns and adjectives into verb forms. 'Verbs' like 'honestied', 'paperbacked', 'storied', 'slowmotioned' and 'jigsawed', 'furied', 'apparitions', 'stanzaing', even 'cromwelled' punctuate the formal 'decorums' from beginning to end of this work.[42]

It is inevitably at the level of language that the negotiations between Irish and 'the English tradition' are most fully enacted in *Cromwell*, and it is at this level that the 'breakthrough' which the book brought in Irish poetry is most richly suggestive.[43] In its parodic-travestying heteroglot method, the book is intensely political, deploying its situation between cultures as a means to undermine all homogenizing versions of stories, myths and authoritarian meanings. Bakhtin claimed that the dialogic, heteroglot discourses of the novel attained a similar importance:

> ...it is possible to objectivize one's own particular language, its internal form, the peculiarities of its world view, its specific linguistic habitus, only in the light of another language belonging to someone else, which is almost as much 'one's own' as one's native language.[44]

Within the colonial situation between Britain and Ireland, such objectivity is made tragically possible, and the impulse to travesty and 'make one's own' what has been brutally imposed is correlatively vibrant for Kennelly. Much of *Cromwell* is made up of a pastiche discourse founded upon the Protestant empirical language to be found in Cromwell's speeches and letters:

> I have no rhetoric, no wit, no words.
> The dispensations of God upon me
> Require I speak not words, but Things...

Cromwell says at the start of 'Oliver Speaks to his Countrymen'.[45] The parsimoniousness of this relation to language smashes against the polymorphic colloquialism of *Cromwell*'s epic pretensions. It is in the encounter between this Puritan plain style and the garrulousness associated with Buffún and the Irish 'characters' that the poetic style of the book, its ludicrous synthesis and its laughter, lies.[46]

In one poem, 'Stones and Pebbles and the Language of Heaven', Kennelly highlights the language question in order to delineate the traditional polarity in which England (in the figure of suave, gentlemanly, honest Oliver) perceives itself as a civilized nation whereas the Irish are perceived as barbaric:

> 'I must confess, Buffún,' honestied Oliver
> 'Your native language strikes me as barbarous,
> Rude in the mouth, agony on the ear...'.[47]

Bakhtin emphazises the pre-literary and orality as both the means for transmitting the parodic-travestying tradition and its chief characteristic.[48] The Joycean ebullience of *Cromwell* relishes capturing oral, non-literary voices rather than those of inscribed poetic tradition.

Because of this, in many ways, rather than 'qualifying' theoretical 'buzz words' like 'colonialism', the hybridization of language in the book fits standard patterns of post-colonial theory as it has been understood by theorists working through adapted and somewhat simplified versions of Bakhtin's ideas. *Cromwell*'s constant playing fast and loose with grammar and punctuation as a means of countering the ordered utterances of the oppressor Cromwell and of the English tradition echoes what have been seen as 'normal' responses to post-colonial situations. 'Dedication', the poem in which the decorum of Ed Spenser's language is violently debunked, is preceded by two of the more surreal poems which the book contains, poems in which the contortions of the language and the odd wrenchings of syntactic connections serve to undermine our sense of the conventional order of things. 'Mum's Tongue' opens 'Mum's tongue snaked after me/I ran three different roads at once'; 'A Sound of Breaking' 'It was forgiveness in the voice I heard/God alone knows how many years after,/Drifting down that rainy street.'[49]

Bill Ashcroft, Gareth Griffiths and Helen Tiffin have argued that such hybridization in which the dominant language of the oppressor (in Kennelly's book embodied in Cromwell's 'speeches' or 'letters') is decontextualized, disjointed and contorted by the colonized people (here represented by Buffún or the other voices' anarchic surrealism) is a standard feature of 'all post-colonial texts'. Of course, vernacularization and hybridization are common in poems from Ireland both North and South and from both communities, from those influenced by Joyce's linguistic ideas like Heaney and Kinsella, to those interested in the vernacular, dialect and colloquialisms of the street, like Tom Paulin, Paul Durcan and Kennelly. As Ashcroft, Griffiths and Tiffin claim:

> ...the syncretic and hybridized nature of post-colonial experience refutes the privileged position of a standard code in the language and any monocentric view of human experience....[There is a] creative potential [in] intersecting languages when the syntactic and grammatical rules of one language are overlaid on another, and of the way in which cross-cultural literature reveals how meanings work.[50]

In this view, the verve and energy of the literature from post-colonial countries like the Republic derives from the ways in which the 'writing abrogates the privileged centrality of English' by using language 'to signify difference, while also employing a sameness which allows it to be understood.'[51]

In this sense, for these three theorists, the focus on the 'language question' is crucial within post-colonial literature. Language itself becomes the implicit subject of all post-colonial texts. The literary work becomes the 'field of intersection...the field within which the word announces its purpose':

> The 'world' as it exists 'in' language is an unfolding reality which owes its relationship to language to the fact that language interprets the world in practice, not to some imputed referentiality.
>
> Language exists, therefore, neither before the fact nor after the fact but in the fact. Language constitutes reality....[52]

But this is to push Bakhtin's ideas about the heteroglot, dialogic force of parodic-travestying literature which exists on various boundary lines to an almost absurd postmodern Derridean extreme in which everything becomes textual. There is, to say the least, something banal and dangerously totalizing about such manoeuvres, one which threatens to see all literatures from countries sharing a common former oppressor as the same. Specific cultures and histories continue to be denied under the aegis of this new 'enlightened' theoretical practice as they were formally by imperialist powers. Even if we might agree that since the only way we can judge the authenticity of histories and experiences is through language – that language is slippery, duplicitous, and therefore that the attempt to form a judgement about it is ultimately doomed – surely this should not be allowed to eradicate difference and the struggle to define all experiences? It is just this specificity which for Bakhtin himself guaranteed the energetic validity of all utterances:

> The living utterance, having taken meaning and shape at a particular historical moment in a socially specific environment, cannot fail to brush up against thousands of living dialogic threads, woven by socio-ideological consciousness around the given object of an utterance; it cannot fail to become an active participant in social dialogue.[53]

One achievement of Kennelly's carnivalesque method in *Cromwell* is that it includes the whole range of social potential within itself and therefore has much which appeals to different sectors of its audience – hence, perhaps, the work's popularity in Ireland. 'Cromwell' is both manager of Drogheda United and, in 'An Expert Teacher', the assured and self-serving pugilistic refutor of Milton's premises in setting out upon his own epic journey, *Paradise Lost*: '"God's ways need not be justified", Oliver said./ Protestants were massacred in 1641.'[54]

So, if *Cromwell* qualifies post-colonial 'buzz words', it does so in ways which reveal the totalizing narrowness of key tenets of that theory yet which do not necessarily confirm the kinds of internal poetic divisions within the island of Ireland as Longley wants them to. While in many ways it conforms to the view of post-colonial texts held by some theorists, in others *Cromwell* conforms to a fuller sense of Bakhtin's original argument, holding itself in creative dialogue with a wide contemporary audience, especially with one which has experienced the book's multifarious embodiments of violence on its home ground. And that is tragically true of the whole island.

This is one effect of the poem's perpetual present, that it is all-involving and difficult to stand back from, and so it breaks the bounds of the critical/oral split which Kennelly recognizes in himself. And the inclusiveness of the book's idiom does not prevent it from opening a lively social dialogue by attacking specific contemporary social ills. As Terence Brown has shown in his *Ireland: A Social and Cultural History 1922–1985* by quoting from Kennelly's earlier poem 'Westland Row' on emigration from Ireland, his is poetry which is often concerned to provide a contemporary insight into perennial cultural trends in his country.[55] In 'Dublin: A Portrait', Kennelly has painted an excoriating attack on the city where he lives and works in terms which further go to the heart of his poetic concerns involving questions of authenticity and definition:

> There the herds of eloquent phonies,
> Dark realities kept in the dark,
> Squalor stinking at many a corner
> Poverty showing an iron hand;
> There the tinker sprawls on the pavement,
> Servile victim of those whose pence
> He begs like a dog....[56]

Kennelly transposes such social involvement into a literary-historical issue by calling another poem about the prostitutes who parade by the polluted Grand Canal in Dublin 'The Celtic Twilight'. In this second case, Kennelly signals the way in which Yeats's high literary and cultural ambitions have been reduced to squalid realities in the contemporary Republic, which has become a 'night/Of lurid women and predatory men/Who must inflict but cannot share/Each other's pain.'[57]

In the phantasmagoric world of *Cromwell*, the criticism aimed at those contemporary social trends which keep part of the population in poverty is caught up in the swirl of Ireland's perennial suffering from hunger, famine, fever and disease. The series of sonnets centred around events associated with the Great Hunger is followed by 'Points', a poem in which a 'tinker-girl' is sent out to rob tourists in Dublin of their purses and wallets:

> The fleeced tourist groans. The girl is gone.
> Tonight, at least, she knows she won't be kicked
> Though brothers wade knee-deep through brothers' blood.[58]

It would be difficult to fit a precise historical moment to this 'story' as to many such in the book. But it has a clear contemporary reference to the time of Kennelly's writing. In the mid to late 1970s, as Brown notes, Jack Lynch's Fianna Fáil party became heavily indebted to foreign governments in order to try and respark the domestic economy into life. By the early 1980s the failure of this economic wager became apparent. Foreign indebtedness rose from only £78 million in 1978 to £6703 million in 1983, the year of *Cromwell's* publication in Ireland. Many lost their jobs and were forced into poverty; unemployment rose by 77 per cent from 1979 to 1982. As a result, crime increased rapidly during these years, particularly in Dublin itself.[59]

One of the violences which Kennelly is particularly concerned to expose throughout the history of the country is, then, that of perennial poverty. Christopher Hill argues that the colonization of Ireland, as Cromwell saw it, was commercially calculating; there was money to be gained from selling off conquered Irish land, something which remains a submerged element in Kennelly's concern with money in various parts of *Cromwell*. Yet, in an extension of this exploration of the pain caused by all authority, Kennelly is also anxious to reveal the complicity of the Catholic Church in slaughter. In many ways, he is true to the historical record in showing how the Church suffered at that time. Beside the financial implications, Hill maintains that it was the political associations of Irish Catholicism which provided the particular motivation for Cromwell's conquest. It is these political associations which formed Cromwell's justification for hanging priests and shooting officers whereas – apart from the dreadful sackings of Drogheda and Wexford – other ranks and civilians were usually given quarter.[60] But Kennelly's concern to portray the 'tragic mess' of Ireland's violent history does not, however, allow this particularity of motivation and target to impinge upon his detailed listing of atrocities. He draws upon other of his sources than Hill to show the violence perpetrated not just at the instigation of, but also by, the Catholic clergy. In 'An Enlightened Man', Father Paddy Maguire, the man of the title, reveals the results of forgiving the sins of all who rebel against the oppressor in ways which dramatize the pathology of licensed 'holy war':

> Kill, says he, all Protestants in the land.
> That's why God planted you here.
> Strip every manjack of them then... .

He then orders his men to open the Protestants' bibles on their privates and to piss on them. 'An Enlightened Man' immediately follows the 'epistle' poem 'The Catholic Bishops to the People of Ireland', in which the bishops have, in temperate language, exhorted their people to resist the English invader: 'we beseech/The gentry and inhabitants of this island,/Praying that God may save them from evil.../To oppose the foe of our religion and King.'[61] That clash between the two adjacent poems reveals a deeper unease about the role of the church in contemporary times.

The early 1980s had seen a severe retrenchment by the Catholic Church in Ireland to counter the accelerating secularization of the country (Brown notes a 1973–4 survey showing that 25 per cent of single people had forsaken religious obligation altogether[62]), with a successful campaign to alter the constitution so that abortion would never be allowable in Ireland and with a hard line taken against divorce. *The Book of Judas*, of course, treats biblical material in parodic manner throughout; the freedom from the *ecclesiastical* element among the laws and authority from which the carnival temporarily breaks free is crucial in Bakhtin's reading of it. But the poems in *Cromwell* which reveal the savagery with which the priesthood relished their role in the resistance perhaps shows once again Kennelly's distrust of fine words which hide other agendas – in both contemporary Ireland and in Ireland's past – fine words which both cover and generate complicity in the inevitably violent nature of history. Such scepticism clearly reflects the mood amongst the young in the South, however, and presumably adds to the book's success there.

Yet it is the wider sweep of history which predominates, and which highlights the violence of Ireland's history North and South through Kennelly's dubious submersion of historical specificity by juxtaposing material from both the Irish Civil War and from contemporary atrocities in the North. As 'Gusto' bleakly delineates it, 'The Catholic bombed the Protestant's home/The Protestant bombed the Catholics home...' and so on and so on, a merry dance of death.[63] But it is precisely in this round, as in the continual Bakhtinian splitting of the self into many voices and the perpetual cataloguing of atrocities throughout history, that the immediate implication of *Cromwell* with its cultural moment, its social origins is revealed. This implication casts further doubt on how far the work might be taken as signalling a 'breakthrough' from 'cultural traumas', a 'transcendence' of the history of Ireland.

Cromwell is a truly modern poem. Its hallucinatory comic-horrific recounting of horrors, its abrupt and energetic colloquialism, impiety and coarseness make it streetwise. Its anachronisms deflate all sense that poetry, even historical poetry, might be remote from its contemporary audience: 'Hunger', for instance, describes a person with flesh turning black and then turns to 'Us, at home, so remote from caring/For you, we stuff our bellies full' – a smugness which is the voice of an Anglo-Irish landowner from the 1840s, or us now reading of that history, or the well-off in relation to contemporary poverty on Dublin streets.[64] All of these sentiments and tones presumably added to the book's appeal and popularity. But it is the deployment of the phantasmagoric, parodic nightmare vision of Buffún as the framer of the book which establishes the historical determinism of violence in Ireland, the sense that – *pace* Longley and Brown – this is a nightmare from which he can never wake.

This has immediate aesthetic and poetic implications for the book. What tends to happen when reading it is that the cataloguing of violence becomes blurred and therefore blind to its own partiality or sectarianism as Johnstone found it to be. There is a curious levelling effect, not only of idiom and tone, but more particularly between the historical layers of the poem. We are not sure at various points from which period of Irish history the particular incidents are derived; the overall impression is that the history is uniform, and it is hard to judge just what it is that the Cromwell material is doing alongside the later incidents. With so many poems that simply retail torture, murder, rape, pillage etc. alongside so many that are fantastic-parodic flights, all sense of the distinctiveness of the single poem is lost. This is one negative aspect of what is in other ways enlivening in the book, the fact that the poems seek to do nothing more than to recount or report, eschewing all 'poetic' language. Often the 'simple' tone of the reporting in *Cromwell* treads a thin line between a shocking plainness which only intensifies the enormity of what is being described, and a deadening rhythmic lameness which merely submerges its effects.

At the end of 'The Soldiers', for instance, 'Blood continues to run in the streets/Warmer now than it ever ran in human veins/Because soldiers have set fire to the city.'[65] Whereas in 'Some People' the lineation is compelling in shocking the reader into a recognition of a brute reality which refutes aestheticization, the naïve lineation here strikes an awkward tone. Such writing hardly warrants the name of poetry, and yet it is consonant with so many other such effects in the book producing a wearied sense of historical inevitability. The determinism of Kennelly's reading of history makes, therefore, for an amazingly uneven and sometimes flat poetry in *Cromwell*.

With the Bakhtinian breakdown of all hierarchies of order and judgement in the book any one speech or incident becomes alarmingly interchangeable with any other, and the images of violence merely, like the bodies, pile up. Violence has become consumerized, any one incident of it without especial value. As the Dublin-based philosopher and cultural critic, Richard Kearney, has argued:

> The consumerization of [cultural artifacts under postmodernity] does not spring from nowhere. It is symptomatic of an ideology of empty imitation ultimately related to the dominant economic system of consumerism that has now achieved almost worldwide proportions.[66]

As Terence Brown has shown, the 1960s and 1970s marked a period of rapid economic expansion in the Republic, which, although it was beginning to slow in the early 1980s, had indelibly changed Irish social and cultural life. There was a 'modernizing virus' active which had been sparked by the economic expansion programmes of Sean Lemass in the early part of the period and which continued with the foreign loans of the latter part, tying the country with negative results into that worldwide economic system. Rapid urbanization and industrialization took place which led to a 'swift advance' in consumerist values. By 1978, 83 per cent of all Irish homes had television and were nightly subjected to a welter of commercials for cars, houses and foreign holidays. Irish society enjoyed a 'rapid rise in its standard of living [which]...marked [15 years of change] as in no other period of modern history.'[67] Yet the South is not distinctive in this; as my opening chapter showed, the North under Terence O'Neill underwent similar rapid expansion with divisive sectarian results. In portraying the results of modern violence, *Cromwell* sees the whole island as a uniform place.

It is finally in the wholehearted embracing of consumerist values, the integration of such a welter of horrifying incidents within the swirling restlessness of the book, that Kennelly's ethical and irretrievably *political* ambitions, his political treatment of history, lie – not simply for the South but for the whole island of Ireland. By bringing such consumerization to bear upon Irish history 'packed with horrors and persecutions' the interchangeable images of horror amount to a totalized view which is inescapable. And it is a view which, presumably, found a place especially among the more secularly minded young in the new consumer-conscious South in which it was a bestseller. In the 'many voices' of Buffún's nightmare we find the exploitation of, or adaptation of, these modern values in relation to the matter of Ireland treated as a united country. Picking up on the themes of hunger which stand so strongly for the country's historical deprivation in this poem, Buffún is literally consumed and self-consumed in the last poem of the book by history, by the historical figures striving to come alive by 'Finding their food in me, chewing hungrily.'

Cromwell is finally, then, a parable of consumption of the present by the past and of the past by the present. Kennelly embraces the levelling, deadening effects of this, whatever negative effects they might have aesthetically. As Kearney puts it in his counter-arguments which seek to redeem postmodernism from its consumerist implications:

> Viewed in this perspective, postmodernism may be reinterpreted as an opportunity to experiment with a radical pluralism which combines a wide variety of historical traditions and projects them in a manner which answers the particular needs of each particular culture.[68]

It is in this light that the historical nightmare of *Cromwell* focuses its concerns, not in relation to, or accommodation of, 'the English tradition' which instigated a transhistorical violence in Ireland. The Bakhtinian carnivalesque space is always temporary and related to the social dialogue of its historical moment. In the buffoonish nightmare space which *Cromwell* creates, Kennelly sustains a dialogue with Ireland's historical experience in all its inevitability, plays with it, exploits it and entertains in the process.

6

'Reconciliation Under Duress': The Architecture of Seamus Heaney's Recent Poetry

The relationship between Seamus Heaney's poetry and the politics and history of Ireland has been the subject of much debate there. His international prominence has led critics North and South to question what version of his home ground it is that has gained him so many admirers abroad, and why his poetry is so appealing to an audience with little knowledge of Irish history or interest in its politics. Heaney has been accused of adopting a form of political quietism, one which does not offend a British or American audience of his work by making public declarations of dissatisfaction at the wrongs suffered on the part of the minority community in the North or on the part of Ireland historically. He has *equally* been accused of using that quietism to offer slyly an explicitly nationalist agenda, one which presumably appeals to left-thinking liberals from abroad looking for a native voice to echo their own righteous feelings of horror at the historical brutality of colonization.

It is his position in between such radically opposing readings which makes Heaney's poetry, and his statements about other Irish poets, central to the concerns of this book. That radical opposition is inherent in Heaney's own thinking; he has asserted on the one hand (as I discussed in my first chapter) that it is the modernity of Francis Ledwidge's writing, his refusal 'to bury his head in the local sand', which paradoxically makes that writing relevant to Irish people living in a similar period of historical transition at present. On the other hand, he has claimed that (as the end of 'Punishment' from *North* famously puts it[1]) he understands 'the exact/and tribal, intimate revenge' taken by his community in response to betrayals of it. These oppositions set Heaney's work at that abrupt divide between native tradition and a broader, discontinuous modernist writing which is the focus of my discussions of other poet's negotiations with both their literary forebears and with recent politics and history.

Out of these dual possibilities, there emerges in Heaney's later poetry a piercing lyric intensity which registers the (often recollected) moment yet also goes beyond the bounds of the lyric, opens it to change in ways correlative to, hampered by and countering conditions in the North of Ireland since 1969. In many ways what I want to trace here is the movement of the poetry towards a modernist continuous present tense, one which is able to register the shocks and thwartings as well as the counterbalancing hope and courage consonant with the conditions which prevailed there until 1994.

Further, of all the poets discussed in this book, it is Heaney who has sought to debate and theorize the relations between poetry and its informing circumstances most thoroughly, and his terms in doing so have consistently focused my own sense of these issues. In the pieces collected as *The Government of the Tongue* in 1988, in his lectures gathered as *The Place of Writing* in 1989, and in his lectures as Oxford Professor of Poetry, *The Redress of Poetry*, collected in 1995, Heaney has carefully striven to negotiate a way between two demands on poetry: one for the poet, particularly from cultures like his own which have suffered historical repression, to make a relevant, committed response to painful circumstance; the other an approach which asserts the continued freedom of the individual creative artist to create works which are true to the demands of their own particular vision and conscience, regardless of the importance of that vision to their society's concerns. These contradictory demands are superbly captured in the rhythmically wavering final line of Heaney's poem 'The Disappearing Island', where, having seen the island which his people had sought to colonize suddenly flip over, casting everything into the sea, the narrator says that 'All I believe that happened there was vision.'[2] The amount of emphasis which is given to that 'I believe' involves the reader in questions of faith and credibility which disturb irresolvably the relation between the individual and notions of common fate or sanctioned destiny. The narrator (actually St Brendan the Navigator in the annals) might be either a specially gifted envisager of redeeming truth behind surprising and ungovernable reality or a self-deluded, insignificant fool. As I will show, Heaney's negotiation between historical pattern and a defeating, deluding arbitrariness has increasingly dared ideas of potential giftedness and destiny in order to mediate between the two possibilities.

Perplexed irresolvability has itself been a keynote of the divergent negative responses to Heaney's work in his own island. That critical polarization can, perhaps, be most economically portrayed through a couple of typical examples which bring out the underlying areas of debate around the poetry. Accusations of a political quietism which underlies the poetry's international appeal came to a head with Desmond Fennell's notorious attack, which appeared as a pamphlet in Ireland, 'Whatever You Say, Say Nothing. Why Seamus Heaney Is No. 1'. Fennell relates the New Critical practices of Helen Vendler, the main fosterer and promoter of Heaney's work in America ('But I myself', she writes, 'think aesthetic value, properly understood, quite enough to claim for a poem'), with the inevitable quietism which arises from Heaney's repetition of those practices in his own prose and poetry. Fennell claims that Heaney is both wary of writing poetry which aims to break its balanced, unified, lyric bounds and also of speaking out publically on behalf of his repressed minority. Heaney has instead in this view chosen to promote a Vendlerian, mystical approach which sees poetry as a symbolic force to set against the world's wrongs:

> Heaney knows that his belief that public speech is dangerous and potentially harmful has prevented him from doing good to his people, or to people generally, in the ways that such good can be done by publically-speaking poetry. He knows that by keeping to 'safe' issues and by 'saying nothing' he has, in the world's terms, done good, positively, only to himself...what Bernadette McAliskey said years ago of John Hume and his moderate nationalist party, the SDLP – that they had 'ridden to power on the backs of the IRA' – might, with much truth, be said of himself.[3]

Heaney, with his reticent approach, has, according to Fennell, consciously made himself the darling of a mainly academic international poetry-reading audience, one which appreciates the way in which he manages to integrate and bring to resolution even the most partial and (politically) intractable materials. Fennell's attack is based on the sense that Heaney has thrived from recent historical and political conditions without ever acting himself or getting his hands dirty. His poetry provides enough nudges to its audience to remind them of the painful conditions of his own and his people's experience without ever fully encountering or dramatizing those conditions in his work.

The counter-view to this disappointed nationalism might be taken as that of John Wilson Foster, a counter-view with its own political perspective in this context, since Foster has sought in his work to speak up on behalf of what he calls 'the voicelessness of Ulster unionist culture.' In his essay 'Heaney's Redress', Foster argues on the basis of *North* that, despite its internal rhetoric of balance (for example, Heaney also accuses himself of conniving in 'civilized outrage' at the end of 'Punishment'), Heaney's is a deeply political poetic. Beneath Heaney's ambivalence, Foster finds a refusal to condemn violence from his own Catholic side which makes his work 'in an Irish sense profoundly political':

> Whatever purity and aloofness his poetry achieves in future, it cannot but be seen as a kind of sovereignty wrested out of subjection or home rule, thereby implicating Irish politics and the empowering, the growing confidence of Irish nationalist culture...in the relationship with Britain and Protestant Ulster.[4]

Again, then, Heaney is accused of maintaining a have-it-both-ways quietism, but in this there lies for Foster a not-so-well-hidden agenda, one which offers tacit support to nationalist paramilitaries while also offering to those ignorant of the 'Irish sense' of such matters an apparently unresolved, unaligned and therefore acceptable surface.[5] And these binaries appear in other critical responses also – Douglas Sealy describes Heaney's 'worried probings into the question of his own guilt and responsibility' as being to the fore in his work and so chides him for sometimes blundering by writing poetry which is 'more political than poetical'; Gerald Dawe finds the poetry 'inherently traditional' and claims that Heaney is an *un*political poet, though his work 'may have political implications....'[6]

Both sides of this argument find in Heaney, then, a lyric reticence which some critics think either culpable or somehow dishonest. And it is true that Heaney's work, unlike that of the generation of writers above him who were more directly affected by modernist ideas, shows little of the direct response to circumstance or specific events in the North to be found in their poetry. He has written no equivalent of *Butcher's Dozen, An Ulster Reckoning* or of the sections of *The Rough Field* called 'The New Siege', 'Patriotic Suite' or 'A Severed Head'. Further, his work after the 1970s has shown little inclination to explore that historically determined violence which Kennelly represents in *Cromwell* and *The Book of Judas* – perhaps because, as James Simmons has argued, the result of such 'argument' in Heaney's earlier work had led him into 'callow moralising' and 'some crude allegories'.[7]

Beyond this, Heaney has himself consistently and angrily refuted what he sees as a fairly crude Marxist reading of poems, one which describes them as products of society or history collectively rather than as creations of the individual artist. When describing his play for Field Day, *The Cure at Troy*, on BBC Radio 4's *Kaleidoscope* programme, he drew a strong distinction between political writing and works of art:

> ...political writing usually ignores the responsibility for...sanctity and the person and it concentrates upon hectoring about a system. It blames a machinery rather than undertakes to examine a psyche....It is a deep misunderstanding to think that a work of art is a poultice for society and will heal it the way a poultice heals wounds. It's more a magic dance performed adjacent to a society in the hope that it would have palliative but not necessarily curative effects.[8]

Art, therefore, explores the individual psyche (and lyric poetry, Heaney's own form, is perhaps the most extreme case of this); but its efficacy with relation to social ills is less certain. Heaney seems to have accepted, as he wittly puts it in the otherwise melancholy 'Sandstone Keepsake' from *Station Island* (1984), that he exists both literally (in his post-early 1970s home in the South) and imaginatively in a 'free state of image and allusion'. He is 'not about to set times wrong or right', but is instead 'one of the venerators', someone with a continuing sense of sanctity denied to the political hectorers.[9]

Fennell would, of course, sneer at this as Vendlerian mysticism, yet, as the somehow regretful tone of that poem demonstrates, Heaney's relation to his times is not as unequivocal as his strong rejection of political readings of art might otherwise suggest. This dilemma was being diagnosed by reviewers of Heaney's work in Ireland from at least as far back as *North* itself in 1975. Rivers Carew wrote then in the *Irish University Review*:

> ...the reader is...aware of an unease as to what role is proper to the poet in the present Northern Ireland situation. There is

evidently in Heaney, as earlier in Yeats, a certain nostalgia for action; and what is finally exposed in the fine concluding poem, 'Exposure', is a sense of opportunities missed.[10]

The terms of Carew's review are those used by Heaney himself in the introductory essay of *The Government of the Tongue* 13 years later. In the interestingly titled 'The Interesting Case of Nero, Chekov's Cognac and a Knocker', Heaney describes an evening in Belfast in 1972 when he was on his way to a recording studio to put together a tape of poems and songs with a friend. A number of bombs went off in the city, and, as a result, the tape never got made. The notion of beginning to sing while others were suffering was deplored by the poet and his friend. But Heaney in this essay questions his response at the time. He displays what Carew calls 'a certain nostalgia for action' in the several pages in which he discusses Wilfred Owen, who went as an officer to the trenches of the First World War the better to warn, as Heaney sees it, the world about the evils of conflict: 'He connived in what he deplored so that he could deplore what he connived in: he earned the right to his lines by going up the line.'[11]

And yet Heaney is immediately suspicious of this, seemingly wanting to claim that an actual experience of the conditions he was compelled to write against made Owen's poetry 'over-insistent, a bit explicit' – led, in other words, to some degree of *artistic* failure on Owen's part. In the latter part of the essay, Heaney turns away from such failure to celebrate the work of Osip Mandelstam, who, despite the repressive conditions of Stalin's Russia in which he lived, felt that 'the essential thing about lyric poetry...was its unlooked-for joy in being itself':

> ...unlike Owen who had a messianic and socially redemptive message to impart, Mandelstam had no immediate social aim. Utterance itself was self-justifying and creative, like nature. ...For him, obedience to poetic impulse was obedience to conscience; lyric action constituted radical witness...witness to the necessity of what he called 'breathing freely', even at the price of his death... .[12]

The freedom of breath, which the lyric poet can achieve in contradistinction to that repressive governing which society crudely enforces upon writing and speech, is not for Heaney, however, totally without efficacy. More recently, when describing the importance of Hugh MacDiarmid's *A Drunk Man Looks at the Thistle* for Scots culture, Heaney claims that poems are as public as they are personal:

> They act like their society's immunity systems, going to attack whatever unhealthy or debilitating forces are at work in the body politic. And in this, they manifest poetry's high potential, its function as an agent of possible transformation, of evolution towards the more radiant and generous life which the imagination desires.

MacDiarmid's poem, he concludes, 'was a magnificent intervention by creative power into an historical situation.'[13] Art, then, even if it does not necessarily or definitely bring about social transformation, at least offers a vision of possible order and harmony which might counter social sickness in whatever form it manifests itself. If it does not offer a poultice to society, yet it might in its wholeness suggest other ways of being which will later come to redress the wrongs which society inflicts on the individual, or which one nation inflicts on another.

Heaney's sense of these issues is, then, complex, and his terms never so hard and fast as they seem when taken within the single context of the occasion of their utterance. The absolute distinction which he makes in the radio interview between 'political writing' and 'works of art' is modulated in response to reading *The Drunk Man Looks at the Thistle*, a work which has, in his view, an afterlife as well as an immediate political impact. There is in the description of both Mandelstam's and MacDiarmid's achievement an inherent organicist poetic ('like nature', 'evolution') which is common, as my first chapter showed, to Vendlerian 'aesthetic' readings of poetry; but, in the MacDiarmid description with its traditional notion of the 'body politic', society itself is an organism to which poetry as 'immunity system' can play a salving role. All of the prose pieces gathered in both *The Government of the Tongue* and *The Redress of Poetry* are anxious to celebrate a Keatsian 'fine excess', in which the lyric voice of poetry is seen to supersede the conditions of its fashioning and demands upon it to deliver a 'social...message'. Yet at the same time, Heaney continues to hold that social conditions are *not* disconnected from the poem's space. Those conditions can both instigate a poetic response, as in MacDiarmid's wry celebration of his national symbol as a way of countering his country's continuing occupation from the South, and the conditions can also in their turn possibly be transformed by the poetry's intervention.

And Heaney's own poetry from relatively early on has shown an unease with the kinds of traditional, organic independence, coherence and reconciliation frequently envisaged in his prose. Indeed, the poetry emerges as more unsettled, contingent and modern than the traditional terms of Heaney's celebratory prose might seem to allow. This sense that, in its envisaging of an order which counters the world's disorder, the poem might become exemplary and promissory, is something which has been actively under question from at least the mid-1970s. The so-called 'Bog poems' in *North* frequently switch back and forth between on the one hand presenting the victims of Iron Age sacrificial rites as simply dead bodies, and on the other seeing them as artifacts, even almost as works of art. This adds an extremely self-conscious element to the imaginative parallels which Heaney seeks to establish between the ancient victims and those of the violence in contemporary Ireland. In 'The Graubelle Man' these tensions are at their most explicit when the corpse comes to seem a perfected thing in Heaney's mind, a thing

> hung in the scales
> with beauty and atrocity:
> with the Dying Gaul
> too strictly compassed

> on his shield,
> with the actual weight
> of each hooded victim,
> slashed and dumped.[14]

The poem meditatively and circumspectly circles between the Yeatsian poles of Art and Life, firstly seeming to deny the possibility of seeing the Graubelle man as simply another corpse in his beautiful repose. But, with the comparison of the body with the Dying Gaul, there comes a recognition of the constraint involved in the creation of works of art, not least in the creation of similes like this which threaten to denature and at the same time aestheticize the specific thing being described. The Dying Gaul is 'too strictly compassed'. The poem ends, then, by adding to the 'scales' the random victims of the violence in the Iron Age and implicitly also in contemporary Ireland, with their 'actual weight' standing over against any translation of them into works of art.

Despite its seeming assurance in dealing with the relation between these elements, then, 'The Graubelle Man' carries some of that unease about how to view the victims of violence which mirrors an unease in the question of how the poet should describe them, where he should best stand in relation to them. The ending of the poem shares something of the randomness of the killings itself. It seems a breaking-off, a simple interruption of the cycle whereby victims can be transformed into works of art only to have their 'actual weight' revealed again in the very act of compassing or constraining them. There *is* no resolution – the poem enacts the Frostian notion that it should be merely a 'momentary stay against confusion', which Heaney quotes in his later *The Government of the Tongue* essay as an apt description of the promissory function of artistic order.

What seems crucial in relation to Heaney's later debates about the relation between art, history and politics, and in relation to the divergent readings of his work, is the way the Graubelle man – and presumably 'The Graubelle Man', the poem – serve as mediators between, and counterweights to, diametrically opposed forces. He is 'hung in the scales/with beauty and atrocity'. Such terminology of weights and balances finds prevalent and various form in the more recent prose and poetry. In describing the notion of the redress of poetry in his inaugural lecture as Oxford Professor of Poetry, Heaney drew upon Simone Weil's *Gravity and Grace*, and head-spinningly said of it:

> ...her whole book is informed by the idea of counterweighting, of balancing out the forces, of redress-tilting the scales of reality towards some transcendent equilibrium. And in the activity of poetry too, there is a tendency to place a counter-reality in the scales – a reality which may be only imagined but which nevertheless has weight because it is imagined within the gravitational pull of the actual and can therefore hold its own and balance out against the historical situation.[15]

He then ends the lecture by discussing a poem in which dual forces are contradictorily operative – George Herbert's 'The Pulley'. Something of this vocabulary had, in the 1987 collection *The Haw Lantern*, served to establish Heaney's own 'in-betweenness'; as 'Terminus' has it:

Two buckets were easier carried than one.
I grew up in between...

Baronies, parishes met where I was born.[16]

That last line establishes the 'gravitational pull' of Heaney's position from the start as one on the border between the baronial British
colonizers and the local parish-based population. Something of that
awkward, difficult state would, in another parable-poem in this collection, 'From the Republic of Conscience', have seemed to have
heightened and informed Heaney's sense of personal responsibility, and of the contradictory demands made upon him as a poet in a
situation between divided cultures:

> I came back from that frugal republic
> with my two arms the one length, the customs woman
> having insisted my allowance was myself.[17]

The returns upon the self which the lyric poet makes are, therefore, both the result of the divisions within his or her society (the
forces which have to be 'counterweighted'), and also enforce
poetry's moral 'conscience' towards it. The balance and equal
weighting which the poet must achieve seems to be gained as the
result of some responsibility towards the conditions of his background; it is not simply a matter of purely formal or aesthetic
resolution.

In the first pamphlet publication of his 'The Redress of Poetry'
lecture, Heaney captured the dual relation which poetry must
sustain in relation to reality in a neatly balanced phrase:

> Poetry...whether it belongs to an old political dispensation or
> aspires to express a new one, has to be a model of active con-
> sciousness. It has to be able to withstand as well as to envisage,
> and in order to do so it must contain within itself the co-
> ordinates of the reality which surrounds it and out of which it is
> generated.[18]

Poetry must both stand against 'reality' which continues beside it
and which it must 'contain', and it must also look beyond the conditions and found its own 'reality'. It is the complex interaction of

these two demands which underlies Heaney's negotiations with both the political and historical 'reality' on his own ground, and also his negotiations in these essays with his principal literary fore-bears – indeed the two strains of thought are for him inextricable.

From the perspective of the divided 'reality' in the North of Ireland, Heaney's withstanding, envisaging redress shares much with the ethos of the Field Day Theatre Company of which he was a director. Reflecting the 'leaven' associated with 'the nascent ex-pectation of better things, on both sides' from the mid-1960s, and the more active Civil Rights movement slightly later, Field Day evolved an ethos which saw (as I described it in my first chapter) in an idealized, imaginary 'fifth province' a place in which sectarian divisions might be resolved.[19] Under this dispensation, as in Heaney's lectures, a poem seeks to resist partiality and to create an equilibrium in which all perspectives might be respected. 'From the Canton of Expectation' in *The Haw Lantern* allegorically captures the mood of Heaney's generation in its greater hope about change compared to earlier, resigned and passive ones:

> Our faith in winning by enduring most
> they made anathema, intelligences
> brightened and unmannerly as crowbars.

Once more this new 'grammar of imperatives' leads Heaney to that 'nostalgia for action' which Carew noted – 'I yearn for ham-merblows on clinkered planks' – and, somewhat surprisingly, seems to hope for a leader who will seize the moment of revolution when it happens.[20] The poem presents from the outside a simple if violence-hinting parable of the virtues of education and the changes it might bring to past traditions; this is furthered by the plain descriptive style of the poem. Yet it is a poem which, despite its seeming neutrality, is, 'in the Irish sense' as Foster would have it, profoundly political, one which demands that the culture of the Catholic minority be treated on equal terms with that of the major-ity (the earlier 'rebel anthem' and speech by a man 'who fought in the brotherhood' describe, however obliquely, nationalist meet-ings). Despite its seemingly scrupulous refusal to provide images which will enliven our sense of its relevance to the historical situa-tion in Ireland, this poem, like others in this collection, carries a freight from those historical actualities which makes it more problematically burdened than Heaney's clear prose warnings against such readings might suggest.

That burden of complex reference and its consequent stylistic and formal effects is further illuminated by Heaney's literary discussion about earlier poets in what he sees as similar conditions, suggesting again the union for him of the aesthetic with the political. That literary discussion has immediate (and, as ever with Heaney, *literal*) formal consequences for the way in which Heaney's own later poetry seeks both to 'withstand and envisage' – consequences which form the focus of my discussion in this chapter.

Heaney has centred this kind of debate between politics and transcendence in poetry on two figures, Mandelstam and Yeats.[21] In the course of his discussions about these issues, Heaney has been forced to modify the natural, biological metaphors which he has increasingly used to describe poetic process (he speaks of 'poetic DNA patterns' several times in 'The Redress of Poetry'), and to develop an architectonics of poetry which performs many of the 'withstanding' functions. In the essay 'Osip and Nadezhda Mandelstam', collected in *The Government of the Tongue*, Heaney notes 'the central importance of Mandelstam's poems about buildings', their 'corroborating force': 'Mandelstam's instinct led him to seek the reliable quarry face and vaulted solidity of buildings.' Further, he discusses Mandelstam's essay, 'Humanism and the Present', in which 'Mandelstam begins by outlining his conception of the ideal society, which naturally turns out to have the same structure as the ideal building or poem.' In other words, by writing poetry, Mandelstam was positing his vision of an ideal society or 'fifth province', as Heaney feels it is 'poetry's high potential' to do.[22] So even within this poet who earlier in the collection of essays he has celebrated as standing 'for the efficacy of song itself, an emblem of the poet as potent sound-wave',[23] Heaney admits a relation between 'the symmetries and pointings of rhyme and stanza'. He sees in Mandelstam's poetic form an imitation of the buildings he is writing about in poems such as 'Hagia Sophia', 'Notre Dame' and 'The Admiralty', and as establishing through that form some future, utopian vision of a just society.[24] Mandelstam is crucial, then, in Heaney's thinking about the ways in which poetic form might relate to the kind of ideal imagined space represented by the notion of a 'fifth province' in Ireland.

Such links, however, become more difficult, more constrained, in Heaney's later writings on Yeats, the other of the main authorizing presences in his recent meditations on poetry and politics. The link between Mandelstam and Yeats is suggested anecdotally in the course of the essay on the Mandelstams. 'A Russian poet once told me', Heaney tells us, 'that the Mandelstam stanza has the impact of late Yeats.' It is in the first of the lectures collected as *The Place of Writing*, 'The Place of Writing: W.B. Yeats and Thoor Ballylee', that Heaney gives his most extensive account of the relation between poetic form and politics in Yeats, and it is an account which plays directly into his own more recent poetic practice. Heaney describes the 'ceremonious action' which Yeats undertook when he bought and restored the Thoor, the immediate sense that Yeats had that here he was consciously creating a 'place of writing'.[25]

Heaney makes much of the fact that the tower was being refurbished and first inhabited by Yeats and his young family at a time of violence and breakdown in both Ireland and Europe – the 1916 Easter Rising in Dublin, the First World War and Russian Revolution, the Civil War in Ireland between 1922 and 1923. He therefore chooses principally to discuss in his essay Yeats's sequence 'Meditations in Times of Civil War', and notes the consonance between the 'pile-up of nouns' at the opening of the poem 'My House' and 'builder's blocks in a course of stonework'; or he describes the stanza form of 'My Descendants' as being like a 'strong-arched room' to further his case that in these poems Yeats strives to 'compound utterance with architecture'. This compounding establishes Yeats's stance towards the violent history of his times, Heaney claims, his indomitability in the face of shocking and impinging actuality. The strong walled tower represents a retreat from a world outside which is threatening and overturning Yeats's own ideals and most cherished hopes for his nation. The poems are ultimately therefore not about history but 'about artistic faith, about trusting images and emblems rather than conventional images of the world, about holding fast, living in a fastness'.[26]

However, in the last pages of the essay, Heaney claims that at the end of his life Yeats was able to admit that such triumphant overbearingness towards historical conditions might itself be questionable. In the last poem which he composed, 'The Black Tower', Yeats includes the ironic, questioning voice of a cook 'who represents an unheroic life force, a scuttling principle of survival and self-preservation' amongst the warriors who are buried in a standing position in the tower 'signifying their eternal vigilance and oath-bound fidelity to the cause that unified them during their lives.' Heaney reads this as hinting at an acknowledged scepticism in Yeats's art about its own aristocratic procedures, although this note is never allowed by the older poet fully to emerge:

> Both tower and poet stand, as Macbeth and Macbeth's castle once stood, suspended in art time, ratified by a prophetic utterance.... But just as the witches equivocated and the world as a wood of trees moved unthinkably to dislodge Macbeth, so in the end the Yeatsian keep of tragic commitment and loyalty is assailed by mutinous doubts about the ultimate value of what there is to keep. Nevertheless, the Yeatsian drama ends with the poet as Macbeth, still pacing the battlements....[27]

This raises questions as to how far the poet can determine and predict the course of history, or give it pattern, which resonate through Heaney's later poetry. It is this sense of acknowledgement, emerging particularly in Yeats's late poems, that the poet should not overbear circumstance or abdicate from the world of pain and injustice which, in the course of *The Place of Writing* lectures, Heaney claims makes for Yeats's modernity. That modernity is founded on the recognition that the struggle to be released through art from what he calls 'the exorbitance of the historical' (an 'exorbitance' which had found literal embodiment in the missed 'comet's pulsing rose' from 'Exposure') might ultimately be an absurd, futile one. The tower walls might be thick and strong, but the mocking voices might already be within.[28]

To take up the terms of Rivers Carew's review of *North* again, Heaney might be said to have later made a virtue of what was a mark of unsureness in his earlier work – that unease about his role and correlative Yeatsian nostalgia for some more active role to play in relation to history, a sense in 'Exposure' of 'opportunities missed'. That unease is famously central to Heaney's own poem on events around Bloody Sunday, 'Casualty'. The poem discovers a complexity of feeling between familial bond and entrapment in the funeral for the 13 killed by paratroops: 'we were braced and bound/Like brothers in a ring.' But then 'Casualty' turns away to its own victim, a drinking friend who was blown up after breaking the IRA curfew subsequent to Bloody Sunday. Heaney questions his friend's culpability in transgressing tribal solidarity but can find no answers. 'I missed his funeral'; Heaney is again away from events. He recalls fishing trips with the man in which, as in poetry, 'you find a rhythm/Working you', but ends by asking the man to question him again.[29]

The poem, a revision of Yeats's own 'The Fisherman' in the light of this communally shocking event, veers uncertainly between the suffering caused to the 'tribe' in the deaths on Bloody Sunday and those questions of the responsibility of the individual victim for his death. Heaney is properly hesitant before such events and concerned about the relation of 'my tentative art' to them. But 'Casualty' dramatizes the supreme unease with which Heaney in the first part of his career handles the 'actuality' of suffering among his own people. The consolations of poetry seem awkwardly tacked on to the poem's ending, working through analogy rather than overt defence. As Patrick Crotty wrote in a retrospective review of these poems, by the time of 'Casualty' the earlier analogies which Heaney had found to parallel the violence in the North, as in the collection of that title, have fallen away, and 'the analogies no longer console.'[30]

Yet such hesitancy and uncertainty about the role which poetry might play becomes in Heaney's poetry of the 1980s and early 1990s an opportunity in itself. By recognizing his distance from the history of the North Heaney resists the need to overbear circumstance and to force an order upon historical unpredictability in his poetic forms. Rather, his poetry can remain more modernistically and formally attuned to the world of pain by paradoxically relaxing the need to 'withstand' the shocks of historical circumstance.

In other words, within these later arguments about the relation of poetry to the circumstances of its making, Heaney has discovered inspiration, as Thomas Kinsella had earlier, in James Joyce's assertion that (as Heaney has paraphrased it) 'departure from Ireland and inspection of the country from the outside was the surest way of getting to the core of Irish experience.'[31] His own distance from the conflict on his native ground in the North might also be turned to advantage in making his work more simply and directly responsive to the central issues of its divided history.

As a consequence of this discovery, Yeats's suitability as a model for a native poet engaged with his country's history has come under question in Heaney's own poetry.[32] 'The Master' from *Station Island* does not name Yeats, but brings with it a welter of Yeatsian paraphernalia. The master dwells 'like a rook in an unroofed tower'; he has in his hand a 'book of withholding.../Each character blocked on the parchment.' The idiom of the poem even dares a cod-Macbeth style, looking forward to Heaney's later prose analogies in *The Place of Writing*. The master's tower is a 'coign of seclusion', a deliberate misquotation of the 'coign of vantage' which Banquo describes Macbeth's castle to be. The idiom itself suggests that the later poet is alluding to, but also appropriating for his own purposes, classic images; it is a quirky, scuttling, vulnerable style similar to that appropriated for the neutrally allegorical poems of Heaney's next collection, *The Haw Lantern*. 'The Master' ends by acknowledging the vulnerability which witnessing the intransigence of the older poet brings, 'How flimsy I felt climbing down'.[33] This poem, then, acknowledges the power of the Yeatsian poetic project, the anxieties it produces on the Irish poet coming after. But it refuses the sense that there is anything mysterious about the Yeatsian poetic, despite Yeats's own attempts to make it seem so in works like *A Vision*. The master's book shows 'just the old rules', and so Heaney seems to want to see Yeats as a deeply traditional poet, one whose tower establishes him in relation to his times but which is out of key with them. The belated poet's style is allusive and playful, if also flimsier, and ultimately the older poet has little to teach him.

In a more recent poem which Heaney has written about Yeats (which appears as an untitled xxii in the 'Squarings' sequence in *Seeing Things*, but which originally appeared in the *TLS* as 'Small Fantasia for W.B.'), the assault on the Yeatsian tower and its withholding is more directly questioning still:

> What's the use of a held note or held line
> That cannot be assailed for reassurance?
> (Set questions for the ghost of W.B.)[34]

This seems to question the humanity in the perfection of the art which Yeats strove for, and recognizes that there might be no 'use' at all in the aristocratic stance which Yeats adopted towards the matter of his times, that the architecture of the Yeatsian stanza might be ultimately uninhabitable.

What emerges in these two poems, then, is the potential architectonics of a poetry which is the reverse of that embodied in Yeats's foundation of Thoor Ballylee as a symbolic place of writing. In its place might be established a modernist-ironic yet also Mandelstamian poetic of self-delighting utterance which is yet a radical witness to both the divisions on its own territory and which also might build its own vision of an ideal society superseding those divisions. I would suggest it is paradoxically the case that when Heaney's poetry is seemingly at its greatest distance from the historical and political circumstances out of which it is written that it reveals the greatest duress brought about by those circumstances for the Irish poet; that it is when he is at his freest, at his most impulsive and improvisatory, that he resists that urge to build forms against those violent circumstances, resists the easy, 'organic' reconciliation between opposed values which Vendlerian critics, some of his own pronouncements on the efficacy of poetry and some of his own earlier poetry seem to offer.

In its claim that there must be a necessary aesthetic distance from the contemporary in order for the reconciliatory 'fifth province' to be imagined in the work of art, Heaney's later thinking about these issues is reminiscent of Adorno's disagreements with the arguments from Lukács and Sartre that art must be socially realistic and politically committed. Indeed, that distance is a definition for Adorno of the work of art's modernism and also of its efficacy. Heaney's own arguments against simplistically political readings of poetry carry something of a similar burden to these earlier debates about the relation of aesthetics to politics, and of their resolutions; I would like, therefore, to explore now the illuminating parallels between the poet's and the philosopher's ideas.

In the essay 'Reconciliation Under Duress', Adorno defends the idealist tendency in modernist art against the social realism demanded of a text by Lukács in *The Meaning of Contemporary Realism*. Rather, for Adorno, it is in the seemingly abstract space of the work of art that the impact of the social basis of its originatory idea is felt. 'The truth of the matter', he claims:

> is that except where art goes against its own nature and simply duplicates existence, its task *vis-à-vis* that which merely exists, is to be its essence and image....Art and reality can only converge if art crystallizes out its own formal laws, not by passively accepting objects as they come. ...Art is the negative knowledge of the actual world.[35]

In the terms of Heaney's debates about Mandelstam and Yeats we see him establishing the formal laws of his later poetry. His flimsy, improvisational style and (as I will later show) form in these poems acts as a kind of 'negative knowledge' of the intransigent world of Yeats's poems from Thoor Ballylee. Adorno argues that the reconciliation between divergent elements which art's duress can bring about is achieved by the formal demands which are made upon the individual consciousness in creating the work of art:

> ...the solitary consciousness potentially destroys and transcends itself by revealing itself in works of art as the hidden truth common to all men....They objectify themselves by immersing themselves totally...in the laws of their own forms, laws which are aesthetically rooted in their own social content.[36]

Adorno would never deny that transcendent works of art do not everywhere bear the marks of the empirical reality out of which they are created; the artist does not create out of nothing. What he does attack, though, is the politically committed art of a Brecht, which he has to deny as bad art. Adorno favours a difficult, distanced, modernist work of art like that by Joyce or Beckett:

> The notion of a 'message' in art, even when politically radical, already contains an accommodation to the world: the stance of the lecturer conceals a clandestine entente with the listeners who could only be rescued from deception by refusing it....Even in the most sublimated work of art there is a hidden 'it should be otherwise'....The true moment of volition, however, is mediated through nothing other than the form of the work itself, whose crystallization becomes an analogy of what that other condition should be. As eminently constructed and produced objects, works of art, including literary ones, point to a practice from which they abstain: the creation of a just life.[37]

Heaney's defence of the 'subtleties' of poetry, its distance from the partial, partisan, infected language of contemporary political debate, shares much of this defence of modernist art against the demands of realism and commitment. In this it is a poetry which is potentially at least more engaged, if not committed, than the internal rhetoric of balancings, scales, etc. in both the criticism and the poetry might at first suggest.

The notion that it is through the seemingly remotest literature or position that the closest engagement with current concerns occurs is to the fore in the version of Sophocles's *Philoctetes* which Heaney made for the Field Day Theatre Company and which he called *The Cure at Troy*. Philoctetes is a wounded hero who has been marooned on the island of Lemnos for 10 years by Odysseus and Menelaus because the stench from his suppurating foot is too much to bear; the play's action involves the attempts to persuade him to return and fight for the Greeks at Troy, as they now realize that they need the aid of the bow which was given to Philoctetes by Hercules if they are to win the Trojan war. The main action of the play is involved with the attempts, deceptive and reasoned, to persuade Philoctetes to rejoin the common cause, or at least to get his bow off of him. But Philoctetes proves recalcitrant, he sees through all these attempts, and in turn gets a promise that he will be taken home to Greece. At this point the Chorus intervenes with a vision of the common sufferings of humanity in which Heaney interposes some jarringly contemporary lines:

> Human beings suffer,
> They torture one another,
> They get hurt and get hard.
> No poem or play or song
> Can fully right a wrong
> Inflicted and endured.
>
> The innocent in gaols
> Beat on their bars together.
> A hunger-striker's father
> Stands in the graveyard dumb.
> The police widow in veils
> Faints in the funeral home.
>
> History says, *Don't hope*
> *On this side of the grave.*
> But then, once in a lifetime
> The longed-for tidal wave
> Of justice can rise up,
> And hope and history rhyme.
> So hope for a great sea-change
> On the far side of revenge.[38]

This might be taken to encapsulate somewhat lumpenly the political relevance of the play to modern Ireland, a plea, based on the suffering common to both communities, for reconciliation, a greater understanding and charity in the face of bitter, entrenched divisions. But it remains unclear where that 'great sea-change' is to arise from – again there is a vague 'nostalgia for action' as there is in 'From the Canton of Expectation' – and the echoes from Shakespeare's *Julius Caesar* serve somewhat to ironize rather than to reinforce the hope.[39] More directly, the sentiments uttered by the Chorus here draw on lines of Auden's, the famous ending of 'Spain 1937' ('History to the defeated/May say Alas but cannot help or pardon') and the equally famous, but presumably especially alluring lines for Heaney, from 'In Memory of W.B. Yeats':

> ...mad Ireland hurt you into poetry.
> Now Ireland has her madness and her weather still,
> For poetry makes nothing happen: it survives
> In the valley of its saying where executives
> Would never want to tamper; it flows south
> From ranches of isolation and the busy griefs,
> Raw towns that we believe and die in; it survives,
> A way of happening, a mouth.[40]

Lines such as these from Auden, an earlier wrestler with Yeatsian poetic responsibilities, clearly find their echo in Heaney's debates about the efficacy of poetry, and, in their dislocation and strangeness ('it flows south/From ranches of isolation') establish Auden as a shadowy figure behind the improvisational idiom in Heaney's later poetry.[41]

But the rough, rigorous definition of the survival of poetry, as something which makes nothing happen but which is in itself a way of happening, is seemingly contradicted at the end of Auden's elegy to Yeats as he enjoins the poet 'With your unconstraining voice/Still persuade us to rejoice/...Sing of human unsuccess/In a rapture of distress'. This, in its grand melodiousness, suggests that the sheer musicality of poetry has much to teach humanity and can alleviate conditions. The crux of the issue is contained in the questions posed in Auden's brief poem 'Orpheus', 'What does the song hope for?.../To be bewildered and happy,/Or most of all the knowledge of life?'[42] These two possibilities of withstanding and envisaging are what Heaney's own later work is both fraught and freighted with. The knowledge in this last Chorus from *The Cure at Troy* that poetry makes nothing happen and that the experience of history – not least Irish history – has led to hope being impossible this side of the grave, goes along with the countering, contrary hope for the 'great sea-change'. There remains within this story of Philoctetes's pain an Adornoian 'it should be otherwise' alongside once more a feeling that the individual, however maimed, can make a difference in bringing things to a resolution.

Yet as these sentiments are being sung by the Chorus, Philoctetes himself remains unconvinced and unreconciled to his people's cause, and only becomes so after the *deus ex machina* intervention of Hercules in the form of a volcanic eruption. This is, again, a matter of duress and the forced reconciliation through stagecraft of the seemingly arbitrary with the destined (why does the god only intervene *now*?). Through this intervention, the equivalent of the enforcement of art's formal unity, Heaney points to the fact that the 'crystallization', in Adorno's term, which is necessary to bring about Philoctetes's forgiveness in these painful circumstances is starkly arbitrary. Artistic form itself partakes of that temporary and surprising reconciliation between the arbitrariness and irresolution of circumstance and some shaping destiny whose designs and 'formal laws' are palpable.

The architectonics of poetry which Heaney develops in *Seeing Things* as a negative image of the forbidding, unassailable Yeatsian tower play between these two poles of pattern and what he calls in one poem 'the music of the arbitrary' as a way of reconciling the (often painful) uncertainties of history with a tentative, contingent and even ghostly form. The book's opening version of part of Virgil's *Aeneid* Book VI, in which Aeneas is instructed that in order to enter the underworld to visit his dead father he must pluck the golden bough, dares notions of giftedness and destiny which might redound on the poet himself: 'If fate has called you,/The bough will come away easily, of its own accord.'[43] Of course, the golden bough passage is – via J.G. Frazer –- important to whatever structure T.S. Eliot's *The Waste Land* might be claimed to have. Heaney mixes his sources. He has Aeneas echo Eliot's Tiresias by saying 'already I have seen and foresuffered all'. Yet Eliot's poem inevitably – such is the extreme disjunctiveness and desolation of its vision of its time – escapes its author's own mythic designs upon it ('These fragments I have shored against my ruins... Hieronymo's mad againe.'[44]). In its turn, Heaney's version of the Virgil myth governs the presiding attention of the book, his hope to conjure the presence of his recently dead father through poetry. But it is a structuring myth which holds only arbitrarily and sporadically through the book, amid other poems concerned with going beyond, crossing over, passing through, and translation from one state to another – all of which hold force within the reconciliations with history, the envisagings of idealized societies and the formal crystallizations which the poems continually negotiate.

The various memorials to his father which *Seeing Things* contains makes it a painful companion in loss to Heaney's previous volume *The Haw Lantern* which centred upon elegiac sonnets for his mother, 'Clearances'. The notion in the title of those sonnets of a compensatory space which opens when the 'pure change' happens at the death of a parent finds an integrational formal correlative in the later book. Architectural images are so to the fore throughout *Seeing Things* that their Mandelstamian relation to its poetic forms and thence potentially to an imagined society are everywhere evident. In the first part of the collection, Heaney establishes the cottage at Glanmore which had given the idyllic, pastoral note in *Field Work* as his own 'place of writing'.[45] The sonnet sequence 'Glanmore Revisited' picks up on the themes of the earlier 'Glanmore Sonnets' and celebrates the return to the place. Clearance occurs with exhilaration when a skylight is put into the hutch-like old ceiling of the cottage:

> But when the slates came off, extravagant
> Sky entered and held surprise wide open.[46]

It is this sense of the wonder and surprise of a new framed openness which runs through these poems in the first part of the book, a belated learning 'to credit marvels' as another sonnet, 'Fosterling', has it. The airiness of this place seems consciously if tacitly posed against the thick stone bulwarks of Thoor Ballylee – it is a place of light and healing (the skylight being put in reminds him of the Biblical story in which the sick man takes up his bed and walks away) rather than entrenchment against the 'exorbitance of the historical'.

What is crucial for the developing sense in Heaney's poems of the relation of the writing to the personal, political and historical grounds out of which it is written is the licence which Glanmore as a place of writing allows him. It is a licence to be literally 'extravagant', to wander beyond and also within boundaries in ways consonant with that sense that the modern writer inherits a 'gapped...discontinuous tradition' as Thomas Kinsella famously described it. The first part of the book shows Heaney handling traditional form, particularly rhymed quatrains, with great finesse, and in greater numbers, than in any of his previous collections. Yet within those tight forms there is a constant playfulness which translates and metamorphoses the poems' objects of focus – ash plant, pitchfork, basket of chestnuts, biretta – into wonderful and strange marvels, even fantastically exorbitant ones as in the case of the pitchfork envisaged 'sailing past/Evenly, imperturbably through space'.[47]

Such transmutations suggest the influence of *Seeing Things*'s dedicatee, Derek Mahon, in Heaney's recent thinking about poetic form and space. Mahon is perhaps the most technically accomplished of contemporary Irish poets, and his poetic is deeply metamorphic, discovering the numinous among the detritus of modern life. His poetry is also burdened by a modern belatedness and sense of exile which can be seen as correlative to Heaney's:

> What coarse god
> Was the gear-box in the rain
> Beside the road?
>
> What nereid the unsinkable
> Coca-Cola
> Knocking the icy rocks?...
>
> It is so long
> Since my own transformation
> Into a stone,
>
> I often forget
> That there was a time
> Before my name
>
> Was mud in the mouths
> Of the Danube,
> A dirty word in Rome.[48]

These lines, from 'Ovid in Tomis', 'spoken' by the author of the *Metamorphoses* in exile, capture that dual flux and lifeless but potentially liberating stasis which combine in Mahon's work. These are complicating qualities which Mahon shares with his forebear in the Northern Protestant tradition, Louis MacNeice. Heaney has himself described the relation between the dilemmas of these two poets' work and its occasional releases in ways which bear upon his own methods in *Seeing Things*:

> ...their vision of the predicament of their own spirit, which is often an analogue for and an exfoliation out of the balked predicament of their [Northern Unionist] group, is typically couched in terms of release or absolution. In Mahon's poems, we have a constant recourse to the resolved stillness of painting or to timeless receptive moments of epiphany.[49]

'The Biretta', Heaney's surprising poem about the square cap worn by Catholic priests, puts its object through several changes – from actual instances recalled from his own past as serving boy at the altar (it 'put the wind up me and my generation', presumably because of the strict rule priests enforced and the expectation that Catholic boys might take up the vocation), to a paper boat, to the boat in the first lines of Dante's *Purgatorio*, to a bronze age boat, to the 'one/In Matthew Lawless's painting, *The Sick Call*'. But this last transformation brings the flight of the imagination comically back to reality, which is then itself instantly and unexpectedly resolved into notions of aptness and order:

> In which case, however, his reverence wears a hat.
> Undaunting, half domestic, loved in crises,
> He sits listening as each long oar dips and rises,
> Sad for his worthy life and fit for it.[50]

This allusion to a painting, then, finally combines (in a way which exploits possibilities shared across the religious divide despite 'predicament') Mahonian stillness and continuity with a sense of proper and unlikely reverence for the mundane as potentially a redemptive and absolving quality. The 'fitness' of the poem's resolution depends upon its formally contained and containing Adornoian 'crystallization', yet it is a form within which anything is possible and that fact leads us to credit whatever does take place. The relation of form to content in this and the other quatrain poems is both apt but partly fortuitous, toying with both its readers' expectations and its own content.

Such a constant and marvellous sense that 'it should be otherwise' marks the impact of the later Yeats's modernist sense on *Seeing Things*. It also suggests the positive importance for Heaney's more recent thinking about poetry of Louis MacNeice. MacNeice remained primarily a Yeatsian formalist whose sense of flux, as in 'Variation on Heraclitus' ('Even the walls are flowing, even the ceiling,/Nor only in terms of physics'[51]), led him to experiment in works like *Autumn Journal* with the open structures of modernist poems like *The Waste Land*. MacNeice's modern internationalism presumably furthers his appeal to Mahon and to later Heaney, in the last of whose *Redress of Poetry* lectures MacNeice emerges as a potential prophet of a Northern Ireland 'struggling to be born'. MacNeice was an Ulster-born Protestant who chose to live much of the time in England, but his imagination was fired also by the western landscapes of Ireland from which his ancestors came (in this sense he shares in Kinsella's notion of gapped traditions). His poetry effectively straddles both traditions in the island, therefore – 'his sense of cultural diversity and historical consequence within the country never congealed into a red and green map', as Heaney puts it.[52]

It is in the second part of *Seeing Things* that the formal consequences of that MacNeicean interweaving of flux and pattern are most prominent in Heaney's work. This part of the collection is made up of the 48 poems under the general title 'Squarings'. The title describes the shadowy architecture which shapes the sequence as a whole, as each poem is broken down into four stanzas of three lines, and there are twelve poems in each of the four sections. At this level, then, the 'structure' is clearly some parodic, less mystical, version of Dante's founded on the number three in the *Commedia*, and is reminiscent within recent Irish poetry of the numerological structuring of some of Thomas Kinsella's sequences. In terms of its 'structure', then, the sequence shares in the virtues of the house which we are told, significantly and comically in poem xxxiii, that his father planned and which Heaney found himself thinking of on the day of his father's death: '"Plain, big, straight, ordinary, you know,"/A paradigm of rigour and correction,//Rebuke to fanciness and shrine to limit…'.[53] The sequence as a whole, therefore, seems planned and deliberately limited, but within it there is much that is counterposed, impulsive and arbitrary.

The ordering of the poems often seems to operate through pairings which juxtapose one poem taking one view of a situation with a poem which takes an opposed view, and the dislocations are allowed to stand as such, with no arbitration or mediation between them. So, in the opening two poems, there is an opposition between the first poem on a ruined cottage or hovel and the second poem which suggests that the cottage should be renovated, done up. Each poem explores the virtues of its occasion, the first 'Shifting brilliancies.../Bare wallstead and a cold hearth rained into – /Bright puddle where the soul-free cloud-life roams.' The second poem, however, is more admonitory, suggesting the need for security against the world, and surprisingly and enigmatically in its final lines demanding both silence and a probity in writing or speaking:

> Sink every impulse like a bolt. Secure
> The bastion of sensation. Do not waver
> Into language. Do not waver in it.[54]

And the paradox remains unresolved, 'the music of the arbitrary', as poem v calls it, simply moves on. There is no correlation between the ghostly architecture and space which the sequence opens up for itself, and the moments of its flimsy imagined existence in time. Poem x offers an encapsulation of the two architectures:

> Ultimate
>
> Fathomableness, ultimate
> Stony up-againstness: could you reconcile
> What was diaphanous there with what was massive?[55]

Here, as elsewhere, the arbitrariness is manifest in line length and vocabulary ('Fathomableness', 'up-againstness'). What the rhetorical nature of these questions, their lack of resolution, illustrates is Heaney's refusal now to enforce or envisage a reconciliation between opposed conditions, or to exert the formal duress necessary to do so. Rather he strives to dramatize the duress involved in that very irresolvability. The very freedom and airiness of the 'music of the arbitrary' is, then, the cause of the sequence's celebration, but also a dramatization of its irredeemable condition.

That openness and openendedness serves to maintain the tense of the sequence as that of a continuous present, one that refuses to settle into any partial resolutions or to fix itself in any one moment of past or hoped-for future. The acceptance in the first poem that 'there is no next-time-round', that there is no life beyond this one, both frees the sequence into the present and traps it within it. The poems serve as glosses to some other, more continuous and resolved sense of things which is never realized. So, although there are various static models of memory offered in the sequence ('Memory as a building or city' in xix, or the many poems recalling incidents from the poet's past), the 'sweet transience' of the whole is what is given licence, and 'I re-enter the swim, riding or quelling//The very currents memory is composed of' (xli).[56]

What the sequence recognizes, then, is that as a response to the duress of circumstance, be it political, historical or personal, it is necessary to relish the drama of movement and the possibilities of change, and in this the poetry might both parallel the historical moment and act as parable to it. History is not escapable-from and therefore it contains everything, it is impossible to be partial within it. But this in its turn leaves the Mandelstamian consonance between the poetic architecture and an envisaged ideal state or 'fifth province' uncertain and unrealized; the poetic form remains consciously if randomly shaped, but is something into which anything and everything, all memories, ideas, images and traditions, can flow. The airy, arbitrary form of these poems both seems to accept but also to deny that 'crystallization' which Adorno speaks of art making upon circumstance, and so leaves everything uncertain beyond the time of its own happening.

Transcendence, or, to take up the pun in the book's title, 'vision', might be possible locally in the single poem, but not absolutely. Heaney's glosses share much of the abstraction of Adorno's modernist art, but also complicate it by setting that abstraction within an (equally modernist) continuous present, one in which Adorno's 'true moment of volition' is exposed in its full contingency. Heaney accepts in this work, then, a poetic like MacNeice's which, he has written, 'is unlikely to set about the enterprise of building up since his poetical body-clock is all set...to run down'.[57] In this, the redress offered by Heaney's later poetry manifests both the liberation and the unbearableness in Paul de Man's discussion of literary modernity. De Man paraphrases a definition of modernity by Nietzsche like this:

Moments of genuine humanity are moments at which all anteriority vanishes, annihilated by the power of an absolute forgetting. Although such a radical rejection of history may be illusory or unfair to the achievements of the past, it nevertheless remains justified as necessary to the fulfilment of our human destiny and as the condition for action.

De Man concentrates on the blindness, the illusion, involved in this forgetting, since forgetting is a common condition of all writing: 'When [writers] assert their own modernity, they are bound to discover their dependence on similar assertions made by their literary predecessors; their claim to being a new beginning turns out to be the repetition of a claim that has always already been made.'[58] Hence the duress felt by Heaney with regard to Yeats, the struggle to define and sustain his own modernity (poem xxxvii relates poems to 'different states of mind//At different times'[59]). But it is the possibilities which that struggle opens up which are manifest in the subliminal architecture of 'Squarings' for the first time truly in Heaney's work.

Within the willed provisionality of the sequence there is no consonance between the poetry's architecture and the voice moving through it; rather the poem's space serves to capture a Heraclitean presence as orality which allows the autobiographical to flow into the Dantean, the historical, and suggestions that, against the exacerbations of the ordinary individual, social and political life, nothing is established timelessly, all might change:

Everything flows. Even a solid man...

Can sprout wings at the ankle and grow feet
As the god of fair days, stone posts, roads and cross-roads....[60]

This is an astounding, one-off example within the run of the sequence of poetry outstripping conditions by revealing how conditions might outstrip themselves, how the mysteriousness of demotic speech re-echoes through literary myth and history. 'In so far as poetry is an extension of the mind's extreme recognitions, [it] is felt to enjoin a flight beyond the pale', Heaney writes in the pamphlet version of *The Redress of Poetry*, suggesting the need to go beyond whatever place or tradition one is born into, while also invoking the need to escape beyond the colonizers' sphere of influence.[61] In 'Squarings' his own poetry is at last beginning to enjoin that flight in all its personal, political and historical resonances. Poetry's 'way of happening' emerges as a model of active consciousness whose 'negative knowledge of the actual world' simultaneously commands our political attention and mocks its own presumption in doing so.

7

Letters from the Alphabet: Carson's and Muldoon's Contigent Poetics

Like Seamus Heaney's later work, the poetry of Ciaran Carson and Paul Muldoon from the generation following his has increasingly foregrounded notions of contingency. In 'Revised Version', one of the prose passages inserted into the middle section of *Belfast Confetti*, Carson relates the way in which the city, as seen in a book of photographs, has changed across history to the way in which the city is constantly changing in his own experience, 'For everything is contingent and provisional; and the subjunctive mood of these images is tensed to the ifs and buts, the yeas and nays of Belfast's history.'[1] In the opening poem of the long sequence which forms the second part of his 1994 *The Annals of Chile*, Muldoon envisages the gradual sweeping away of everything on the land by the streaming yarrow plant which gives the sequence its title. That knowledge dawns as the recognition:

> ...that the row
> of kale would shortly be overwhelmed by these pink
> and cream blooms, that all of us
>
> would be overwhelmed....[2]

This awareness of the transitory, of an external force which will break everything and everyone down, obviously counters all notions of tradition, permanence and absoluteness. The pressure of history as flux is brought to bear by these poets upon the seemingly permanent or the 'true'. In the process, the self – be it of cities or of people – is rendered contingent and provisional, and language appears to have no determinate relation either to that self or to 'reality'. Language is no longer a transparent medium between self and world as it was for pre-Saussureans or pre-Wittgensteinians. Rather, words themselves are open to change and to history, independently of the self and 'reality' which are in their turn changing. Everything is speculative and at the sway of possible events ('ifs and buts'); all 'meaning' is about to give way or to be 'overwhelmed' through the processes of temporality and history.

The relation of the self to the world, of the private to the public, both become radically unpredictable once the old, stable 'truths' of self, reality and language have been countermanded. The later Wittgenstein's 'ordinary language' philosophy, a philosophy which is crucial for such perspectives of contingency, sees language rather as a useful tool than as a medium; he shares with Saussure the sense that it is only in a specific historical or communal context that it can have 'meaning'. It is this context for contingency which I wish to explore in relation to Carson and Muldoon.

In each of these poets, this sense of everything, everywhere remaining permanently impermanent has an obvious, self-conscious reference to their poetic and its praxis. This very self-consciousness has in its turn led critics both in Ireland and beyond to see their work as 'postmodernist', as countering the kinds of mythic writing favoured in the work of Seamus Heaney, the Heaney of *North* particularly. To generalize broadly, such criticism rejects all 'grand narratives' which impose totalizing patterns on history or on the world through myth, and so welcome writing which they see as pulling those narratives apart and revealing the (usually politically) reactionary drives underlying them. As such, all writing for them is inherently textual, a matter of responding to earlier formulations of those narratives. To take but two examples of this kind of response to the work of these poets: Colm Tóibín, in reviewing *Belfast Confetti* for *The Irish Review*, observed that:

> Writing, for Carson, in so many of his poems, is a way of reading. Experience for him is a 'fount of broken type'. For Carson idiom is only a step on a road elsewhere...history is here being deconstructed as text, symbol, sign.... Each poem becomes a deconstruction of itself.[3]

John Goodby, writing in the same journal on Muldoon's *Madoc: A Mystery*, said that the book's 'self-proclaimed parasitic status invites us to read it as an exemplary postmodern work', and perversely and presumptuously claimed that the work 'confirms postmodern critical theory precisely by its elaborate "denials" of theory, demonstrating that all literature is intertextual, parasitic and parodic.'[4]

Both Carson and Muldoon do indeed display that intertextuality in their work, not least in their wry allusions to Heaney himself.[5] Yet that very textuality seems insufficient to describe the particular energizing and motivating forces behind the poetry, nor to account for the formal choices made by the poets. Further, these critics cloud, by partially refusing it altogether, the precise relation which the poetry makes with its circumstances and context. While not wanting to suggest that this deconstructive postmodernity is necessarily ahistorical in these reviewers' readings of the poetry (Tóibín says that 'History is association, part of the mind's method of connecting and disconnecting'), it is clear that they find in the work a comedic, envisaged end of history's impingement upon the text. In order for history to be 'deconstructed', there is a sense in which history's 'construction' is known about in every way, that it can be kept at a distance from the ludic concerns of the particular text, and from its negotiations with earlier texts which are nullified or killed off by them. It is these unaddressed questions around history which I want to explore in what follows.

The ahistorical view might seem justified by the knowingness of Muldoon's poem called 'History', which begins 'Where and when exactly did we first have sex?/Do you remember?', before speculating about the various places home and abroad where it might have happened, and ending (perhaps) in the room where Louis MacNeice wrote his poem 'Snow'.[6] 'History' here is a wholly personal and intimate thing, and one which wryly feeds into questions of poetic influence rather than into public event. Yet it would be too ungenerous a reading to see this as the last word, to imply that Muldoon somehow does not *care* about his country's historical plight. Rather, the mock-retreat into the personal world of relationship in the poem needs seeing as a reflection of historical pressures which have made the communal and the political poetic 'no-go' areas. The poem is also proposing that most people's lives, even in the North of Ireland during the 1970s, are not chronicled in terms of the latest explosion, or, for that matter, of the latest poem.

In an interview with Alan Jenkins, Muldoon has speculated that the sense of suspicion and uncertainty which he was brought up with might have helped impel both his and others' writing: 'There's so much good writing now from Northern Ireland, perhaps it's to

do with that element of uncertainty, of not being sure who one is –
or being only too sure, and not liking it.'[7] The sectarian divide in
the North, with its demands upon allegiance and partiality, might
rather be seen as generating that uncertain 'postmodern' irresolvability seen by the critics, as well as the 'intertextual' allusion to
earlier poets who have wrestled with the problems of responsibility
and of the relation of poetry to politics and history.

I want in this chapter to contend that the contingency and sense
of its continuity with their situation which is shared by Paul
Muldoon and Ciaran Carson is in fact generated by the speaking
voice, the vernacular of their 'home ground', rather than fostered
by the textual vagaries so favoured by postmodernist critics of their
work.[8] The internationalism and academicism of the parodic approach blocks the poetry's immediate vocal verve. It is this sense of
voice as speech which informs the relation which their poetry
makes between the public and the private, between the lyric, politics and history. Carson himself made this point when in interview
he cited Muldoon as the poet amongst his peers with whom he felt
the most affinity:

> Even though Muldoon's method is very different to mine, he's
> writing about the here-and-now, with a cleverness and facility
> which constantly amazes me. For all the technical skill...the
> poetry comes from a demotic notion of the world. It arises from
> ordinary speech, and the peculiarity, the vitality and strangeness
> of ordinary speech....It doesn't pay homage to notional ideas of
> Ireland, to the received myths. It includes the myths, of course,
> and then sets them up against pub-talk and slabbering.

In contrast to the textual basis emphasized by postmodernism, the
poetry celebrates rather the voice as presence, as a way of capturing
the 'here-and-now'. Such a sense of the innovatory potential of the
present-as-speech is, rather, closer to Walter Benjamin's notion of
'now-time'. As Jürgen Habermas has described it, 'now-time'
stands in for an irrefutable modernity, one conscious of its place in
history: 'Inasmuch as we appropriate past experiences with an orientation to the future, the authentic present is preserved as the
locus of continuing tradition and of innovation at once; the one is
not possible without the other'[9]. Against on the one hand an empty,
inactive historicism which sees the past as finished and imprisoned
in museums, and, on the other hand, a sense of history as purely

progress, Benjamin argues instead for a more responsible and attuned attitude to history, one which recognizes its continuing impact upon the present and so the future. In Carson's terms, myths are constantly being re-energized through their transformation in the slabber of speech.

It is at this point that Carson's and Muldoon's poetry moves closer to recognizing the authority of the poet they are often seen as 'deconstructing'. In describing the time which he shared with Muldoon as a student at Queen's University, Belfast, Carson says:

> Heaney was a big force, naturally, and we all felt his presence, and I think all Ulster poets of my generation must have been influenced by his example. Because before Heaney, there was precious little, certainly nothing like a poetry which had some tie-up with our own vernacular, with ordinary Ulster speech.[10]

Whatever the ideological differences which these writers might have with Heaney's methods at certain stages of his career – and Carson has provided the classic dissent for his generation from the 'mythic method' of *North*[11] – it is the presence of the vernacular in his work which released their own writing. That oral inheritance from an immediate forebear has freed the poetry of Carson and Muldoon from the *formal* anxieties of influence which governed the Yeatsian inheritance for the earlier poets I have been discussing, and removed much of that anxiousness about the relation of the poetry to the history of their times which had underpinned those earlier negotiations. There is little of that architectural interest to be found in their work which I examined in my previous chapters.

Both writers have used poetic forms which are suited to the orality they favour. Muldoon has written in a huge variety of forms, from long-breathed 'sonnet' sequences like 'The More a Man Has the More a Man Wants', to the gallimaufry of fragments and more developed forms in *Madoc*. His permissive and surprising rhymes and assonance (as most famously deployed perhaps in 'Sushi': (*'Is it not the height of arrogance/to propose that God's no more arcane/than the smack of oregano,/orgone/...the mines of Arigna,/the poems of Louis Aragon?'*[12]) keeps the aural qualities of words to the fore in his work. Although it has a literary source in the work of the American poet C.K. Williams, Carson's deployment of extremely long poetic lines is also geared to the rhythms of traditional Irish storytelling, as the acknowledgement of gratitude to John Campbell of Mullaghbawn at the start of *The Irish for No*, his first collection to use that long line, shows.

Beyond the immediately formal impact of the vernacular on their writing, there is a strong sense in each of these poets that what the presence of the voice demands is a realism in the face of historical event as opposed to a mythic (textual?) falsification of it.[13] In 'Exposure' Heaney famously characterizes himself in the South of Ireland as 'a wood-kerne//Escaped from the massacre'; Carson replies:

> No-one really escapes from the massacre, of course – the only way you can do that is by falsifying issues, by applying wrong notions of history instead of seeing what's before your eyes....[14]

Carson remains wholly aware of historical determinism, sceptical of myth and of poetry's claims to have transcended the reality out of which it has arisen, while at the same time positing the value of the individual voice and action against competing claims. 'Whether you want to change your face or not's up to yourself', 'Two to Tango' in his 1994 *First Language* begins, 'But the bunk of history/They'll make up for you.' This leads to an imperative impetus at the end of the poem:

> One side says this, the other that. You work it out for yourself and
> walk between the story lines.
> What's true is what you do. Keep your head down. Know
> yourself. Ignore the starry skies.[15]

Such Heaney-like quietism and Polonius-like advice derives ultimately from a determinism founded on the divided communities of Ulster, the sense that against that history the individual can only take his or her own line, to his or her own self be true: a lyric emphasis upon the personal and the private again. This recognition suggests that, rather than seeking a strictly 'postmodernist' description for the strategies of this kind of poetry, Richard Rorty's recent explorations of contingency and social 'solidarity' offer some more appropriate ideas, not least in their championing of a poetic perspective upon 'actual history'.

Rorty's two collections of philosophical papers, *Contingency, irony and solidarity* and *Essays on Heidegger and Others* consistently

counter what he perceives as a tendency towards transcendental-
ism in Derrida himself with a more historicist perspective:

> The trouble with making a big deal out of language, meaning, in-
> tentionality, the play of signifiers, or *différence* is that...one starts
> reifying language...instead of seeing convenient divisions within
> a toolbox – divisions between batches of linguistic tools useful
> for different purposes.[16]

Rorty's late-Wittgensteinian, pragmatist sense of language recognizes that when faced with the tension derived from two opposing
demands such as those posed by Irish history, the retreat into a personal language such as that which seemingly occurs in Muldoon's
'History' or at the end of 'Two to Tango' is the courageous step to
take. This for him is the final exemplary status which the later work
of Derrida holds for its readers. Having been trapped between on
the one hand the urge to theorize and on the other the ironic sense
that all theorization is absurd, the later Derrida in Rorty's view
privatizes his thinking:

> ...I take Derrida's importance to lie in his having had the courage
> to give up the attempt to unite the private and the public, to stop
> trying to bring together a quest for private autonomy and an
> attempt at public resonance and utility. He privatizes the
> sublime, having learnt from the fate of his predecessors that the
> public can never be more than beautiful.[17]

Yet this seeming retreat into the privacy of a personal language is
not at all an escape from history, since, under the pragmatist aegis,
such privacy is one more potentially useful tool which history has
provided for future thinkers to use or to ignore as they wish.
Ultimately, therefore, there are no private languages since we are as
a community involved in particular language games; Rorty constantly reminds us of the essential ethnocentricity presupposed in
Wittgenstein's argument in maintaining this point:

> ...his argument that you cannot give meaning to a word or a
> poem by confronting it with a nonlinguistic meaning, something
> other than a bunch of already used words or a bunch of already
> written poems. Every poem, to paraphrase Wittgenstein, presup-
> poses a lot of stage-setting in culture.[18]

True, Rorty's sense of context is often as non-specific as 'Europe', 'the West' or 'Western democracies', and suggests a freedom of connection not available to the communities divided by religion in the North of Ireland. But this Wittgensteinian alertness to the use-value of language within community does not deny – indeed it might be said to further – the restriction of the language game within a more specific community or nation.

Poetry for Rorty performs an important role in 'dealing with blind impresses...common to the members of some historically conditioned community'. He underscores his sense of the contingency of history by seizing upon and repeating throughout his books Nietzsche's definition of 'truth' as 'a mobile army of metaphors'.[19] Metaphors are by definition unparaphraseable, they are a breaking off of a conversation, in which all the terms are known through habitual use, and a taking of it into an undefined area. 'Uttering a sentence without a fixed place in a language game is, as the positivists rightly have said, to utter something which is neither true nor false':

> But this is not to say that it may not, in time, *become* a truth-value candidate...the sentence may be repeated, caught up, bandied about. Then it will gradually acquire a habitual use, a familiar place in the language game. It will thereby have ceased to be a metaphor....[20]

It is through the arrival of a new set of metaphors that history can be seen to change, and those metaphors will not necessarily be understood at the time of their creation since they have no place within current language games. Within the field of literature, Rorty sees the Romantic poets as having had the most revolutionary effects. The move from an eighteenth century art of imitation to that of self-creation in the nineteenth which they brought about still holds in his view for the twentieth century, with the added knowledge that post-Nietzsche and post-Freud, selfhood itself is – like language – contingent.

But, when describing the likely provenance of these new metaphors, Rorty's earlier assertion that 'the world does not speak. Only we do' is crucial:

> The world can, once we have programmed ourselves with a language, cause us to hold beliefs. But it cannot propose a language

for us to speak. Only other human beings can do that. The real-
ization that the world does not tell us what language games to
play should not, however, lead us to say that a decision about
which to play is arbitrary, nor to say that it is the expression of
something deep within us...the notions of criteria and
choice...are no longer in point when it comes to changes from
one language game to another. Europe did not *decide* to accept
the idiom of Romantic poetry....[21]

Or, in Carson's words, 'Ignore the starry skies'. It is, for Rorty, the
recognition of the need to change by individual poets which leads
them to seek to revise vocabularies that have become redundant,
and which might lead them in the process to devise metaphors
which in their turn alter their society's way of perceiving the world.
For Carson and Muldoon, that sense of new possibility which owes
something to Heaney's use of the vernacular in his poetry liberates
their ironic, contingent relation to things. What we find in their
work, under the historical pressure of the violence in the North
which, until 1994, had punctuated all their adult lives, is an exploitation of 'ordinary Ulster speech' relative to history and 'what's
before your eyes' with the kinds of result manifested by 'ordinary
language' philosophy.

Muldoon has said that the age difference between himself and
Heaney is crucial in establishing the early difference between their
poetry:

There's no tribe in Ireland for which I would feel comfortable as
a spokesman. I wonder who would, who does, who is? I think
Seamus Heaney flirted...with the idea of it for a while. Seamus is
so well known, is a public figure, that these are concerns that
impinge more upon him. He did become associated, for example,
with the Northern Catholic nationalist position. I was brought up
in that society with a similar background to Seamus. But things
have changed a bit in the ten or fifteen years between us. Ireland
has changed; well, certainly, it *had* changed. But I don't think
even Seamus flirts with that now. From what I can work out from
his recent poems, I think Seamus is now much more interested in
the idea of the free agent....[22]

Carson and Muldoon, because younger, would not have been as
attuned to the build-up towards the Civil Rights movement, with

the hope for true change in their country which it brought, across the 1960s. As such, that sense of possible joint action which is shared by Heaney and Field Day is alien to them (although it is true that the more outspokenly politically committed Tom Paulin, who is of their generation, was one of Field Day's directors). Further, Belfast, where Muldoon and Carson have lived and worked for much of their adult lives, had despite the violence from the early 1980s a renewed cultural and commercial life. Largely supported by huge grants from Westminster, the city became a buzzing, modern consumer centre. Tremendous poverty remained, particularly in Catholic areas. But the new cosmopolitanism sat uneasily with the traditional divisions which underlay the violence. Out of these contradictory circumstances it became difficult to write a poetry true to 'what's before your eyes' and also claiming to speak on behalf of any single community or tradition.[23]

These contradictions and complexities have increasingly found their way into Ciaran Carson's poetry, which has become more of a surprising and joyous babble as time has gone on. *First Language* initially seems to be a gift for a purely postmodernist reading. Its foregrounding of issues around language itself (signalled so playfully in the opening poem which is in Irish yet is called '*La Je-Ne-Sais-Quoi*'), immediately raises issues of audience, of community and communication, and of translation (for the first time in Carson's career, the book contains versions of Ovid, Rimbaud, Baudelaire and a poem 'From the Welsh'). Irish is Carson's 'first language', a fact that, as he has said in interview, gave him early a perspective on the world which was aware of the detachment of language from things:

> To a child, things are what they are. But even then, a tinge of the exotic or the strange still comes through. I think that from a very early age I was aware that to say a thing in one language was different from saying it in another; that there was always a gap between the form and the reality, the thing expressed.[24]

This is a perception which is familiar to post-Saussurean theorists also, but is consonant with Rorty's description of the playfulness which derives from the ironist's ability 'to appreciate the power of redescribing, the power of language to make new and different things possible and important'.[25] To this degree, it would be possible to say that in *First Language* Carson has simply found a new and

more extreme way to describe his perennial themes. What he perceives in the interview to be the case *between* languages has earlier
been the case between different of his poems, which in *The Irish For
No* and *Belfast Confetti* read like versions of each other.

Indeed, the preoccupation with language and with grammar as
providing particular metaphors or analogies for the violence in the
city have recurred in the earlier work. In *The Irish For No*, the poem
'Belfast Confetti' opens 'Suddenly as the riot squad moved in, it
was raining exclamation marks,/Nuts, bolts, nails, car-keys. A
fount of broken type' (the 'confetti' being the local name for the
bricks thrown at the troops).[26] In the *collection* of poems *Belfast
Confetti*, 'Night Out' describes how an evening's drinking in the city
amounts to a grammar: 'So the sentence of the night/Is punctuated
through and through by rounds of drink, of bullets, of applause.'[27]
Carson's poems, from within this violent context, often seem to be
simply variations on a theme, to repeat themselves in ways which
give a sense of the claustrophobia of life in the city. All seems imprisoned and incapable of altering the conditions. Within this paradigm, history itself seems to have become scripted, offering a
pattern of itself which might make sense, but which might, on the
other hand, be entirely random and meaningless. Under this perspective, even the bases of the current, post-1969, outbreak of civil
strife fail to add up:

> The ambient light of yesterday is amplified by talk of might-
>   have-beens,
> Making 69 – the year – look like quotation marks, comment-
>   ators commentating on
>
> The flash-point of the current Trouble, though there's any
>   God's amount
> Of Nines and Sixes: 1916, 1690, The Nine Hundred Years'
>   War, whatever.
>
> Or maybe we can go back to the Year Dot (...).[28]

Yet it is in wry moments like this that the witty metaphorical life
of the poems, which associates punctuation marks with violence,
crosses the line from the (postmodernist) textual to the rhythms of
speech. The almost constant reference to dots and dashes in the
poems, a morse of the streets, reflects what Carson has called in

interview the 'kind of staccato, yakky Belfast speech that goes 'tat-tat-tat-tat-tat', like that; I'm trying to get it down.' The poetry's *way* of talking is close to 'the *way* of talking in Belfast which is very ironic, dark and sarcastic – when you talk about things which are apparently awful and you...try and laugh about the whole thing.'[29] The subject matter and the voice speaking the poems elide the one into the other, the uncertain 'whatevers' and 'maybes' which are the shrugging speculation of the poetic energy also containing the 'meaning' of the sentences. Phrases like 'quotation marks, comm...' or the demotic 'any God's amount/Of' make much of the interplay of inflection which the linguist James Milroy has isolated as being specific to the idiom of Belfast English (and Ulster English generally), as opposed to that English spoken on the mainland; an inflection between 'o' sounds produced at the back of the throat and 'a' sounds produced at the front.[30] The heavy alliteration, in its turn, ensures that the yakky staccato is sustained and sustaining of the cadences across the poem.

But of course, it remains true that what the vernacular in these poems is obsessive about is the *textual* marks of grammar, the dots, hyphens, colons and quotation marks which reflect violent life as it is in Belfast. Carson is making complex play upon the way in which the vernacular contains, unspoken, those marks which are made to contain sentences textually, while at the same time freeing the grammar from the page into the streets. Indeed, it is telling that, in this oral-centred poetry, the marks of the *written* text are associated with violence. As Rorty has said in following through Derrida's attempts to break with the old narratives in the tradition of philosophy:

> So, he may infer, we must break away from meaning, thought of in the Wittgenstein-Saussure way as a play of *inferential* differences, to something like what Heidegger called 'force', the result of a play of *non*inferential differences, the play of *sounds*....[31]

Carson's range of dots, exclamation marks and hyphens register nothing other than the violent and the surprising, the remoteness and alienations of what's 'out there anyway'.[32] Since history offers no *inferential* connections, connections which give the words used a meaning ('or maybe we can go back to the Year Dot'), then the *non*-inferential becomes the true method of writing and speaking, the two together becoming the only 'truth'.[33]

In *First Language*'s development from the earlier work, the non-inferentiality of language is at an extreme. With its central motif of the tower of Babel, the book parades its almost-anti-logic in a way that the closing 'The Ballad of HMS *Belfast*' suggests is essential to the place itself:

> Ice to Archangel, tea to China, coals to Tyne: such would be
>   our cargo.
> We'd confound the speculator's markets and their
>   exchequered, logical embargo.[34]

The poem seems both to be authorized by, and to repeat or bring home, the version of Rimbaud, 'Drunken Boat', from earlier in the book. Again, there is no sense of escape into new subjects or possibilities. HMS *Belfast* is revealed at the end of the 'Ballad' to be 'the prison ship *Belfast*.'

These concerns all coalesce in the second poem of *First Language*, 'Second Language'. For some of its length, the poem is a clear re-working of Heaney's allegorical treatment of his own learning of language in his poem 'Alphabets'. But where Heaney treats his learning of various languages, Latin, Greek, Gaelic, the 'learned' language of literature, as a process of continuity which links him back to his own 'pre-reflective' state,[35] Carson, whose second language is of course English, charts a much more bizarre and fantastic course which muddles up historical processes and so is perhaps true to the bizarre, contradictory conditions in Belfast. The Latin which he 'inhales' in church is followed by the 'Pharonic unguents' of his glue for assembling balsawood planes. Within the divagations of this poem, even the irredeemable present (that 'here-and-now' he attributed to Muldoon's writing) must be alert to such possible escapes and erasings:

> What comes next is next, and no one knows the *che sera* of it,
>   but must allow
> The *Tipp-Ex* present at the fingertips. Listen now: an angel
>   whispers of the here-and-now.[36]

In this highly involuted poetry, the repeated sounds '*Tipp*/tips' 'ips/list' 'ing/ang' 'an/ang' 'tips/whisp' 'now/now' finally confirm Carson's sense of history as at the same time discontinuous and as, in Belfast, a series of minor variations on set themes. The increased obliqueness of *First Language*, its heightened non-inferentiality, derives from an exacerbated sense of what's 'out there anyway'; the greater complexity of Carson's echoes and assonances in the book form the determination to keep the casual speaking voice alive against such suddenly and violently punctuated conditions.[37]

In his subsequent work, *Letters from the Alphabet*, a still greater emphasis on the drunken-drugged-hallucinatory ('B' is 'like...a tab of mescaline', in 'E' 'She handed him the hip-flask' and so on[38]) serves to determine both the unpredictable, jarring leaps in the slabber of speech, and also the surreal way in which language has become divorced from individual speakers. Several poems mention karaoke machines, from which the original singer's voice has been erased; and, as 'F' has it, the feeling 'that everything was dubbed://The *mise en scène*, the plot, the lines'. Such dubbing is consonant with the way in which spokespeople from groups banned by the British government had to have their lines spoken by actors on television after the broadcasting ban issued by Margaret Thatcher. But, once more, Carson continues to recognize the significance of language in determining political allegiance. 'H' dramatizes the voice of a prisoner from the H-Block ('An actor spoke for him in almost-perfect lip-synch') and ponders on the community-dividing pronunciations of the letter itself as 'aitch' or 'haitch', before concluding that:

> Everything is in the ways
> You say them. Like, the prison that we call Long Kesh
> is to the Powers-that-Be *The Maze*.

The contingency of *Letters from the Alphabet* ('everything is *ad hoc*' ('J')) is added to by the fact that the poems were produced at a rate of nearly one a day. Paul Muldoon's short collection, *The Prince of the Quotidian*, takes a similar route to, and fix on, the transitory. The book dramatizes its very 'inconsequentiality' by being a poetic journal of January 1992, an enterprise which advertises spontaneity and randomness. Yet, within this seemingly unshaped gathering of work, Muldoon is all the time counter-asserting various kinds of continuity under different conditions. The epigraph quotes a letter from Wolfe Tone about his move to Princeton, thinking that he might become an American farmer; the leader of the United Irishmen therefore provides a tongue-in-cheek precedent for our poet-hero's sojourn as a university professor in the same place nearly two hundred years later. The quotation picks up on the surprising way in which 'Madoc – A Mystery', Muldoon's long sequence which forms the bulk of *Madoc* (a sequence which imagines that Coleridge and Southey had indeed undertaken their 'Pantisocratic' scheme to set up a utopian community on the banks of the River Susquehanna), related to events on his native ground. '[Ptolemy]''s map does, after all, locate 'Ulster' just south of 'Athens' on the river.[39] *The Prince of the Quotidian* sees Muldoon objecting that he, along with '"Louisa May" Walcott', is not – contrary to an article by one of Field Day's directors Seamus Deane – in exile, since he is free to travel anywhere as he pleases.[40]

Indeed, the greater freedom and immediacy which the quotidian scheme of the book gives him seems to allow Muldoon to speak out more openly about his complex sense of the relation of events to art's seemingly sanitized 'freedoms'. While recounting a concert by the Irish pianist Barry Douglas, Muldoon also attacks the 'casuistry' by which some would hold that the good health of a country's art proves that all is not rotten in the state:

> amid the cheers and the cries of 'Bravo'
> I hear the howls of seven dead
>
> at a crossroads between Omagh and long Cookstown.[41]

(Note the 'o' and 'a' interplay which literally pick up those 'cries' in 'Bravo' as longer howling syllables in the last line.) For all his inveterate 'postmodern' textual allusiveness and distance from Field Day's island-based readings of history, therefore, Muldoon is claiming a realism in his work, an openness to shocking events on his home ground, which mirrors that of Carson.

Edna Longley has been anxious to assert Muldoon's relevance in this. Against those, including Deane, who have seen him as a postmodernist, Longley claims in a review of *Madoc* that Muldoon's insistence on the 'relativity of perception' is simply a true reflection of Northern Irish society:

> Muldoon's relativism does not go so far as to exclude all value-judgements. His poetry is sometimes discussed as 'post-modernist collage'. ...Although *Madoc* sometimes looks like collage...[it] is essentially a socio-political parable with a *stratum* of literary criticism.[42]

In this light *Madoc*, with its portrayal of the failure of Coleridge's and Southey's imagined utopianism, might be read as a criticism of the mixture of politics and idealism which had been set out in Ireland by Field Day during the 1980s. The expedition becomes dissipated in retrenchment and mystery as Coleridge and Southey end up following their own personal concerns rather than attending to the ideals of their enterprise. The continuity between the imaginary context of the poem and Ireland's contemporary history is in fact made to coalesce within the critique offered in the poem. The whole enterprise of 'Madoc – A Mystery' is centred upon 'Ulster', and dated to the time of the United Irishmen uprising in Ireland which broke down into squabbles among its leaders. Yet that uprising gave imaginative energy to the Field Day poets' enterprise – as represented by Tom Paulin's 1983 *Liberty Tree* and Seamus Heaney's 'Wolfe Tone' from *The Haw Lantern*.[43] Once more, Muldoon seems to put his finger in the individualist side of the scales, distrusting communal action of whatever kind, and, like Carson, keeping his head down and working it out for himself.

Against Field Day's attachment to an 'old' solution to seemingly intractable situations, that of imagined transcendence in a 'fifth province', Muldoon has claimed to hold to a more modest aim in writing – 'to discover through language some little revision, however slight.'[44] His stance is that of ironists as described by Rorty:

> who are inclined to...see the choice between vocabularies as made neither within a neutral and universal metavocabulary nor by an attempt to fight one's way past appearances to the real, but simply by playing the new off against the old.[45]

Yet, to turn again, Muldoon has recently also dramatized the awkward way in which the 'new' rests against deeper political and sectarian concerns. This is literally the case in his 1995 play *Six Honest Serving Men*. A good proportion of the play juxtaposes scenes among an IRA cell who are trying to work out who has been responsible for killing 'the Chief' with other scenes in which a woman, Kate, who awaits her lover from among the cell, reads about the goods on offer from an in-flight magazine (e.g. '"The hiker's dream. Add a new dimension to your hiking or climbing experience with Avocet's Vertech Alpine."'[46]). The juxtapositions are entirely random, and what emerges from the play is a queasy sense in which the two orders of experience are surreally incompatible – that the 'modern' lacks the bewildered anger and mistrust of the terrorists, but that it also makes their struggle seem dated and irrelevant.

However, this simple yet loving (and often rappingly staccato) listing of objects, as in Kate's reading of the magazine, has often formed a vital element in Muldoon's later poetry. Throughout 'Madoc – A Mystery', Muldoon derives much energy for the speaking voice from the simple listing of objects in his poetic 'world'. As suits that philosopher, the poem '[Hobbes]' reveals this nominalism explicitly. Coleridge, we are told, can no more argue from an object to its platonic idea, 'than from

> ...powder-horns, muskets,
> paddles, pumpkins,
> thingums, thingammies,
> bear-oil against mosquitoes...
>
> ...to anything beyond their names.[47]

The inclusion of the comic (and in the terms of the interview quoted above, for Muldoon North of Ireland) 'uncertainty' in 'thingums, thingammies' highlights the fact that naming involves memory, and also that, under the pressure of a clamant, nasty, brutish reality, memory is faulty. The words needed to recount fail. As with the 'poetic refrain' 'de dum, de dum' used throughout the sequence, there is an acknowledgement that sound itself carries the voice through the work, almost regardless of the sense.

Nominalism, a continual listing of nouns, remains the staple strategy of Muldoon's poetry, its energizing basis, and it often allows him to exploit his *penchant* for rarified vocabulary – e.g. 'marlinspikes, wimbles', 'shalloon-lined galligaskins', 'two big-horn fleeces/sewn into their own rumens'.[48] He undermines our sense of the immediate expressibility of the 'authentic' – these nouns could not be said not to refer, but to discover what it is they refer to is to needlessly disrupt the vocal delight there is in giving the lists in the first place. Muldoon wryly includes in the sequence the famous letter from Coleridge to Cottle expressing his concern that Southey might begin to rely too much on 'story & event' in his poems to the 'neglect of those lofty imaginings that are peculiar to, & definitive of, the POET.'[49] But in presenting his own poetic 'mystery' in such a chaotic fashion, Muldoon paradoxically also recognizes the intractability of the given world to 'lofty imaginings'. This remains true even at the level of the ghostly ordering of the book. The suggested titles given to each poem are the names of philosophers, and cumulatively the book adds up to a 'history' of Western philosophy. Yet there is nothing cumulative or evolutionary about the 'ideas' conveyed; the very fragmentedness of the structure refuses the patterning or totalizing presence of a single system of 'thought'.

The 'relevance' of 'Madoc – A Mystery' is clear, its spiralling down to non-achievement and confusion both a mirroring of revolutionary attempts to change history in Ireland, like that by the United Irishmen, and a warning about the relevance of idealism such as that of Field Day's which attempts to step outside history for solutions. Muldoon's reading of history, like Carson's, is deeply determinist, one in which there is a variety of chaoses which hold little hope for the reader, but which countermandingly delight in the accumulation of objects and *words* which are thereby thrown into the foreground. Some of Muldoon's vocabulary fails to communicate to a contemporary audience, but in this he is simply reconciling himself to the 'public-private split' in languages that Rorty maintains an ironic imagination must: 'the part of a liberal ironist's final vocabulary which has to do with public action is never going to be subsumed under, or subsume, the rest of her final vocabulary.'[50] 'But where (I wonder myself) do I stand,

> In relation to a table and chair,
> The quince-tree I forgot to mention,
> That suburban street, the door, the yard –
> All made up as I went along
> As things that people live among

Muldoon famously had his narrator ask in 'Lunch with Pancho Villa',[51] and he has made a career of this unsettled relation to energetically rehearsed 'real' things which never subsume one another.

In *The Annals of Chile* these qualities, which are close in their nominalism at times to Beckett's relish for obscure and obsolete words, become prominent in Muldoon's boldest and most moving exploitation of the world as its contents to date, the elegy for the artist Mary Farl Powers, 'Incantata' (Beckett for the first time in Muldoon's work forms a presence in this poem). In an extraordinarily sustained and controlled ending of the poem, the world after

the death of his friend is seen to break down into a babbling mean-
inglessness. That breakdown is an answer to Powers's own
Thomist belief that 'in everything there is an order,/that the things
of the world sing out in a great oratorio'. The elegy is inspired by a
thought of Powers as Muldoon peels a potato; she had refused all
treatment for her cancer other than the homeopathic:

> The fact that you were determined to cut yourself off in your
>   prime
> because it was *pre*-determined has my eyes abrim:
> I crouch with Belacqua
> and Lucky and Pozzo in the Acacacac-
> ademy of Anthropopopometry, trying to make sense of the
>   '*quaquaqua*'
> of that potato-mouth; that mouth as prim
> and proper as it's full of self-opprobrium,
> with its '*quaquaqua*', with its 'Quoiquoiquoiquoiquoiquoi-
>   quoiq'.

This stammering sound is 'all that's left' we're told, after the death.
Yet the stammering, left over, forms an astounding 'sentence'
which fills seven pages:

> That's all that's left of the voice of Enrico Caruso
> from all that's left of an opera-house somewhere in Matto
> Grosso,
>   all that's left of the hogweed and horehound and cuckoo-pint,
> of the eighteen soldiers dead at Warrenpoint,
> of the Black Church clique and the Graphic studio claque,
> of the many moons of glasses on a tray,
> of the brewery-carts drawn by moon-booted drays,
> of those jump-suits worn under your bottle-green worsted
> cloaks....[52]

This is a summatory exploitation of those Frostian 'sentence
sounds' which Muldoon early on in his career said he admired.[53] It
is a miraculous containment of a life through its myriad details, and
amounts to an magnificent welter in which incidents from the
recent violence in the North of Ireland are held syntactically in
with, but remain as distinct from, all the other details, and all are
contained with the summary, alliteratively variational staccato

rubble of a person's past. As with the 'structuring' philosophical 'history' of 'Madoc – A Mystery', the Thomism which Powers held to the end is both confirmed by the intricate grammar of Muldoon's sentence and denied by its 'chaotic' detail, which is in its turn controlled or suggested by the sustained rhyme scheme. The seemingly casual rhythms of speech play off against the intricately rigid structure of the poem. The narrative of the individual life (and in this lies its consonance with other of Muldoon's histories) is constantly interrupted but made fascinating by the 'random' details it contains.

This process is accelerated in 'Yarrow', the long sequence which makes up the second part of the book. The polylingual parodying of the noble, heroic deeds of warfare in the sequence (through recounting his childhood wargames) and of romance (through the recounting of early sexual experience) continues Muldoon's attack on all idealisms. The poetry is obsessed by demotic measures of time which reinvigorate the telling – 'that was the year', 'for thirty years' 'it was now too late', etc. – and which fail to amount to a fixed sense of history at all, mixed as they are with fragmented, bizarre memories. A constant butt of Muldoon's irony across his career has been his old tutor Seamus Heaney and 'Yarrow', with its 150 poems varying between two, three and four three-line stanzas, is surely an attempted outdoing of Heaney's airily architectural 'Squarings'. The various references to Sylvia Plath (the year referred to in the sequence is 1963, that of Plath's death) obviously question Heaney's conclusions about her in an essay of the late 1980s. The question 'How to read the last line/in that last poem?' humorously has Muldoon worrying about the inferentiality of poetry in order to resist Heaney's reading of 'Edge' as a given, as 'being' in itself – something which is anathema to Muldoon's nominalist poetic.[54] Elsewhere, reading again gains a literalism, in this case a childishly smutty one, as Yeats's late Romantic Celtic Twilight symbolism of the dark rose and other lines proclaiming poetic grandeur are seen as pure smut: 'how dare you misread//his line about how they "all gave tongue"...?'[55]

But, as with Heaney's weightlessness in *The Haw Lantern* and *Seeing Things*, *The Annals of Chile*'s (often childish) exuberance and freedom is gained in response to loss; the loss of Powers in the first part of the book and of Plath and the poet's mother in the second part (the whole collection is dedicated to his mother's memory). In its chaotic and confused sexuality, in its druggy flights, as in its boy's own adventure stories in which the young Muldoon plays a variety of roles, the skittish 'freedom' of 'Yarrow' laments and operates in the absence of those feminine presences and the values they sustained. In one poem which follows another containing that description of giving tongue, Muldoon's mother herself chips in in order to celebrate the political vision of Yeats, who had been dismissed as '*Il Duce* of Drumcliff' in the earlier poem puerilely spotting the sex in the symbols. Ma sets up her own 'September 1913'-like lament for the lost nationalist heroes, among whom she includes the founder of Sinn Féin, Arthur Griffith.[56] Her remembered mispronunciation of his name as 'Arthur Griffin' recalls Heaney's 'Clearances' sonnet recollecting his own mother's affected inadequacy when 'pronouncing words "beyond her"'. In her presence, 'I'd *naw* and *aye*', Heaney recounts:

> And decently relapse into the wrong
> Grammar which kept us allied and at bay.[57]

This sense in Heaney of a familial warmth and strength in a shared language which is yet the definer of a culturally hampered and inadequate position underwrites also the skewed, disjunctive, hallucinatory poetry of the later Carson and Muldoon. That oral contingency which frees the poetry from both standard English forms and political absolutism in its reading of history also registers an inability to flee any further, a need to make a stand on what little ground poetry has in these conditions.[58] 'Nevermore', as 'Ma' says in this Muldoon poem, 'will the soul clap its hands/for sheer joy' as it did for Yeats. This frees the poetry into playful flight from all attachments, while also continuing a dialogue in its speaking slabber with the divisions and painful, punctuating events in the North of Ireland.

Notes

CHAPTER 1   INTRODUCTION: MAKING HISTORY?

1.   *Irish Times*, Weekend Section, September 3, 1994. 'Ceasefire' has sub-
      sequently been reprinted in Longley's collection *The Ghost Orchid*
      (London: Jonathan Cape, 1995, p. 39). The poem continues Longley's
      discovery in the classics, and in Homer particularly, of passages and
      incidents pertinent to the present. His collection before *The Ghost
      Orchid*, *Gorse Fires* (London: Secker & Warburg, 1991), also contains
      moving, freely translated excerpts which press upon events in the
      North of Ireland.
2.   'Ulysses, Order, and Myth', *Selected Prose of T.S. Eliot*, edited with an
      introduction by Frank Kermode (London: Faber, 1975), p. 177.
3.   *Modernisms: A Literary Guide* (London: Macmillan, 1995), p. 167.
4.   *Transitions: Narratives in Modern Irish Culture* (Manchester University
      Press, 1988), p. 9.
5.   Jonathan Bardon, *A History of Ulster* (Belfast: Blackstaff Press, 1992),
      pp. 662–90.
6.   'The Irish Writer', *Davis, Mangan, Ferguson? Tradition and the Irish
      Writer*, writings by W.B. Yeats and Thomas Kinsella (Dublin: Dolmen
      Press, 1970), p. 66.
7.   *Francis Ledwidge: Selected Poems* (Dublin: New Island Books, 1992), p. 11.
8.   *Field Work* (London: Faber, 1979), p. 60.
9.   *Station Island* (London: Faber, 1984), p. 37.
10.   'An Ulster Twilight', *Krino*, No. 5, Spring 1988, p. 100.
11.   Dublin: The Dedalus Press, 1994; London: Anvil Press, 1993. In the
      poem 'Irish Cuttings' from the latter collection, O'Driscoll has written
      a horrific and modern version of the *aisling* or vision poem in which
      Ireland is described as a young maiden, as an old farmer is blown up
      by a booby-trapped bomb in a copy of *Playboy* (p. 16).
12.   'Squarings', xli, *Seeing Things* (London: Faber, 1991), p. 101.
13.   *Guide to Kulchur* (London: Peter Owen, 1952 reprint), pp. 60, 83.
14.   *Selected Prose of T.S. Eliot*, p. 38.
15.   'Nineteen Hundred and Nineteen', *The Collected Poems of W.B. Yeats*
      (London: Macmillan, 1979 edition), p. 233.
16.   Padraic Fallon, *Collected Poems* (Manchester/Loughcrew: Carcanet/
      Gallery Press, 1990), p. 16.
17.   Terence Brown's Field Day pamphlet, 'The Whole Protestant
      Community: the making of a historical myth', dramatizes the circular
      and entrapping dominance of history on both sides of the religious
      divide: 'Since history is to be understood as a series of events occur-
      ring as time passes but [also] as a permanently existing reality to
      which appeal can be made in order to endorse contemporary political
      deeds, a sense of historical repetition is inevitable' (Derry: Field Day
      Theatre Company, 1985, p. 6).

18. *The Music of What Happens: Poems, Poets, Critics* (Cambridge, Mass.: Harvard University Press, 1988), pp. 3, 2, 149.
19. See Chapter 6 below for a discussion of these issues in Heaney's writing. It is possible to discover, at least subliminally, some kind of reciprocal influence between Vendler's and Heaney's critical thinking about the uniqueness of the aesthetic. Heaney's lectures given as Oxford Professor of Poetry, collected as *The Redress of Poetry* (Faber: London, 1995), more readily acknowledge the pressure of historical context upon a poem than Vendler does. But ultimately (and rather repetitively) each lecture concludes by defending and celebrating the Keatsian 'fine excess' of poetry, its flight beyond all such forming conditions, and the renewal that that flight can offer the individual reader: '...there is always a kind of homeopathic benefit', he claims, in experiencing the rhythmic life of the poem, which 'furthers the range of the mind's and the body's pleasures' and helps the reader the better to know him or herself (p. 37). Heaney's surprising celebration of the work of George Herbert (work so integral to the native English tradition) in the opening lecture establishing the idea of redress holding throughout the series perhaps also reveals the effect of Vendler's critical work on his own thinking. Vendler's *The Poetry of George Herbert* appeared in 1975, her book on Keats, of whom she finds Heaney the natural successor, in 1988.
20. 'A More Social Voice: "Field Work"', in *The Art of Seamus Heaney*, edited and introduced by Tony Curtis (Bridgend: Poetry Wales Press 1982 (1985, 2nd edition)), pp. 104, 115. In describing how Heaney in other poems seems to seek to more directly involve himself in Irish 'facts of life', Curtis adopts a presumptuous holistic approach. He claims that the pastoral imagery in 'The Strand at Lough Beg' and 'Casualty' prove that 'For peace to return to Ulster the people have to re-establish the rhythm of the natural world' (p. 115). His reading of Heaney's casual reference to the fact that a hammer and a cracked jug were standing on a windowsill in 'At the Water's Edge' is even more inflationary in its desperate assertion of the poem as site of a unity of being unimpinged upon by those harsh 'facts': 'They are the male and female, the sense of belonging to a place, trees, water, construction and survival; they have the symbolic force for which Heaney has travelled...he is again in touch with the elemental, the basic possibilities of life...' (p. 110). Writing from within the North of Ireland, Robert Welch has recently also accepted the space of the poem as one in which Heaney's transactions work to translate ordinary 'doings' into 'a different order of experience by the aura of mystery'. Poetry therefore offers a language which is freed from the intransigent and divisive tug of those 'doings': on Heaney's 'Bone Dreams', Welch writes that 'There is a conflict between Ireland and England; it often seems insoluble to the mind trained in the discourses of politics, negotiation, opposition. It may be, in fact, insoluble. But a poem such as this witnesses to a space human creativity can create where history is set aside and the problem is viewed objectively' (*Changing States: Transformations in Modern Irish Writing* (London: Routledge, 1993),

pp. 260, 254). The nature of such objectivity is revealed when Welch claims that 'the country of writing is a country of movement...Inside it things flow together in a unity which can accommodate', alongside various mythic figures, 'Catholics, Presbyterians' (p. 283); the precise means by which the 'discourses' about ordinary worldly 'doings' are translated in the space of the poem remains in Welch's commentary mysterious, however.

21. Terry Eagleton has argued that organicist ideas have historically had little impact in Ireland, and that in this lies one of the main distinctions between that country and England: 'From Burke and Coleridge to Arnold and Eliot, a dominant ideological device in Britain is to transmute history itself into a seamless evolutionary continuum.... Society itself, in this view, becomes a marvellous aesthetic organism, self-generating and self-contained. This is a much rarer sort of discourse in Ireland.' He attributes this rareness to the apocalyptic laying waste of the Irish countryside during the years of the Great Hunger: '...in the British context history becomes Nature, in Ireland Nature becomes history. And this both in the sense that, in a largely pre-industrial society, the land is the prime determinant of human life, and in the sense that in the Famine history appears with all the brute, aleatory power of a seismic upheaval, thus writing large the course of much Irish history' (*Heathcliff and the Great Hunger: Studies in Irish Culture* (London: Verso, 1995), pp. 4, 11). Several poems on the Famine, including 'At a Potato Digging' and 'For the Commander of the "Eliza"', contribute to the anxious, terminal pastoralism conveyed in the title of Seamus Heaney's first collection, *Death of a Naturalist* (London: Faber, 1966). The impact of the Famine on the historical vision of Thomas Kinsella and of Brendan Kennelly forms an important feature in my discussions of them below.

22. *Fortnight*, No. 174, December 1979–January 1980.

23. 'Edna Longley in conversation with Carol Rumens', *Krino* No. 15, Spring 1994, p. 10.

24. *Poetry in the Wars* (Newcastle upon Tyne: Bloodaxe Books, 1986), p. 196.

25. Ibid., p. 185.

26. *The Living Stream: Literature and Revisionism in Ireland* (Newcastle upon Tyne: Bloodaxe Books, 1994), p. 62. I discuss the particular impact of Longley's stance on her reading of individual poets – and, in her battles with Field Day, her surprising championing of the Republic's Brendan Kennelly and Paul Durcan – in Chapter 5 below.

27. Ibid., pp. 194, 260.

28. *The Music of What Happens*, p. 5

29. *The Living Stream*, p. 267.

30. *Aesthetic Theory*, trans. C. Lenhardt, edited by Gretel Adorno and Rolf Tiedemann (London: RKP, 1986 paperback edition), p. 491.

31. Ibid., p. 261.

32. Ibid., pp. 30, 35.

33. Edna Longley is, as the opening chapter of *Poetry in the Wars* shows, vehemently opposed to 'Modernist-based or biased criticism' whose

'formalist emphases' she considers 'largely redundant in the presence of [poetry] where form has always been the *sine qua non*.' Against what she sees as the unnecessary disjunctions and emphases of modernism, its tendency to 'collapse history or anticipate the millenium', Longley favours a more 'evolutionary' approach: 'the history of forms comments on social conditions, and its pace cannot be forced' (pp. 13–15). Longley's rejection of modernism here echoes the terms of the distinction she draws between Protestant and Catholic imagery as displayed on murals and banners in the essay 'The Rising, the Somme and Irish Memory': '...Orange insignia work as reminders which are also warnings. They are not icons, but *exempla* or history-lessons: a heritage-pack as survival-kit. Republican iconography, on the other hand, merges memory into aspiration. It has yet to enter history as such' (in *Revising the Rising*, edited by Máirín Ní Dhonnchadha and Theo Dorgan (Field Day, Derry, 1991), p. 37. The essay is reprinted in *The Living Stream*.

34. 'The Birth', *The Annals of Chile* (London: Faber, 1994), p. 31.
35. *Ireland's Field Day* (London: Hutchinson, 1985), p. vii.
36. As displayed in Deane's pamphlet, 'Heroic Styles: The Tradition of An Idea' and Richard Kearney's 'Myth and Motherland'.
37. Quoted in Elmer Andrews, 'The Fifth Province' in *The Achievement of Brian Friel*, edited by Alan Peacock (Gerrards Cross: Colin Smythe, 1993), p. 242. The poet and critic Tom Paulin, another of Field Day's directors, defined the idea in his own terms when setting out the bases of his seemingly eclectic critical stance in the Introduction to his first collection of essays: 'My...position... assumes the existence of a non-sectarian, republican state which comprises the whole island of Ireland.' He then associates that ideal with a similar concept from another director, Seamus Heaney (*Ireland & the English Crisis* (Newcastle upon Tyne: Bloodaxe Books, 1985), p. 17).
38. 'Heroic Styles: The Tradition of an Idea', p. 58.
39. As the first pamphlet, Tom Paulin's 'A New Look at the Language Question' , signalled, for Field Day the literary is inextricably bound up with linguistic issues. This emphasis encouraged some of the early pamphleteers including Deane to draw upon linguistic theory and semiotics to leaven their arguments. An early defender of Field Day against its attackers (and principally Longley whose calls for 'rationality' and 'neutrality' he saw as repeating British stereotypes about Ireland) seized upon this as the central *raison d'être* of their work: 'Critics of Field Day, ironically, have reduced the issue to politics. If we examine the[ir] particular idealism...it is clear that the overriding issue is language itself.' He then goes on to quote Friel in support of his argument: 'I think that is how the political problem of this island is going to be solved. It's going to be solved by language in some kind of way' (Joe McMinn, 'In Defence of Field Day: Talking Among the Ruins', *Fortnight*, No. 224, 9–22 September 1985, p. 20). Peter Sirr contended in an *Irish Times* review of the collected first six pamphlets: 'If the whole Field Day enterprise is about anything, it is about the refusal to see aesthetics and politics as anything other than

inextricably linked, and often close enough to be morally accountable to each other' ('Art, Politics and Polemic', review of *Ireland's Field Day*, Saturday, 22 June 1985, Weekend Section, p. 4).

40. 'The Man From God Knows Where', an interview with Fintan O'Toole, *In Dublin*, No. 165, 1982, p. 23.

41. 'On Irish Expressionist Painting', *The Irish Review*, No. 4, 1988, p. 36.

42. *The Government of the Tongue* (London: Faber, 1988), p. xxi. The events in the late 1960s also brought about an urgent politicization of Brian Friel's work. His early plays had dealt with perennial themes of Irish historical deprivation and diaspora. In the early 1970s Friel's writing directly addressed events. *The Freedom of the City* (a title which plays upon notions of British civic pride but also the Free Derry declared by protesters in 1968–9), was first performed in 1973. The play is set around a Derry Civil Rights march in 1970 but carries clear resonances of Bloody Sunday. Three marchers become separated from their colleagues during tear gas attacks and inadvertently enjoy the luxuries on offer in the Guildhall Mayor's chamber, the heart of Unionist power. They do not know that the building has been surrounded, though, and on their exit are shot dead by troops. The play includes the professional, pompous voice of a sociologist commenting on the roots of the Civil Rights movement and linking them to international trends, the priest giving a funeral sermon over the victims, and, framing the whole, an enquiry which whitewashes the killings of the three in terms recalling those of the Widgery enquiry which exonerated the action of the paratroops on Bloody Sunday (Widgery is also the instigation of Kinsella's *Butcher's Dozen*). *The Freedom of the City* provides a complex view of the motivations of the movement, of those who are seeking to use it for their own political ends, and of the social and class-based issues which gave the movement its impetus.

43. *A History of Ulster*, p. 653. My description of the rise of the Civil Rights movement is indebted to his full account on pp. 643–89 of this book.

44. *Preoccupations: Selected Prose 1968–1978* (London: Faber, 1980), p. 56.

45. 'To Bind the Northern to the Southern Stars: Field Day in Derry and Dublin', *The Irish Review*, No. 4, Spring 1988, p. 57. Typically within such debates, these very qualities have been celebrated by another critic, Eamonn Hughes, as the possibility which the Company offers. Writing of Friel's own *Translations*, Hughes argues that 'The attitude...to history is, in effect, "mourn, and then onwards"....This is an attitude...which will allow for pluralism...[which] leaves the way open for a new approach to history in Ireland, an approach which would allow for the release of human potential in and through history, an approach which must be called "charismatic humanism"'. ('"To Define your Dissent": The Plays and Polemics of the Field Day Theatre Company', *Theatre Research International*, Vol. 15, No. 1, Spring 1990, p. 76).

46. *Selected Plays* (London: Faber, 1984), p. 429.

47. Loughcrew Gallery Press, 1992, p. 112. Paul Muldoon has mocked the ambition behind Friel's translation, which the publisher's blurb describes as 'an act of love' which hoped to make Chekov, who had

previously only been available in American and English translations, more accessible to Irish audiences. Muldoon derides the 'vershin' done by 'Monsignor Friel' for its pains to 'prove that Chekov was more Irish/than a rush...' (*The Prince of the Quotidian* (Loughcrew: Gallery Press, 1994, p. 22). In truth, the level of 'Irishness' in Friel's translation is low, restricted only to an odd use of colloquial phrases, and those are, worryingly, mostly spoken by the servants.

48. 'For Liberation: Brian Friel and the Use of Memory', in *The Achievement of Brian Friel*, pp. 230, 234.

49. I discuss Seamus Heaney's dramatic contribution to Field Day, the 1990 *The Cure at Troy*, in my chapter on him below. Only Thomas Kilroy's 1986 production *Double Cross* seems to elude the terms of this dilemma between the personal and the national or communal, by showing how the traitors Brendan Bracken and William Joyce (Lord Haw Haw) managed to transgress the restrictive codes which the oppressor and the oppressed, Ireland and England, share with each other. But the Lady Journalist 'commenting' on Joyce's trial ends suggesting that nothing has been changed by the individual traitor's action: 'It was as if they had taken the idea of England to some terrible logical meaning of their own which England itself could never tolerate' (London: Faber, 1986, p. 79).

50. 8 February 1986, Weekend Section, p. 5.

51. 'An Outside Look at Irish Poetry', a review of Dillon Johnston, *Irish Poetry After Joyce*, 5 April 1986, Weekend Section, p. 4. Boland spends much of her review chiding the exclusion of poetry from the South of Ireland from Johnston's argument in favour of the more obviously 'relevant' and newsworthy poetry from the North: 'I can no more believe now that all Irish poetry emanates from the North than I believed 20 years ago that it issued from the South. What I do believe, increasingly, is that as long as poets allow others to think it comes from one or the other...then something is wrong and very wrong. That is one sure way of allowing the wounding and wounded national experience we are involved in to exact a terrible price from the healing tradition of Irish poetry....We are poets first, and then Irish poets.' Debates around whether the political border between North and South is matched by a poetic one are, of course, highly contentious and politicized in themselves. Edna Longley has argued in the Galway magazine *Krino* that 'the cultural, formal, and sociolinguistic dynamics of...'Northern' poems differ from ['Southern' ones] ('Misplaced Figures on a Partial Map', p. 99). In an earlier issue of the same magazine, Terence Brown had argued that, despite the prominence accorded to 'Northern' poets by the political situation in the North, 'in fact the north as a clearly defined cultural entity does not exist. Heaney has in fact written more of his poetry in Wicklow and Dublin than in the North and it shows in his preoccupations and development' (*Krino*, No. 2, Autumn 1986, p. 20).

52. *The Magdalene Sermon* (Loughcrew: Gallery Press, 1989), p. 11.

53. 'The Real Thing', *The Brazen Serpent* (Loughcrew: Gallery Press, 1994), p. 16.

54. 'An Ulster Twilight?', p. 102. Clyde argues forcefully that McGuckian's poetic marks the only bright light for the future of poetry in the North. As the quotation from this article given earlier in the main text suggests, he feels that the male poets have reached an impasse, that their preoccupation with issues of territory, language and history had proved both politically divisive and imaginatively deadening, monotonously refusing to accept a pluralism which already exists in the North. McGuckian's experimentalism offers at least an ambition to break the standard modes, as he sees it.
55. Loughcrew: Gallery Press, 1994, pp. 82–3.
56. Manchester: Carcanet, 1995, pp. xiv, xv, 114.
57. Ibid., p. 148. Edna Longley has attacked this association by Boland because, as she sees it, it is not revisionist enough. Boland, Longley writes, fails herself, because she 'recycles the literary cliché from which she desires to escape.' Boland's attention upon the plight of woman has, in other words, deflected her attention from the solidly male nationalist ideas from which she refuses to be set apart (*The Living Stream*, p. 188). But this seems a reductive and slightly mean reading of the struggle towards eloquence which Boland describes, a struggle in which the traditional male versions of nationalism are a particular cause of pain and difficulty for her.
58. *Selected Poems* (Manchester Carcanet, 1989), p. 18.
59. *Object Lessons*, p. 178.
60. *Selected Poems*, pp. 27, 30.
61. Manchester: Carcanet, 1990, pp. 31–2.
62. Manchester: Carcanet, 1994, p. 7.
63. Ibid., p. 10.
64. *Outside History*, p. 45.
65. *Object Lessons*, pp. 24–5.
66. Ibid., pp. 188–9.

CHAPTER 2   JOHN HEWITT: AN HONEST ULSTERMAN'S 'POEMOSAICS'

1. *Preoccupations: Selected Prose 1968–1978* (London: Faber, 1980), p. 207.
2. *Ancestral Voices: The Selected Prose of John Hewitt*, edited by Tom Clyde (Belfast: Blackstaff Press, 1987), p. 78.
3. *The Collected Poems of John Hewitt*, edited by Frank Ormsby (Belfast: Blackstaff Press, 1991), p. xviii. Hereafter designated as *Collected Poems*.
4. *Collected Poems* contains poems modelled on the work of each of these precursors: Edward Thomas in 'The Neglected Lane'; Robert Frost in 'The Hired Lad's Farewell'; Ezra Pound in 'Mauberley's son: a summary'; T.S. Eliot in 'Tiphead'; W.H. Auden in 'Prelude to an ode for Barnum'.
5. *Collected Poems*, p. 365.
6. Heaney has acknowledged the 'original and epoch-making... significant extension of the imagining faculty' contained in Hewitt's

1940s notion of regionalism which I discuss later in this chapter. But Heaney recognizes the ultimate failure of that idea due to Hewitt's inability to fully 'include the Irish dimension' in his vision. As a response to this failure, Heaney proposes a new map of Ireland which seeks to include all traditions equally within it ('Frontiers of Writing', *The Redress of Poetry* (London: Faber, 1995), pp 195–203).

7.   'History Men', review of Hewitt's *Freehold, inter alia,* in *The Irish Review,* No. 1, 1986, p. 114.

8.   *The Honest Ulsterman,* No. 8, December 1968, p. 24.

9.   *Collected Poems,* p. 98.

10. Ibid., p. 97.

11. Hewitt wrote that it was William Morris who had for him 'most movingly evoked the quality of the Good Society in his *News from Nowhere*' (*Ancestral Voices,* p. 152). The vision of Coventry given in this poem is close to that of London as an ordered garden-city in Morris's utopian romance. Morris earns an equally significant role in Raymond Williams's tracing of the intractable relation between an organicized, ideal community derived from Romanticism and the actualities of Victorian industrial society, since he sought to attach the general values of that tradition to 'an actual and growing social force: that of the organized working class' (*Culture and Society 1780–1950* (Harmondsworth: Penguin, 1982), p. 153). Hewitt's socialist poetic often awkwardly mediates between similar idealism and pragmatism; the relation of it to the terms of Williams's own ideas about ideal communities I will discuss below.

12. Seamus Deane has given a version of the history of this polarization and recorded some of its repressive effects in Ireland in his Field Day pamphlet 'Civilians and Barbarians' which is reprinted in *Ireland's Field Day* (London: Hutchinson, 1985, pp. 33–44).

13. Quoted in *Collected Poems,* p. 588. Hewitt had arrived in Coventry in March 1957 to take up the position of art director at the Herbert Art Gallery and Museum. The move from his natal city had been instigated by his rejection for the post of director of the Belfast Museum and Art Gallery in 1953. He had been deputy director there for three years but his application for promotion was rejected, as he argued in the section of his autobiography called 'From Chairmen and Committee Men, Good Lord Deliver Us', because of his socialist sympathies and because of his having close friends who were Catholics (*Ancestral Voices,* pp. 48–55). In this immediate sense Coventry is 'tolerant' when compared to his own city, Belfast.

14. *Collected Poems,* p. 570.

15. Ibid., p. 8. Among those who have accepted Hewitt's own rhetoric of the 'comfortable pace' are John Wilson Foster, who draws a contrast between Hewitt's work and that of John Montague which plays upon the title of Montague's 1972 collection that I will discuss later: 'One cannot imagine Hewitt inhabiting the rough field...' ('The Dissidence of Dissent: John Hewitt and W.R. Rodgers', *Across the Roaring Hill: The Protestant Imagination in Modern Ireland,* edited by Gerald Dawe and Edna Longley (Belfast: Blackstaff Press, 1985), p. 144); Tom Clyde in

his review of Hewitt's *Freehold*, who speaks of 'sensitivity to others, his commitment to democracy and equality, his rationalism and his tolerance' (*The Irish Review*, No. 1, 1986, p. 114); Frank Ormsby in his summary remarks in the Introduction to the *Collected Poems*, which note and take as apt Hewitt's repeated 'confident claim[s] for the strength of the quiet voice, for all its apparent fragility' (p. lxxii).

16. *Collected Poems*, pp. 313–14.
17. Quoted in *Collected Poems*, p. 610. Hewitt's few attempts to write in the 'obscure' modernist style, like the 1956 'Those Swans Remember', are embarrassing, however.
18. *Ancestral Voices*, p. 80.
19. *Collected Poems*, p. 19.
20. Ibid., p. 191.
21. *Ancestral Voices*, p. 152.
22. Ibid., p. 122. Martin Mooney has argued in '"A Native Mode": language and regionalism in the poetry of John Hewitt' that it is this phrase which marks 'Regionalism's value to Hewitt the middle-class socialist' (*The Irish Review*, No. 3, 1988, p. 69). As well as the renewed currency which Hewitt's idea attained in the late 1960s, which I now go on to discuss, it has more recently surfaced in the thinking of Edna Longley (in *The Living Stream* (Newcastle upon Tyne: Bloodaxe Books, 1994, p. 195) and also of John Wilson Foster, whose *Colonial Consequences: Essays in Irish Literature and Culture* (Dublin: Lilliput Press, 1991) ends by advocating 'radical regionalism' – Ulster as a separate region in the European context.
23. No. 1, May 1968, p. 3.
24. Ibid., pp. 36–8. Nietzsche's essay 'On the Use and Misuse of History for Life' is discussed by Paul de Man in his 'Literary History and Literary Modernity'. De Man concludes his essay in a manner strikingly similar to Simmons's, that 'the bases for historical knowledge are not empirical facts but written texts' (*Blindness and Insight: Essays in the Rhetoric of Contemporary Criticism* (London: Methuen, 1983), p. 165).
25. *Ancestral Voices*, p. 121.
26. Ibid., pp. 115–116.
27. *The Collected Poems of W.B. Yeats* (London: Macmillan, 1979), p. 369.
28. The myth of the 'ground-hugger' Antaeus and of Hercules, who tries to deprive him of his strength by lifting him into the air, provides Seamus Heaney with his framing and structuring idea in his book most directly addressing the political situation, *North* (London: Faber, 1975).
29. *Collected Poems*, p. 91.
30. Ibid., p. 21.
31. Hewitt gives lavish praise to Austin Clarke's experimental 'hybrid begot of normal English and Gaelic metres' at the end of his essay 'Irish Poets, Learn Your Trade', but never attempted such experiments himself (see *Ancestral Voices*, pp. 82–6). His poem 'Gloss, On the Difficulties of Translation' reveals his inability to capture the sound qualities of Gaelic in his own work: 'the intricate wordplay/...is beyond my grasp' (*Collected Poems*, p. 129).

32. Ibid., pp. 95–6.
33. *Ancestral Voices*, p. 79. This assertion of Yeats the skilled craftsman against Yeats the maker of myths and symbols is very much in tune with Hewitt's interest in that other group of poet-artisans, a collection of whose work he edited in 1974 as *Rhyming Weavers and Other Country Poets of Antrim and Down*. These artisans were part of the United Irishmen rebellion in 1798, when both communities rose up against British rule, and provide Hewitt with a further model for the uniting of a poetic with a political ideal.
34. *Collected Poems*, pp. 70, 72.
35. *Station Island* (London: Faber, 1984), p. 110.
36. *Ancestral Voices*, p. 80.
37. *Collected Poems*, p. 327.
38. London: Chatto & Windus, 1961, p. 26.
39. Ibid., pp. 23, 25.
40. *Culture and Society 1780–1950*, p. 301.
41. *The Long Revolution*, p. 33.
42. *Collected Poems*, p. 228.
43. Between 1931 and 1939, unemployment in Ulster stood at an average 27 per cent (see Jonathan Bardon, *A History of Ulster* (Belfast: The Blackstaff Press, 1992), p. 529). By the time Hewitt was writing 'Ars Poetica', however, unemployment had 'all but disappeared' in a postwar boom in which there was also comparative peace under secure Unionist rule. Bardon calls 1945–63 'The Quiet Years' (p. 587); Hewitt's poem is clearly to that extent retrospective, showing his continuing socialist and community concerns even at times when the causes for them had receded somewhat. In linking the question of labour with the national question, Hewitt is here following the example of one of his heroes, as he describes it in the essay 'James Hope, Weaver, of Templepatrick': '[Hope's] message for his own age was that Ireland could not be free until Irish workers, trusting only themselves, and through their own class effort, achieved economic justice throughout the land; that the national struggle was emphatically a class struggle. And his message is still true after the lapse of a hundred years' (*Ancestral Voices*, p. 137).
44. *Collected Poems*, p. 229.
45. *Ancestral Voices*, p. 114. Hewitt has himself recognized the debilities brought about by the lack in Northern Ireland of that communal artisan activity which had produced great art in cities like Florence: 'the potential artist here has lacked the strong body of traditional usage inherent in the urban milieu. There could have been no group or class sharing the diffused wisdom of settled masters....Suffering from the deficiency in these urban benefits, the Irish (like the Welsh) can produce poets, story-tellers, singers, actors, whose activities can be fostered in small poor communities and carried on by single individuals, wherever they may find themselves... (*Ancestral Voices*, p. 88).
46. *The Living Stream*, pp. 95–6.
47. *Collected Poems*, p. 4.

48. Jonathan Bardon, *A History of Ulster*, p. 617.
49. *Collected Poems*, p. 12. The ancestors of these Antrim farmers had been some of the most dedicated recruits to the cause of that historical force in Irish history which had drawn the two sides of the nation together in order to resist British occupation, the United Irishmen. Hewitt has not pursued this historical precedent for his ideal of a free, tolerant Ulster society in his poetry, but has in his discussions of the Rhyming Weavers from the area and in 'The Longest Campaign' (*Ancestral Voices*, p. 126–33). The United Irishmen have provided an important precedent for the political thinking of the next generations of poets, like Tom Paulin in *Liberty Tree* (London: Faber, 1983), Paul Muldoon in *Madoc* (London: Faber, 1990) and Seamus Heaney in 'Wolfe Tone' from *The Haw Lantern*.
50. *Collected Poems*, p. 25.
51. Ibid., p. 60. 'O Country People' (p. 73) despairingly admits that, because of his life in Belfast, Hewitt was destined to be for ever alienated from the central focus of his imagination: 'even a lifetime among you shall leave me strange/for I could not change enough and will not change'.
52. Ibid., p. 245. The graffiti seen as having significance here recalls the 1951 essay 'Painting and Sculpture in Ulster', in which Hewitt maintained that the only folk art to be found in the cities and towns was the mural paintings on the gable ends of houses (*Ancestral Voices*, pp. 105–6).
53. *Collected Poems*, p. 388. Derek Mahon's poem 'Derry Morning' provides a picture of the city which in effect blends the 1930s and 1980s parts of Hewitt's poem: within the ruins of the bombed-out city he sees 'an early crone' whose 'oak-grove vision hesitates' before the destruction. Yet, in this aftermath, 'A strangely pastoral silence rules/The shining roofs and murmuring schools', suggesting that, within this 'fitful revolution', all possibilities are glimpsed momentarily (*Selected Poems* (London/Loughcrew: Viking/Gallery, 1991), p. 123).
54. 'Carrigskeewaun', *Poems 1963–1983* (Harmondsworth: Penguin, 1986), p. 96.
55. This is again a precedent which has since been followed by, amongst others, Tom Paulin in 'The Other Voice' (*The Strange Museum* (London: Faber, 1980), p. 42) and Seamus Heaney in essays in *The Government of the Tongue* (London: Faber, 1988), which I discuss in the chapter on him.
56. This lack of a settled stance in the pamphlet provoked a hostile review in *The Honest Ulsterman* from Frank Ormsby, who felt that 'What we are given are the dithery cries of that vague, watery entity, the Outraged Liberal. If the *Belfast Telegraph*'s editorials were chopped up they couldn't be less authoritative than these poems...' (No. 29, July/August 1971, p. 40). Ormsby's own outrage mirrors the expectation that Hewitt's response will be definitive and contained in magisterial verse which comes through in Bareham's review of the earlier *Collected Poems*.
57. *Collected Poems*, p. 140.

58. Ibid., p. 132.
59. Ibid., p. 134.
60. Jonathan Bardon, *A History of Ulster*, p. 626.
61. *Collected Poems*, pp. 135–7.
62. *The Politics of Modernism: Against the New Conformists*, edited and introduced by Tony Pinkney (London: Verso, 1989), pp. 45–6.
63. Ibid., p. 141.
64. *Collected Poems*, p. 139.
65. Ibid., p. 358.
66. Ibid., pp. 188–9.

CHAPTER 3   THOMAS KINSELLA'S POETIC OF UNEASE

1. *Viewpoints: Poets in Conversation with John Haffenden* (London: Faber, 1981), p. 105.
2. *The Dual Tradition: An Essay on the Poetry and Politics in Ireland* (Manchester: Carcanet, 1995), p. 4. This book collects much of Kinsella's prose, but, except where I especially acknowledge so, I have always returned to the original unedited versions of his essays.
3. *Viewpoints*, p. 106.
4. Terence Brown *Ireland: A Social and Cultural History 1922–1979* (London: Fontana, 1985) pp. 215–16.
5. *Davis, Mangan, Ferguson? Tradition and the Irish Writer*, writings by W.B. Yeats and Thomas Kinsella (Dublin: Dolmen Press, 1970), p. 57.
6. In the poem 'Nightwalker', Kinsella derives a similar idea from memories of his own schooldays: 'And the authorities/Used the National Schools to try to conquer/The Irish national spirit, at the same time/Exterminating what they called our "jargon"/ – The Irish language…' *Poems 1956–1973* (Dublin: Dolmen Press, 1980), p. 110.
7. This sense of isolation even extends to those also writing at the moment: in response to John Haffenden's question 'Do you feel a kinship with other contemporary poets?', Kinsella replied 'The simple answer is: No. I don't feel that there is a group activity afoot in which I play a part, or a creative heave in which maybe two or three poets are engaged' (*Viewpoints*, p. 112).
8. He does his best to repair this loss, however, in the translations which he made from the Irish in *The Tain*, in his *New Oxford Book of Irish Verse*, and in *An Duanaire 1600–1900: Poems of the Dispossessed*.
9. *Davis, Mangan, Ferguson?*, p. 66.
10. Terry Eagleton has argued that it is Ireland's colonization which has made it the home of a particular, political brand of modernism: 'In an increasingly unified world, where all times and places seem indifferently interchangeable, the "no-time" and "no-place" of the disregarded colony, with its fractured history and marginalized space, can become suddenly symbolic of a condition of disinheritance which now seems universal….Modernism…needs a traditional culture

against which to react; but it can also, as in Ireland, turn a fragmented cultural history to its own advantage, exploiting the very absence of a stable system of representation for its own audacious experiments…in Ireland [modernism] is intensified by the boisterous presence of politics' (*Heathcliff and the Great Hunger: Studies in Irish Culture* (London: Verso, 1995), pp. 298–9).

11. *Davis, Mangan, Ferguson?*, pp. 64, 65.
12. The terms of Kinsella's praise for Joyce anticipate those used by writers associated with the Field Day Theatre Company in the early 1980s: by Seamus Deane, for instance, in his essay 'Heroic styles: the tradition of an idea' (*Ireland's Field Day* (London: Hutchinson, 1985), pp. 45ff.); or by Seamus Heaney in his essay 'A tale of two islands' (*Irish Studies 1*, edited by P.J. Drudy (CUP, 1980). Heaney has his persona address Joyce, who emerges as the crucial literary forebear in 'Station Island', as 'Old father' (*Station Island*, p. 93; this line has been dropped, however, for the revised sequence in *New Selected Poems 1966–1987* (London: Faber, 1990)).
13. Brian John persuasively argues for this influence in his essay '"Brothers in the Craft": Thomas Kinsella and the Yeats Inheritance' (*Irish University Review*, Vol. 24, No. 2, Autumn/Winter 1994, pp. 251–63). My argument will be that Yeat's influence has a more complicating and immediate formal impact upon Kinsella's poetic than the terms of John's discussion can allow for.
14. *Poems 1956–1973*, p. 95.
15. Ibid., p. 104. This last line hints at the disgusting piece of xenophobia which follows in the next passage of the poem, when, in describing an interview with two German investors, Kinsella has his persona see that 'A red glare/Plays on their faces, livid with little splashes/Of blazing fat. The oven door closes' (p. 105). Such writing is only partly excused by Kinsella's claims that the Second World War represented the greatest expression of that disjunction and violence which is the modern world, a fulfilment of Yeats's prophecy in 'The Second Coming': 'But it is one thing for Yeats to have foreseen such an upheaval as inevitable, in a schematic way, and even to have given body to his idea as the rough beast slouching toward the place of rebirth, destroying one state in the emergence of another. It is another thing to have participated in the second coming itself, even remotely, as my own generation did, coming to consciousness during the Second World War, in Ireland – to have breathed in the stench and felt the dread as the rough beast emerged out of mass human wills' ('The Divided Mind', in *Irish Poets in English*, edited by Séan Lucy (Cork and Dublin: Mercier Press, 1973), p. 214).
16. OUP, 1994, p. 26.
17. 'Redeeming the Ordinary', a review of *Blood and Family*, Krino, No. 7, 1989, p. 108.
18. *New Poems 1973* (Dublin: Dolmen Press, 1973), p. 60.
19. *Viewpoints*, p. 109.
20. *Poetry Ireland Review*, No. 25, Spring 1989, p. 59.
21. *Viewpoints*, p. 106.

22. Downstream', in *Tracks* No. 7, Thomas Kinsella Issue, edited by John F. Deane (Dublin: Dedalus Press, 1987), p. 23.

23. *Poems 1956–1973*, p. 112. Kinsella quotes these lines among the 'Precedents and Notes' for the 'Out of Ireland' sequence in *Blood and Family* (OUP, 1988), p. 86, so emphasizing their importance in his career.

24. 'The Harvest Bow', *Field Work* (London: Faber, 1979), p. 58.

25. *New Poems 1973*, p. 16.

26. *Irish Poets in English*, p. 209.

27. *Poems 1956–1973*, p. 116. In a later poem, called this time 'Rituals of Departure', in *From Centre City*, Kinsella sets the move away from some kind of source in a more traditional image (although one updated to the twentieth century), as he recalls a return from a family holiday in the West of Ireland, long seen as a repository of a truer, more authentic Irishness. Yet even this is set by Kinsella as part of an inevitable, oft-repeated personal, historical and poetic process – '... remember the detailed care you have had here./And the love. And the other rituals of departure,/their ashes dying along our path' (p. 18).

28. Kinsella invokes the painterly analogy in an earlier poem from *Nightwalker and Other Poems* in which 'Ritual of Departure' first appeared. 'Landscape and Figure' again uses the metaphor of potato blight as a way of describing the blighted history of the country and of all would-be returns to origins – 'He works towards the fruit of Adam', yet 'The protecting flesh/When it falls will melt away in a kind of mud' (*Poems 1956–1973*, p. 82).

29. That there is a compensatory yearning for 'shared histories' by Kinsella is clear, not from the poems, but from several passages in the prose commentaries to them. It is a barely glimpsed healing of rifts that confirms the greatness of the loss brought about by the early death of Kinsella's close friend, the musician Sean O'Riada, which is lamented by two poems in *Fifteen Dead* (Dublin and Oxford: Dolmen Press and OUP, 1979) and also by 'Her Vertical Smile' in *Blood and Family*. O'Riada's discovery and adaptation of traditional Irish music, and the popularity of his performances of that music, stand for the dream of reconciliation between artist and community which underlies much of the anguish of Kinsella's intractable modernism. In the notes to the poems in *Fifteen Dead* he wrote: 'For O'Riada...the traditional "European" relationship between the composer and a select audience appears from the beginning to have been uninspiring. His escape from it...came about, not through any new devices, but through his revival of the old native relationship between Irish traditional music and the Irish community, and his renovation of it for the twentieth century. This enabled him to make the whole nation his audience for a time, and to affect it deeply, without abandoning musical standards' (p. 59). A similar sense of the immediate connection which O'Riada was able to form with the national audience, as well as, in reaction, an exacerbated sense of the troubled relation of the modernist poet to his or her audience, also informs the poems which lament the musician's loss by another of O'Riada's friends, John Montague, as I argue in the next chapter.

30. 'The street becomes a dwelling for the *flaneur*; he is as much at home among the facades of houses as a citizen in his four walls' (*Charles Baudelaire: A Lyric Poet in the Era of High Capitalism* (London: Verso, 1976), p. 37.

31. *New Poems 1956–1973*, p. 56.

32. 'Theses on the Philosophy of History', *Illuminations*, edited by Hannah Arendt, translated by Harry Zohn (London: Fontana/Collins, 1973), p. 264.

33. Benjamin constantly related his theory of the monadic nature of historical materialism with his hope for some Messianic redemption of history from its barbaric progression: 'Where thinking suddenly stops in a constellation pregnant with tensions, it gives that constellation a shock, by which it crystallizes into a monad. A historical materialist approaches a historical subject only where he encounters it as a monad. In this structure he recognises the sign of a Messianic cessation of happening, or, put differently, a revolutionary chance in the fight for the oppressed past.' (Quoted by Terry Eagleton, *Walter Benjamin or Towards a Revolutionary Criticism* (London: Verso and New Left Books, 1981), p. 50.) That transfigurative power is integral to the project of the Field Day Theatre Company and their notion of an imaginary 'fifth province' which I discussed above; Kinsella's more intransigent modernism would seek to qualify such notions immediately.

34. *The Letters of Ezra Pound 1907–1941*, edited by D.D. Paige (London: Faber, 1951), p. 249.

35. *Aesthetic Theory*, translated by C. Lenhardt, edited by Gretal Adorno and Rolf Tiedmann (London: RKP, 1986, paperback edition), p. 491.

36. *New Poems 1973*, pp. 26–7.

37. Ibid., p. 36. Maurice Harmon has traced the origin of this poem to the myths of origin contained in the Irish *Lebor Gabala Erenn*: 'The survivor-persona may be identified with Fintan, one of three men who arrived in Ireland with the prediluvian Cessair and her company of women. When they threatened him, he took refuge on the Hill of the Wave where he sheltered in a cave and survived the Flood....In some accounts the early peoples were thought to have come from the sky, or from the Ocean' (*The Poetry of Thomas Kinsella: 'With darkness for a rest'* (Dublin: Wolfhound Press, 1974), pp. 87–8). Characteristically, Kinsella breaks up the paradoxes and indeterminacies contained in his originatory narrative and presents them directly, heightening his readers' sense of confusion and uncertainty.

38. *One and Other Poems* (Dublin: The Dolmen Press, 1979), p. 15.

39. Harmon has again traced the source of this poem to the *Lebor Gabala* or 'Book of Invasions', to an account of the journey of the Sons of Mil from Finistere in Brittany to Ireland and the founding song of the poet Amhairgin who accompanied the voyage (*The Poetry of Thomas Kinsella*, p. 103). Harmon takes the allegory of the poem to be both 'a declaration of belief in poetry' and an affirmation of 'arrival in Ireland as a state of promise' (p. 88). Yet the rhetorical questions which form Amhairgin's song in Kinsella's reworking of it hardly warrant such

assurance, certainly when it comes to their premonitory sense of violence to come: 'Who/is the word that spoken/the spear springs/and pours out terror?'

40. *Blood and Family*, p. 15.
41. 'The Poems of the Dispossessed Repossessed', *The Government of the Tongue* (London: Faber, 1988), p. 32.
42. *Aesthetic Theory*, p. 32.
43. *One and Other Poems*, p. 51. Richard Kearney has set such division as the defining characteristic of modernism: 'Modernism is essentially a "critical" movement in the philosophical sense of questioning the very notion of *origins*. And as such it challenges the *ideology of identity*....The modernist mind prefers discontinuity to continuity, diversity to unity, conflict to harmony, novelty to heritage' (*Transitions: Narratives in Modern Irish Culture* (Manchester University Press, 1988), p. 12).
44. 'Did you make a conscious decision to renounce received forms and rhyme?' John Haffenden asked him: 'Yes, I kicked the whole scheme asunder at a certain point, realizing that the modern poet has inherited wonderfully enabling free forms. My poems have a form which ought to be felt as a whole, rather than in, e.g., stanzaic explanations. Each poem has a unique shape, contents and development' (*Viewpoints*, p. 108).
45. *Illuminations*, pp. 222–3.
46. *Aesthetic Theory*, pp. 30, 32.
47. *New Poems 1973*, pp. 12, 52.
48. *The Dual Tradition*, p. 76.
49. *Fifteen Dead*, p. 57.
50. True to his sense of the temporality of poetry, Kinsella said in his 1979 commentary that 'I couldn't write the same poem now. The pressures were special, the insult strongly felt, and the timing vital if the response was to matter, in all its kinetic impurity' (p. 57).
51. He has used the form again recently, for more personal and literary reasons, in his vehement attack on Dublin literati in 'Open Court (A Fragment)' in *From Centre City* (pp. 60–4). Seamus Heaney has adopted a similar Dantean schema for the fragmented title sequence of *Station Island* (London: Faber, 1984), in which he explores his own relation as artist to his people's plight.
52. *Fifteen Dead*, p. 14. Maurice Harmon claims that this derision of the report's conclusion forms 'the poem's main device' (*The Poetry of Thomas Kinsella*, p. 106). But this is to limit the range of attitudes which the Dantean frame allows Kinsella to give voice to, without commenting on or prioritizing any one over the others.
53. *Fifteen Dead*, p. 17.
54. Ibid., p. 19.
55. Seamus Heaney adopts a similar stance and acknowledges its modernity, when using Joyce's own words at the end of his poem 'Traditions' in response to MacMorris's question in *Henry V* '"What ish my nation?"': '...sensibly, though so much/later, the wandering Bloom/replied, "Ireland," said Bloom,/"I was born here. Ireland"' (*Wintering Out* (London: Faber 1972), p. 32).

56. Conleth Ellis, 'Above the Salt', *Tracks*, p. 35.
57. *Fifteen Dead*, p. 20.
58. Dennis O'Driscoll, 'Public Vices and Private Voices', *Hibernia*, 21 June 1979; Gerald Dawe, 'In the Violent Zone', *Tracks*, p. 27.
59. *Fortnight*, No. 39, p. 19.
60. *Aesthetic Theory*, p. 28.

CHAPTER 4   A FAILURE TO RETURN: JOHN MONTAGUE'S *THE ROUGH FIELD*

1. *The Figure in the Cave and Other Essays* (Dublin: Lilliput Press, 1989), p. 219. True to the notion of denationalization in the last sentence here, Montague has himself lived and taught in America and France as well as in Ireland. He has published translations from the French of Esteban, Pierre Jean Jouve, Guillevic and Marteau, as well as from the Gaelic.
2. *The Rough Field* (Dublin: Dolmen Press, 1972), back cover.
3. *The Figure in the Cave*, p. 154.
4. *Ibid.* p. 125.
5. *Marxism and Form* (Princeton, NJ: Princeton University Press, 1971), p. 338.
6 Ibid., p. 390.
7. 'An Enduring Succession', review of Montague's *Selected Poems*, *Fortnight*, No. 190, January 1983.
8. Quoted by Terence Brown, *Ireland: A Social and Cultural History 1922–1979* (London: Fontana, 1981), p. 202.
9. *The Bell*, No. 1, October 1940, p. 5.
10. *The Figure in the Cave*, p. 168.
11. This oddness is perhaps partly explained by the discussion in 'The Impact of International Modern Poetry on Irish Writing' of the value of native and international models: 'Again I am not saying that Ezra Pound is necessarily more important than Aodhagen O'Rathaille for an Irish poet (one has to study both) but the complexity and pain of *The Pisan Cantos* are certainly more relevant than another version of the "Preab san Ol"' (*The Figure in the Cave*, p. 216). *The Pisan Cantos* are Pound's most personal poetry – and if they are what Montague thinks of when he refers to Pound, then their importance for his own work in its integration of the personal with history is immediate and obvious. This section of *The Cantos* is a meditation from a holding cell in an American prison camp near Pisa (Pound was being held for broadcasting pro-Mussolini propaganda) on the wreckage of Europe in the aftermath of the Second World War, a meditation interwoven with reflections on Pound's part in that history. It is significant that the 'complexity and pain' which Montague reads in *The Pisan Cantos* makes them relevant to the modern world as he experiences it – something resonant for his own sense of deprivation in the rough field of his country's history.

12. *The Collected Poems of W.B. Yeats* (London: Macmillan, 1979), p. 120.

13. *The Rough Field*, p. 65.

14. *The Collected Poems of W.B. Yeats*, p. 147.

15. *The Rough Field*, p. 64.

16. In the essay 'The Impact of International Modern Poetry on Irish Writing', Yeats's traditionalism, which he held to despite the way his friends and 'juniors' like Pound had helped him learn 'how to make his language more active', ultimately renders him in Montague's eyes less effective as an influence for later poets than those juniors themselves. Further, and this is clearly and oddly crucial for Montague, Yeats is 'little read in Europe' whereas Eliot and Pound are known there (yet what of the translations of Yeats into French by Bonnefoy, into German, into Italian?). Europe as the ultimate court greeted Montague in 1988, when he was translated into French by Deguy, Estaban, Marteau and others. Yet Montague in the essay characteristically returns on himself again and claims presciently that Yeats's later poems, the meditations on politics, violence and history, might prove important for Europe as it moves towards decentralization at the end of the century (*The Figure in the Cave*, p. 210).

17. *The Rough Field*, p. 68.

18. *The Figure in the Cave*, pp. 13, 47.

19. *The Rough Field*, p. 66.

20. Just to illustrate this further, I will list a few of the poems Montague reused from his 1971 collection *Tides* in the collections of the 1970s and early 1980s. So: 'The Wild Dog Rose', which gave its title to the first section of the earlier collection, reappears as the tenth part of *The Rough Field*. 'Omagh Hospital' reappears as the third poem in 'The Leaping Fire', the second part of the poem. 'A Meeting', 'A Dream of July' and 'Tracks' reappear in *The Great Cloak* of 1978. 'Last Journey' and 'What a View' reappear in *The Dead Kingdom*. Montague had a dry run in organizing his poems to bring out their relation to his country's history in his Belfast Festival pamphlet of 1967, *Home Again*.

21. *Tides* Dublin: Dolmen, 1971, p. 2.

22. *Object Lessons* (Manchester: Carcanet 1995), pp. 152–3.

23. *Tides*, p. 18; *The Rough Field*, p. 77.

24. *The Rough Field*, p. 80.

25. Harmondsworth: Penguin, 1992, p. 205.

26. *The Figure in the Cave*, p. 64.

27. 'A Raised Voice: John Montague's *Selected Poems*', *Irish University Review*, Vol. 12, No. 2, Autumn 1982, p. 152.

28. *The Rough Field*, p. 71.

29. 'Glanmore Sonnets' II, *Field Work* (London: Faber, 1979), p. 34.

30. *The Rough Field*, p. 51.

31. Ibid., p. 57.

32. 'The Politics of Theory', *The Ideologies of Theory, Essays 1971–1986*, Volume 2: *The Syntax of History* (London: Routledge, 1988), p. 11.

33. I would be reluctant, however (for reasons which will become clear below), to go as far as Seamus Deane and conclude that 'History, although a potent force in Montague's work is, finally, a maiming

influence': 'It attracts him by the thought of community which it holds within it; it repels him by the spuriousness of the communal sense which it finally offers' (*Celtic Revivals* (London: Faber, 1985), p. 152).

34. *The Figure in the Cave*, p. 75.
35. *The Rough Field*, p. 10.
36. *Marxism and Form*, p. 312.
37. Quoted by Paul de Man in his essay 'Literary History and Literary Modernity', *Blindness and Insight* (London: Routledge, 1989), p. 150. The translation is De Man's own.

CHAPTER 5   HISTORY IS ONLY PART OF IT: BRENDAN KENNELLY'S *CROMWELL*

1. No. 204, May 1984, p. 21. Writing in the American-based *Irish Literary Supplement*, the co-editor of the Dublin magazine *The Crane Bag* Mark Patrick Hederman shared Longley's sense of the cultural importance of the poem: the result of the book 'in terms of contemporary Irish people is devastating.' ('The Monster in the Irish Psyche', Fall 1984, p. 15).
2. More startlingly, the recent Bloodaxe collection of *critical* essays edited by Richard Pine, *Dark Fathers into Light: Brendan Kennelly*, comes with an endorsing Foreword by Michael D. Higgins, TD, Minister for Arts, Culture and the Gaeltacht. The form of the gratitude which Higgins offers is a curious one from a minister of state, since he claims that the importance of Kennelly's work lies in its reminder to us that we share a situation of 'unfreedom'. But the Foreword ends by valuing another quality in Kennelly's work. Higgins praises 'the truth of the thing....Through Brendan Kennelly's work we are reminded that authenticity continually threatens to assert itself' (Newcastle upon Tyne: Bloodaxe Books, 1994, p. 10). Yet, as I show below, it is authenticity itself which is under question in Kennelly's work.
3. 'Q & A With Brendan Kennelly' by Richard Pine, *Irish Literary Supplement*, Spring 1990, p. 21.
4. 'Patrick Kavanagh's Comic Vision', *Journey Into Joy: Selected Prose*, edited by Åke Persson (Newcastle upon Tyne: Bloodaxe Books, 1994), p. 112.
5. *Irish Times*, 19 December 1991.
6. *The Living Stream: Literature and Revisionism in Ireland* (Newcastle upon Tyne: Bloodaxe Books, 1994), pp. 218, 221, 200. In this essay, Longley argues her case by linking the genial influence which Patrick Kavanagh has had upon Kennelly with that he has had on Paul Durcan, and uses this as a means to distinguish between these writers from the South and the more polarized effect which Kavanagh has had upon writers from the North like Heaney. Durcan shares much of Kennelly's popularity and political profile in the South. After his work was quoted by the President-elect Mary

Robinson in her acceptance speech, one newspaper profile called him the 'virtual poet laureate' of Ireland (Eileen Battersby, 'A completely original voice, whether genius or showman', *Irish Times*, 10 November 1990). The either/or in her title reveals that Durcan's work shows some of the indefinable quality which I will discuss in relation to Kennelly's work in this chapter. Durcan shares Kennelly's iconoclasm about all Irish institutions, as shown in his newspaper style titles 'Making Love outside Aras an Uachtaráin' (the President's Mansion) or 'Archbishop of Kerry to Have Abortion'. Durcan has not shown the epic-historical ambition of *Cromwell*, though; when history appears in his lyrics it serves to confirm personal insecurities or to add to that note of skewed bizarreness with which he views the mundane incidents of contemporary Irish life. He sustains a wry sense of his contemporary distance from the country's defining historical moments. So, in 'Bewley's Oriental Café, Westmoreland Street', we are told that 'for me the equivalent of the Easter Rising/Is to be accosted by a woman whom I do not know/And asked by her to keep an eye on her things' (*A Snail In My Prime* (London: HarperCollins, 1993), p. 93).

7. *The Living Stream*, p. 198. Again this begs as many questions as it answers. While it is true that, as Longley notes, in *Wintering Out* part of the readjustment Heaney seeks to make between Irish and English historical and literary inheritances involves an uncertain, querulous vision of 'Edmund Spenser,/dreaming sunlight,/encroached upon by /geniuses who creep/"out of every corner/of the woodes and glennes"' ('Bog Oak' (London: Faber, 1972), p. 15), elsewhere in the collection he also relishes the fact that 'some cherished archaisms/are correct Shakespearean' ('Traditions', p. 31). Further, of course, Heaney has written several sonnet sequences which celebrate (although again with a sense of the excess involved) the blending of the aureate sonorities of the mainland English tradition with a local, native music – not least in the first line of the third of the 'Glanmore Sonnets', 'This evening the cuckoo and corncrake/(So much, too much) consorted at twilight' (*Field Work* (London: Faber, 1979), p. 35).

8. Newcastle upon Tyne: Bloodaxe Books, 1987 edition, p. 81.

9. Not totally, according to 'Poetic Forms and Social Malformations': 'Kennelly's epics do not quite transcend malformation...having recited the trauma, laid out the dossier, he stops short of jurisdiction, of diagnostic or formal closure.' Durcan is more successful at such transcendence, since he is 'interested in personal and sexual relations for their own sake' (ibid., p. 224).

10. *Ireland's Literature: Selected Essays* (Mullingar: Lilliput Press, 1988), p. 255. It is fair to say that not all Irish critics have taken this line, though. As opposed to the 'salutariness' which both Longley and Brown find in *Cromwell*, Jonathan Sawday sees a 'compulsive' exploration of both the British and the Irish national psyches which, rather than aiming at transcendence, leaves things very much as they were: 'If the poem leaves us with a sense of bewilderment, then that...is a common historical legacy, as shared as the legacy which Oliver has

left us' ('Lord Protect Us', *Poetry Ireland Review*, No. 10, Summer 1984, p. 60).

11. *A Time For Voices: Selected Poems 1960–1990* (Newcastle upon Tyne: Bloodaxe Books, 1990), p. 11.

12. Ibid., p. 6.

13. *Breathing Spaces: Early Poems* (Newcastle upon Tyne: Bloodaxe Books, 1992), p. 128.

14. *Cromwell*, p. 49.

15. *The Living Stream*, p 199.

16. *Cromwell*, p. 81.

17. 'Brendan Speaks to Oliver's Countrymen', a review of the first British 1987 Bloodaxe edition of the book, *Krino* No. 5, Spring 1988, p. 166.

18. Kennelly has followed up this interest in exploring drama in his versions of *Medea* (Bloodaxe Books, 1992) and *The Trojan Women* (Bloodaxe Books, 1993). *Cromwell* did itself appear in a staged version which was first performed at the Damer Hall, Dublin in 1986.

19. Newcastle upon Tyne: Bloodaxe Books, 1991, p. 77. *Cromwell* has a similar poem, 'Lettering', which, in response to some graffiti saying 'BOOM WENT MOUNTBATTEN' refuses to give in to 'Public explosions of private indignation' (p. 107).

20. Ibid., pp. 119, 120, 144.

21. *Journey into Joy*, p. 9.

22. 'Speech', *Cromwell*, p. 140.

23. Ibid., p. 51.

24. *Journey into Joy*, p. 10.

25. *God's Englishman: Oliver Cromwell and the English Revolution* (London: Weidenfeld & Nicolson, 1970), p. 122.

26. *Breathing Spaces*, p. 11.

27. *Journey Into Joy*, p. 237. In Yeats's own recollection of how he came upon the notion of the mask as a liberating idea he keeps the personal, the historical and the imaginary in balance in ways which impel the 'breathing space' which Kennelly also finds in it: 'My mind began drifting vaguely towards that doctrine of "the mask" which has convinced me that every passionate man...is, as it were, linked with another age, historical or imaginary, where alone he finds images that rouse his energy. Napoleon was never of his own time, as the naturalistic writers and painters bid all men be, but had some Roman emperor's image in his head...' in *Autobiographies* (London: Macmillan, 1955 (1979 edition)), p. 152.

28. *Cromwell*, p. 160.

29. Ibid., p. 57.

30. Ibid., p. 45.

31. Translated by Helene Iswolsky (Bloomington: Indiana University Press, 1984), p. 39.

32. *Cromwell*, p. 29.

33. Ibid., p. 129; *Irish Times*, 19 December 1991.

34. *Rabelais and his World*, pp. 5, 7, 10, 11.

35. 'Poetry and Violence', *Journey Into Joy*, pp. 36, 42, 43.

36. Ibid., p. 33; 'A View of Irish Poetry', ibid., p. 70.

37. 'Theses on the Philosophy of History', *Illuminations*, edited and with
     an Introduction by Hannah Arendt (London: Fontana, 1973), p. 258;
     'Poetry and Violence', p. 32.
38. *Cromwell*, pp. 70, 87–8.
39. 'The Disappearance and Recovery of Oliver', ibid., p. 148; 'It is charac-
     teristic for the familiar speech of the marketplace [a form of carniva-
     lesque folk humour] to use abusive language, insulting words or
     expressions...', *Rabelais and his World*, p. 16.
40. *Cromwell*, p. 63.
41. Ibid., p. 135.
42. Ibid., pp. 45, 47, 87, 89, 92, 119, 127, 137.
43. The 'many voices' in the book suggest not only that the boundaries
     between poetry and drama are being broken through, but also the
     boundaries between poetry and the novel. Bakhtin saw the develop-
     ment of novelistic discourse as being away from the traditionally mo-
     notonic discourse of poetry, the personal voice of lyric in which
     'consciousness is fully immanent, expressing itself...directly and
     without mediation', to the polyglot language which characterizes nov-
     elistic discourse:

> In essence this discourse is always developed on the boundary
> line between cultures and languages....From our point of
> view...two...factors prove to be of decisive importance: one of
> these is *laughter*, the other *polyglossia*....Parodic-travestying litera-
> ture introduces the permanent corrective of laughter, of a critique
> on the one-sided seriousness of the lofty direct word, the correc-
> tive of reality that is always richer, more fundamental and most
> importantly *too contradictory and heteroglot* to be fit into a high and
> straightforward genre. (*The Dialogic Imagination: Four Essays*,
> edited by Michael Holquist; translated by Caryl Emerson and
> Michael Holquist (Austin, Tex.: University of Texas Press, 1981),
> pp. 50, 55).

44. Ibid., p. 62.
45. *Cromwell*, p. 64.
46. In an earlier poem, 'A Tale for Tourists', Kennelly had dramatized the
     pitfalls in the confrontation between a local culture and a modern in-
     ternational travelling one: 'Mr. Patrick Healy, a grumpy old
     man/Who lived alone,/In a small thatched house/Such as nowadays
     a tourist might call/An authentic expression/Of a dying culture/Was
     considered a most insulting son-of-a-bitch/By his various neighbours'
     (*Breathing Spaces*, p. 33). By telling the story of the neighbours'
     revenge on Healy, Kennelly might seem to be aligning his poetry with
     the oral culture against the tourists' ignorance. But the title of the
     poem shows his awareness that even this kind of alignment is liable to
     be seen as producing work that is merely quaint to outsiders' eyes.
47. *Cromwell*, p. 45.
48. *The Dialogic Imagination*, pp. 50, 58.
49. *Cromwell*, pp. 48–9.

50. *The Empire Writes Back: Theory and Practice in Post-Colonial Literatures* (London: Routledge, 1989), pp. 41, 44.
51. Ibid., p. 51.
52. Ibid., p. 44.
53. 'Discourse in the Novel', *The Dialogic Imagination*, p. 276.
54. *Cromwell*, p. 69.
55. London: Fontana, 1985, p. 237–8.
56. *A Time For Voices*, p. 123.
57. Ibid., p. 119.
58. *Cromwell*, p. 123.
59. *Ireland: A Social and Cultural History*, pp. 326–8. Elsewhere, Kennelly has attacked the entrepreneurial classes who continued to flourish throughout the 1980s despite the economic crisis. As Katie Donovan quotes him as saying at the time of *The Book of Judas*, '"The book has a go at middle-aged men…the smiling man in the suit, nodding here and there like an amateur pope, practising his inner doctrines of infallibility." Kennelly believes that this breed of man – occasionally personified as 'the Pinstripe Pig', who notes "There's money in love" – has taken over Irish society.' Judas is the legendary figure who betrayed 'truth' for money, and in Book Seven of his poem on him, Kennelly has a fine time attacking such capitalists, past and present.
60. Hill argues that the priesthood and the papacy itself had undoubtedly taken the political lead in the revolt which brought about Cromwell's invasion (*God's Englishman*, p. 121).
61. *Cromwell*, pp. 131, 130.
62. *Ireland: A Social and Cultural History*, p. 302.
63. *Cromwell*, p. 128.
64. Ibid., p. 144.
65. Ibid., p. 53.
66. *The Wake of Imagination* (London: Hutchinson, 1988), p. 371.
67. *Ireland: A Social and Cultural History*, pp. 256–60.
68. *The Wake of Imagination*, p. 394.

CHAPTER 6   'RECONCILIATION UNDER DURESS': THE ARCHITECTURE OF SEAMUS HEANEY'S RECENT POETRY

1. *North* (London: Faber, 1975), p. 31.
2. *The Haw Lantern* (London: Faber, 1987), p. 50.
3. Reprinted in *Stand*, Autumn 1991, p. 62.
4. *Colonial Consequences: Essays in Irish Literature and Culture* (Dublin: Lilliput Press, 1991), pp. 276, 175, 199.
5. David Lloyd has found Heaney's writing operating somewhere between the polarities of Fennell's and Foster's positions. He finds the constant return to origins and to childhood places in the poetry typical of the aestheticization of racial archetypes in Irish Romantic nationalism. But he also finds Heaney's constant 'linguistic and metaphorical usages which promise a healing of division' in those

returns premature, a blindness to circumstance. This closure of the lyrics to actuality is, though, for Lloyd what makes them so appealing internationally; their integrationism and resolution makes them ideal in a pedagogical environment which is still founded upon practical criticism (*Anomalous States: Irish Writing and the Post-Colonial Moment* (Dublin: Lilliput Press, 1993), pp. 20, 35). Lloyd's own 'postcolonial' approach seems premature, though, given Heaney's frequent recognition, as exemplified by *North*'s final poem 'Exposure', for example, that he is regretfully at a remove from the (essentially colonial) struggle on his home ground. By the time Lloyd published his book, Heaney's poetry had also shown a good deal of scepticism about the quest for origins, as I will show below. Yet the premature attempt to see all of Ireland as a post-colonial state is very much a part of the later thinking of the Field Day Theatre Company, of which Heaney was a director – in 1988 three pamphlets appeared on the subject of nationalism, colonialism and literature by Edward Said, Terry Eagleton and Frederic Jameson; those pamphlets make no distinction between the situation in the North and that in the South of the island.

6. Douglas Sealey, review of *New Selected Poems*, *Poetry Ireland Review*, No. 29, Summer 1980, pp. 98–100; Gerald Dawe, review of *The Government of the Tongue* from *Honest Ulsterman*, Spring/Summer 1989, reprinted in *How's the Poetry Going?: Literary Politics and Ireland Today* (Belfast: Lagan Press, 1991), p. 58.

7. 'The New Seamus Heaney', review of *Field Work*, *The Honest Ulsterman*, No. 65, February/June 1980, p. 59.

8. 10 October 1990.

9. London: Faber, 1984, p. 20.

10. *Irish University Review*, Vol. 5, No. 2, Autumn 1975, p. 330.

11. *The Government of the Tongue* (London: Faber, 1988), p. xv.

12. Ibid., p. xix.

13. *The Redress of Poetry: Oxford Lectures* (London: Faber, 1995), pp. 114–5.

14. *North*, p. 36.

15. *The Redress of Poetry*, pp. 3–4.

16. *The Haw Lantern*, p. 5.

17. Ibid., p. 13.

18. *The Redress of Poetry* (Oxford: Clarendon Press, 1990), p. 11. In the later collection of the lectures 'It has to be able to withstand and envisage…' has been simplified to 'It should not simplify' (p. 8).

19. 'Parable Island' from *The Haw Lantern* offers a fast and loose description of this position: 'the fork-tongued natives keep repeating/prophecies they pretend not to believe/about a point where all the names converge/underneath the mountain and where (some day)/they are going to start to mine the ore of truth' (p. 10).

20. Ibid., pp. 46–7.

21. This pair of opposed authorities within the debate is a more politically engaged version of Heaney's earlier, more neutrally poetic, craft-based establishment of an opposition between the possibilities offered by Wordsworth and those offered by Yeats. See, for example, 'The Makings

of a Music: Reflections on Wordsworth and Yeats' in *Preoccupations: Selected Prose 1968–1978* (London: Faber, 1980), pp. 61–78.

22. *The Government of the Tongue*, pp. 78, 81.

23. Ibid., p. xx.

24. The use of Eastern European writers like Mandelstam to stand as models for the type of role a modern Irish poet might play in relation to his or her society forms a central idea in *The Government of the Tongue* and earned Heaney several critical reviews of the book in Ireland. W.J. McCormack rightly objected that 'In poetry "conditions" can hardly be classified in any neat way, and certainly not in some binary system....Regarded...as other or different conditions, they gradually appear to be less uniform, less susceptible to generalisation. And the risk Heaney takes in fixing on Milosz or Holub is that the individual writer becomes the basis for generalisation' ('Holy Sinner', *Krino*, No. 6, Autumn 1988, p. 67). Thomas Docherty even accused Heaney of an 'imperialism of thought' in uprooting poems from their cultural, historical and political provenance and claiming their relevance to his own situation ('The Sign of the Cross', *Irish Review*, No. 5, Autumn 1988, p. 114).

25. *The Place of Writing* (Atlanta, Ga.: Scholars Press, 1990), p. 25.

26. Ibid., pp. 27–8.

27. Ibid., pp. 34–5.

28. It is also a recognition which allows Heaney elsewhere to call for greater sympathy for Yeats in the one place where he openly discusses Yeats's fascist sympathies. Heaney enters the case for the opposition, 'Naturally, some political aspects of his work have been particularly assailed', only to immediately integrate the political with other aspects of Yeats's achievement: 'There is surely political meaning, at once realistic and visionary, in his sense of life as an abounding conflict of energies; in his recognition of the necessity as well as the impossibility of the attempt "to hold in a single thought reality and justice", and in his conviction – overriding his sense of hierarchy and election – that even among the Paudeens of this earth, "There cannot be...a single soul that lacks a sweet crystalline cry"' (from Heaney's introduction to his selection from Yeats in the *Field Day Anthology of Irish Writing* (Lawrence Hill: Field Day,1991 Vol. 3, pp. 789–90).

29. *Field Work* (London: Faber, 1979), pp. 21–4.

30. 'Vocal Visitations', review of Heaney's *New Selected Poems*, *The Irish Review*, No. 9, Autumn 1990, p. 103.

31. *The Government of the Tongue*, p. 40. '"Let go, let fly, forget./You've listened long enough. Now strike your note"', Heaney has the ghost of James Joyce tell him at the end of the title sequence of *Station Island* (p. 93). This collection is crucial in the struggle with influence which Heaney can be seen publicly conducting in the earlier collections; his Dantean encounters with the literary and personal figures who have affected his thinking in this central sequence mark his last reckoning with both his own past and with his past ways of writing about the Irish experience.

32. Throughout the late 1970s and early 1980s Heaney was engaged, along with Seamus Deane, in an attempt to reveal the mythologizing and self-mythologizing in Yeats's project as politically and aesthetically dangerous. In 'John Bull's Other Island' (*The Listener*, 29 September, 1977) and 'A tale of two islands: reflections on the Irish Literary Revival' (*Irish Studies 1*, edited by P.J. Drudy, Cambridge University Press, 1980), Heaney argued that 'Yeats created a magnificent and persuasive Ireland of the mind, but a partial one.' In both essays, Heaney favours instead the work of Joyce, which sticks closer to the 'facts of his own bourgeois Catholic experience'. See also Deane's *Celtic Revivals* (London: Faber, 1985) and his 'Heroic styles: the tradition of an idea' in *Ireland's Field Day* (London: Hutchinson, 1985).

33. *Station Island*, p. 110.

34. *Seeing Things* (London: Faber, 1991), p. 78. A slightly different version appeared in the *TLS*, No. 4478, January 27–February 2 1989, p. 76.

35. *Aesthetics and Politics* (London: Verso, 1980), pp. 159–60.

36. Ibid., p. 166.

37. Ibid., pp. 193, 194.

38. London: Faber, 1990, p. 77.

39. The image echoes Brutus's before the Battle of Philippi: 'We, at the height, are ready to decline./There is a tide in the affairs of men/Which, taken at the flood, leads on to fortune;/Omitted, all the voyage of their life/Is bound in shallows and in miseries' (Act 4, Scene 3, ll. 215–91).

40. *The English Auden*, edited by Edward Mendelson (London: Faber, 1977), p. 242.

41. What Heaney describes as 'the stylistic densities and the dislocated geopolitical phantasmagorias of early Auden' ('The Impact of Translation', *The Government of the Tongue*, p. 41) authorize his own experiments in a kind of translatorese version of East European allegory in poems like 'From the Frontier of Writing', 'Parable Island', 'From the Republic of Conscience', 'From the Land of the Unspoken' and 'From the Canton of Expectation' in *The Haw Lantern*. In the essay, Heaney claims that early Auden, with the lack of insularity in the poetry which brought it near to an understanding of the suffering which was taking place in Europe, came closest to establishing a 'native British modernism', which was lost with the victory of the 'Empson/Davie line' after the Second World War.

42. W.H. Auden, *Collected Poems*, edited by Edward Mendelson (London: Faber, 1991), p. 158. Heaney discusses these lines in *The Government of the Tongue*, p. 110.

43. 'The Golden Bough', *Seeing Things*, p. 3. A similar moment in which the giftedness of the poet is seemingly dared is in 'The Sounds of Rain', where he is told '*You are steeped in luck*' (p. 49). Yet 'The Crossing', the version of Dante at the end of the book counterpart to that from Virgil at the beginning, finds the poet still waiting to cross over to the underworld and wittily gives the book over to its readers' evaluation. The 'guide' (Virgil in the original) tells the poet '"No good

spirits ever pass this way/And therefore, if Charon objects to you,/You should understand well what his words imply"' (p. 113).

44. *The Complete Poems and Plays of T.S. Eliot* (London: Faber, 1969), p. 75.
45. Heaney now owns the cottage in which he wrote much of *North* and *Field Work*, and uses it as a study, as he told Blake Morrison (*The Independent on Sunday*, 19 May 1991, p. 27).
46. 'Glanmore Revisited' 7, 'The Skylight', *Seeing Things*, p. 37.
47. Ibid., p. 23.
48. *Selected Poems* (Harmondsworth/Loughcrew: Penguin/Gallery Press, 1993), p. 191.
49. *The Place of Writing*, p. 49.
50. *Seeing Things*, p. 27.
51. *Selected Poems*, edited by Michael Longley (London: Faber, 1988), p. 137.
52. *The Redress of Poetry*, pp. 198–9.
53. *Seeing Things*, p. 91.
54. Ibid., p. 55, 56.
55. Ibid., p. 64.
56. Ibid., p. 101.
57. *The Place of Writing*, p. 47.
58. 'Literary History and Literary Modernity', *Blindness and Insight: Essays in the Rhetoric of Contemporary Criticism* (London: Routledge, 1983), pp. 146, 161.
59. *Seeing Things*, p. 97.
60. 'Squarings', xxvii, ibid., p. 85.
61. *The Redress of Poetry*, p. 4.

CHAPTER 7   LETTERS FROM THE ALPHABET: CARSON'S AND MULDOON'S CONTINGENT POETICS

1. *Belfast Confetti* (Newcastle upon Tyne: Bloodaxe Books, 1990), p. 67.
2. *The Annals of Chile* (London: Faber, 1994), p. 39.
3. 'Like No One Else', *The Irish Review*, No. 8, Spring 1990, pp. 121, 124. In a review of Carson's *First Language* in *The Honest Ulsterman*, Patricia Horton has written of the central image of the book, the Tower of Babel, that 'For Carson the enterprise of Babel is an apt symbol for those grand narratives which obscure difference and lead to generalisation and exclusion. With its aspiration to unity and stability, Babel is analogous to the imperialist desire to dominate and colonise' (No. 99, Spring 95, p. 85).
4. 'Elephantiasis and Essentialism', *The Irish Review*, No. 10, Spring 1991, pp. 133–4. Goodby has been quick to find similar qualities working in later Heaney; as he has said in reviewing *Seeing Things*, the book 'continues the trend away from Heaney's agonizing over his relationship towards his "community".... [This] is the new playful, "postmodern" Heaney encountering old childhood material...as paradigms of the artistic act's liberation of the spirit without the ponderous earlier

parallels of poetry-as-craft' (*Studies*, Vol. 81, No. 324, Winter 1992, p. 449). Clair Wills's *Improprieties: Politics and Sexuality in Northern Irish Poetry* (OUP, 1993) offers the most comprehensive exposition to date of the post-Heaney generation of writers in terms of postmodern ideas. She does not, however, neglect the context of their writing, and argues that to discuss the work of her three central authors, Muldoon, Paulin and McGuckian, it is necessary to develop 'a more nuanced definition of postmodernism as it applies to poetry in particular cultural contexts' (p. 4). Yet in pursuing these dual attentions towards, on the one hand, an international theoretical approach and, on the other, traditions on the poets' home ground, Wills often succeeds in selling the latter short. The dogged postmodernism of her reading even leads her to chide each of her poets for failing to live up to her theoretical ideals, as when she says of Paulin that 'his blindness to the progressive aspects of the destruction of the public space of politics...by a "social" life more broadly conceived, is one sign of [his] failure' (p. 157). Equally troublingly, her insistent Barthesian attention to nomenclature and the Word leads to a deafness about poetry itself, its rhythms and cadences. Her reading of Muldoon's poem 'Chinook', for instance, makes much of what she sees as the solidity conveyed by the poems final *word*, 'Pompeii', but has nothing to say about the bizarreness of the *cadence* in which that word appears – 'relinquishing the table to Pompeii' (p. 207). That emphasis on the single word means that she does not register this or other poems' speaking moments of recognition or tonal contortion.

5. For example Muldoon's comment on his character Gallogly in 'The More a Man Has The More a Man Wants' when he tries to pronounce the local dialect word for the sunken border of a field: '*Sheugh*, he says. *Sheugh.*/He is finding that first "sh"/increasingly difficult to manage' (*Quoof* (London: Faber, 1983), p. 49). This parodically picks up on Heaney's definition of the difference between the Irish and English through pronunciation of the place-name 'Broagh' – 'that last/*gh* the strangers found/difficult to manage' (*Wintering Out* (London: Faber, 1972), p. 27). Carson has questioned the Keatsian fullness of early Heaney by playing upon the title of his second collection in his 'The Irish for No': 'They opened the door into the dark:/*The murmurous haunt of flies on summer eaves.* Empty jam-jars./Mish-mash. Hotch potch' (*The Irish for No* (Newcastle upon Tyne: Bloodaxe Books, 1988), p. 50). There is an excellant discussion of Carson and Heaney, as well as of Carson's sceptical postmodern narratives which are nonetheless 'peculiarly appropriate to a poetry of the contemporary fate of Northern Ireland', in Neil Corcoran's essay 'One Step Forward, Two Steps Back' (*The Chosen Ground: Essays on the Contemporary Poetry of Northern Ireland* (Bridgend: Seren Books, 1992), pp. 213–36).

6. *Why Brownlee Left* (London: Faber, 1980), p. 27. MacNeice's internationalism and his feel for the pull of both traditions in Ireland make him a model for the kind of 'neutral' poetry which Muldoon writes, as it does for that of later Heaney. MacNeice's refusal to think of poetry in terms of 'race-consciousness' in the 'Prologue' derived from a radio

broadcast which Muldoon put in his edition of *The Faber Book of Contemporary Irish Poetry* frees him into treating of any subject, whatever its racial or political resonances: 'I think that the poet is a sensitive instrument designed to record anything which interests his mind or affects his emotion.' (London, 1986, p. 18). But Muldoon, like Heaney, is aware that this does not free the poetry into a self-obsessed, free-playing irresponsibility. In the sequence '7, Middagh Street', Muldoon dramatizes Auden in his 'poetry makes nothing happen' mode, something which I discussed with relation to Heaney in my last chapter. But the last word in the argument goes to 'Louis': 'For poetry *can* make things happen –/not only can, but *must...*'. (*Meeting the British* (London: Faber, 1987, p. 59).

7. *Sunday Times*, 16 December 1986.
8. That contingency and lack of 'all-knowingness' extends for Muldoon to the process of writing itself. He has said in interview that 'I never know when I begin to write a poem what is going to happen, what I quote, unquote, 'have to say', or what it has to say. For myself it's a constant attempt to discover something' ('Lunch with Paul Muldoon...', a conversation with Kevin Smith (*Rhinoceros*, No. 4, 1990), p. 80).
9. 'Modernity's Consciousness of Time', *The Philosophical Discourse of Modernity*, translated by Frederick Lawrence (Cambridge: Polity Press, 1987), p. 13.
10. Ciaran Carson interviewed by Rand Brandes, *The Irish Review*, No. 8, Spring 1990, pp. 89, 79. Muldoon has affirmed in his interview with Alan Jenkins that 'I'm very interested in speech, in the rhythm of speech, and try to keep close to that, so it's important to me that a poem should sound right when it's read – I'd like it to sound as if it had slipped out of nowhere, as if someone had told it to me five minutes ago.'
11. '...the poet seems to have acquired the status of myth, of institution. One can hardly resist the suspicion that *North* itself, as a work of art, has succumbed to this notion; Heaney seems to have moved – unwillingly, perhaps – from being a writer with the gift of precision, to become the laureate of violence – a mythmaker, an anthropologist of ritual killing, an apologist for "the situation", in the last resort, a mystifier' (*The Honest Ulsterman*, No. 50, Winter 1975, p. 183).
12. *Meeting the British*, p. 35.
13. Another poet of the same generation as Muldoon and Carson, Tom Paulin, has shown a similar concern for the vernacular of Ulster, but from within the Protestant tradition. That concern is most fully expressed in his 'A New Look at the Language Question', the first pamphlet produced by Field Day. In his later poetry, Paulin too has made contingency a key concern. In 'History of the Tin Hut', for example, he celebrates the inventor of the Nissen huts which pock the English landscape, huts which 'have a throwaway permanence/a never new-painted sense of duration/that exists anywhere/and belongs nowhere' (*Walking a Line*, London: Faber, 1994, p. 4). Paulin's earlier, aggressive deployment of Ulster dialect words, particularly in his

1987 *Fivemiletown*, however, came close to an essentialism which was politically powerful but poetically strained and awkward, a poetry whose designs were all too palpable.

14. *The Honest Ulsterman*, p. 186.
15. Loughcrew: The Gallery Press, 1993, pp. 18, 20. The sense of binary possibilities which have to be negotiated here, and which haunts other poems in this collection like 'that switch between the *off* and *on*' in 'On Not Remembering Some Lines of a Song' (p. 27), the 'base-of-two conundrum' of the robot bomb-disposal expert in '*Apparat*' (p. 29) or even 'Chancellor of the Exchequer/What-Do-You-Call-Him Clarke/...counting his stars in twos' in '*Opus 14*' (p. 31) – among many others – are reminiscent of Heaney's sense that 'I grew up in between. ...Baronies, parishes met where I was born' in 'Terminus' (*The Haw Lantern* (London: Faber, 1987), p. 5).
16. *Essays on Heidegger and Others* (Cambridge: Cambridge University Press, 1991), p. 4.
17. *Contingency, irony and solidarity* (Cambridge: Cambridge University Press, 1989), p. 125.
18. Ibid., pp. 41–2.
19. Ibid., pp. 38, 17 inter alia.
20. Ibid., p. 18.
21. Ibid., p. 6.
22. 'Q & A: Paul Muldoon', *Irish Literary Supplement*, Fall 1987, p. 36.
23. Jonathan Bardon, *A History of Ulster* (Belfast: Blackstaff Press, 1992), pp. 818–20.
24. Interview with Rand Brandes, p. 77. Muldoon too has a background in Gaelic poetry and has been involved in translating the work of Nuala Ní Dhomhaill. Muldoon's translations appear in the selection *Pharoh's Daughter* (Loughcrew: Gallery Press, 1990) alongside versions by Carson and Heaney among others; and he has worked with Ni Dhomhaill to produce a separate collection, *The Astrakhan Cloak* (Loughcrew: Gallery Press, 1992).
25. *Contingency, irony and solidarity*, p. 39.
26. *The Irish for No*, p. 31.
27. *Belfast Confetti*, p. 77.
28. 'Queen's Gambit', ibid., p. 35.
29. 'It's not so much *about* Belfast as *of* Belfast', interview with Arminta Wallace, *Irish Times*, 13 October 1990.
30. *Regional Accents of English: Belfast* (Belfast: Blackstaff Press, 1981), p. 54. In this again, Carson's use of the vernacular follows the example of Heaney: in various of his early essays and interviews, Heaney has made much of the fact that 'the Ulster accent...strikes the tangent of the consonant rather more than it rolls the circle of the vowel', and that 'a poetic voice is probably very intimately connected with the poet's natural voice, the voice that he hears as the ideal speaker of the lines he is making up' ('Feeling into Words', *Preoccupations: Selected Prose 1968–1978* (London: Faber, 1980), pp. 45, 43). Many of Heaney's own lines from early on make much of this interplay of inflection which for Milroy characterizes the Ulster accent – e.g. 'Old

dough-faced women with black shawls/Drawn down tight kneel in the stalls' (*Death of a Naturalist* (London: Faber, 1966), p. 42.

31. *Essays on Heidegger*, p. 97.
32. Interview with Arminta Wallace.
33. This has its own dangers in making poetry incomprehensible beyond its own immediate circumstance, when taken along with the poems' constant reference to Belfast streets and buildings etc. Such concerns form the core of Fred Johnston's dismissive sentences in his review of *Belfast Confetti*: 'It is a book to be read most comfortably by natives of Belfast; most poems are sprinkled with references and locations few outside the city would recognise or attach importance to. In this sense, it is a parochial book, possessed of a parochial angst' ('A poet in the city', *Irish Times*, 20 January 1990).
34. *First Language*, p. 72.
35. *The Haw Lantern*, p. 3.
36. *First Language*, p. 13.
37. Nuala Ní Dhomhaill has testified to this resource in a review of *The Irish for No*, in which she first approves Walter Ong's argument that Ireland is an 'oral' rather than a 'literate' culture, then enthuses 'It is all here; the long, seemingly haphazard, spoken line; the additive rather than subordinate clauses, the repetition of the just said, the transitions due to memory and association rather than due to any formal or linear logic, the vast reportoire of a good seanchaí [story-teller], captured once and for all, permanently, on the printed page' ('The English for Irish', *The Irish Review* No. 4, Spring 1988, pp. 116–17).
38. Loughcrew: Gallery Press, 1995, unnumbered pages.
39. *Madoc: A Mystery* (London: Faber, 1990), p. 46.
40. Loughcrew: Gallery Press, 1994, p. 36.
41. Ibid., p. 35. Muldoon's resistance to adopting a direct political stance has been many times stated by him. In the interview 'Lunch with Paul Muldoon...', the poet registers his disagreement with a similar consolatory notion held to by Seamus Heaney: 'I've never understood some of these notions about art – "the end of art is peace" [etc.]...none of these ideas mean anything to me' (p. 90). In similar vein, in another interview, Muldoon says to his interlocuter 'It doesn't matter where I stand politically, with a small "p" in terms of Irish politics. My opinion about what should happen in Northern Ireland is no more valuable than yours' ('A Conversation with Paul Muldoon', Michael Donaghy, *Chicago Review*, Vol. 35, No. 1, Autumn 1985, p. 85).
42. 'Way down upon the Susquehanna', *Irish Times*, 3 November 1990.
43. *The Haw Lantern*, p. 44. 'Why should "Field Day" continue to peddle/its "old whines in new bottles?"' Muldoon asks in *The Prince of the Quotidian* (p. 22), quoting a phrase of Edna Longley's.
44. 'Lunch with Paul Muldoon...', p. 80.
45. *Contingency, irony and solidarity*, p. 73.
46. Loughcrew: Gallery Press, 1995, p. 32. There is something similar happening in an earlier poem of Muldoon's, 'The Sightseers', where, recalling a trip his family made to drive round the first roundabout built

in mid-Ulster, Muldoon also recalls that on that occasion his Uncle Pat told a story of being stopped by the brutal B-Specials: 'They held a pistol so hard against his forehead/there was still the mark of an O when he got home' (*Quoof*, p. 15). Once again, the letters of the alphabet force the modern jarringly against sectarian maltreatment.

47. *Madoc*, p. 92.
48. Ibid., pp. 122, 197, 206.
49. Ibid., p. 195.
50. *Contingency, irony and solidarity*, pp. 120–1.
51. *Mules* (London: Faber, 1977), p. 12.
52. *The Annals of Chile*, pp. 20, 21.
53. *Viewpoints: Poets in Conversation with John Haffenden* (London: Faber, 1981), pp. 133–4.
54. Ibid., p. 56. See *The Government of the Tongue* (London: Faber, 1988), p. 164 for Heaney's discussion of the poem. Heaney's reverence for objects is strongly felt. In his talk 'The Sense of the Past', he describes the old nails left on the top of a dresser in his first childhood house '…these objects were living a kind of afterlife and…a previous time was vestigially alive in them. They were not just inert rubbish but dormant energies, meanings that could not quite be deciphered' (*Ulster Local Studies*, Vol. 9, No. 20, Summer 1985, p. 110).
55. *The Annals of Chile*, p. 145.
56. Ibid., p. 165.
57. *The Haw Lantern*, p. 28.
58. Heaney's use of the hunting term 'at bay' in this sonnet counters his resurrection of an obsolete term, also from hunting, to give concluding force to the redress which he claims poetry makes: 'To bring back (the hounds or deer) to the proper course.' That redress is consonant with the unhampered lyric utterance which, in his prose, Heaney argues that poetry possibly has to offer (*The Redress of Poetry: Oxford Lectures* (London: Faber, 1995), p. 15). Muldoon's most famously wry consideration of familial language comes in the title poem of *Quoof*: 'How often have I carried our family word/for the hot water bottle/to a strange bed…?' (p. 17). It is just such relish for private idioms which Tom Paulin sees as one of the strengths of Ulster dialect as opposed to standard English in his 'A New Look at the Language Question': '…every family has its hoard of relished words which express its members' sense of kinship. These words act as a kind of secret sign and serve to exclude the outside world. They constitute a dialect of endearment within the wider dialect' (*Ireland's Field Day* (London: Hutchinson, 1985), p. 16).

Select Bibliography

POETRY, PLAYS AND PROSE COLLECTIONS BY POETS

Eavan Boland
  The Journey and Other Poems. Manchester: Carcanet, 1987.
  Selected Poems. Manchester: Carcanet, 1989.
  Outside History. Manchester: Carcanet, 1990.
  In a Time of Violence. Manchester: Carcanet, 1994.
  Object Lessons. Manchester: Carcanet, 1995.
Ciaran Carson
  The Irish for No. Newcastle upon Tyne: Bloodaxe Books, 1988.
  The New Estate and Other Poems. Loughcrew: Gallery Press, 1988.
  Belfast Confetti. Newcastle upon Tyne: Bloodaxe Books, 1990.
  First Language. Loughcrew: Gallery Books, 1993.
  Letters from The Alphabet. Loughcrew: Gallery Books, 1995.
Paul Durcan
  A Snail in My Prime. London: Harvill, 1993.
Padraic Fallon
  Collected Poems. Edited by Brian Fallon. Loughcrew: Gallery Books, 1990.
Seamus Heaney
  Death of a Naturalist. London: Faber, 1966.
  Door Into the Dark. London: Faber, 1969.
  Wintering Out. London: Faber, 1972.
  North. London: Faber, 1975.
  Field Work. London: Faber, 1979.
  Preoccupations: Selected Prose 1968–1978. London: Faber, 1980.
  Station Island. London: Faber, 1984.
  Sweeney Astray. London: Faber, 1984.
  The Haw Lantern. London: Faber, 1987.
  The Government of the Tongue. London: Faber, 1988.
  The Place of Writing. Atlanta, Ga.: The Scholars Press, 1988.
  New Selected Poems 1966–1987. London: Faber, 1990.
  The Cure at Troy. London: Faber, 1990.
  Seeing Things. London: Faber, 1991.
  The Redress of Poetry: Oxford Lectures. London: Faber, 1995.
  The Spirit Level. London: Faber, 1996.
John Hewitt
  Ancestral Voices: The Selected Prose of John Hewitt, edited by Tom Clyde. Belfast: Blackstaff Press, 1987.
  The Collected Poems of John Hewitt, edited by Frank Ormsby. Belfast: Blackstaff Press, 1991.
Brendan Kennelly
  Cromwell. Newcastle upon Tyne: Bloodaxe Books, 1987.

A Time for Voices: Selected Poems 1960–1990. Newcastle upon Tyne: Bloodaxe Books, 1990.

The Book of Judas. Newcastle upon Tyne: Bloodaxe Books, 1991.

Breathing Spaces: Early Poems. Newcastle upon Tyne: Bloodaxe Books, 1992.

Journey into Joy: Selected Prose, edited Åke Persson. Newcastle upon Tyne: Bloodaxe Books, 1994.

Thomas Kinsella

New Poems 1973. Dublin: Dolmen Press, 1973.

Poems 1956–1973. Dublin: Dolmen Press, 1973.

Fifteen Dead. Dublin: Dolmen Press, 1979.

One and Other Poems. Dublin: Dolmen Press, 1979.

Blood and Family. Oxford: Oxford University Press, 1988.

From Centre City. Oxford: Oxford University Press, 1994.

The Dual Tradition. Manchester: Carcanet, 1995.

Michael Longley

Poems 1963–1983. Harmondsworth: Penguin, 1986.

(ed.) *Louis MacNeice: Selected Poems.* London: Faber, 1988.

Gorse Fires. London: Secker & Warburg, 1991.

Tuppenny Stung. Belfast: Lagan Press, 1994.

Ghost Orchid. London: Cape, 1995.

Medbh McGuckian

Venus and the Rain. Oxford: Oxford University Press, 1984.

On Ballycastle Beach. Oxford: Oxford University Press, 1988.

Marconi's Cottage. Newcastle upon Tyne: Bloodaxe Books, 1992.

The Flower Master and Other Poems. Loughcrew: Gallery Books, 1993.

Captain Lavender. Loughcrew: Gallery Books, 1994.

Derek Mahon

High Time. Loughcrew: Gallery Books, 1985.

(trans.) *Philippe Jaccottet: Selected Poems.* Harmondsworth: Penguin, 1987.

(ed. with Peter Fallon) *The Penguin Book of Contemporary Irish Poetry.* Harmondsworth: Penguin, 1990.

(trans.) *The Bacchae.* Loughcrew: Gallery Books, 1991.

Selected Poems. Harmondsworth: Penguin, 1993.

John Montague

The Rough Field. Dublin: Dolmen Press, 1972.

A Slow Dance. Dublin: Dolmen Press, 1975.

The Great Cloak. Dublin: Dolmen Press, 1978.

Tides. Dublin: Dolmen Press, 1978.

Selected Poems. Oxford: Oxford University Press, 1982.

The Figure in the Cave and Other Essays. Dublin: Lilliput Press, 1989.

Mount Eagle. Newcastle upon Tyne: Bloodaxe Books, 1989.

Paul Muldoon

Mules. London: Faber, 1977.

Why Brownlee Left. London: Faber, 1980.

Quoof. London: Faber, 1983.

(ed.) *The Faber Book of Contemporary Irish Poetry.* London: Faber, 1986.

Meeting the British. London: Faber, 1987.

Madoc: A Mystery. London: Faber, 1990.

Shining Brow. London: Faber, 1993.
The Annals of Chile. London: Faber, 1994.
The Prince of the Quotidian. Loughcrew: Gallery Books, 1994.
Six Honest Serving Men. Loughcrew: Gallery Books, 1995.
Richard Murphy
  New Selected Poems. London: Faber, 1989.
Eiléan Ní Chuilleanáin
  The Magdalene Sermon. Loughcrew: Gallery Books, 1989.
  The Brazen Serpent. Loughcrew: Gallery Books, 1994.
Nuala Ní Dhomhnaill
  Pharaoh's Daughter. Loughcrew: Gallery Books, 1990.
  The Astrakhan Cloak. Loughcrew: Gallery Books, 1992.
Tom Paulin
  A State of Justice. London: Faber, 1977.
  The Strange Museum. London: Faber, 1980.
  Liberty Tree. London: Faber, 1983.
  Ireland & the English Crisis. Newcastle upon Tyne: Bloodaxe Books, 1984.
  The Riot Act. London: Faber, 1985.
  Fivemiletown. London: Faber, 1987.
  Seize the Fire. London: Faber, 1990.
  Minotaur: Poetry and the Nation State. London: Faber, 1992.
  Walking a Line. London: Faber, 1994.
W.B. Yeats
  Collected Poems. London: Macmillan, 1979.

CRITICAL, PHILOSOPHICAL AND HISTORICAL BACKGROUND

Theodor Adorno
  Negative Dialectics, translated by E.B. Ashton. London: Routledge, 1973.
  The Jargon of Authenticity, translated by Knut Tarowski and Frederic Will. London: Routledge, 1973.
  Dialectic of Enlightenment, translated by John Cumming. London: Verso, 1979.
  Aesthetic Theory, translated by C. Lenhardt. London: RKP, 1986.
Elmer Andrews
  The Poetry of Seamus Heaney: All the Realms of Whisper. London: Macmillan, 1988.
  Contemporary Irish Poetry: A Collection of Critical Essays. London: Macmillan, 1992.
  Seamus Heaney: A Collection of Critical Essays. London: Macmillan, 1992.
M.M. Bakhtin
  The Dialogic Imagination, translated by Caryl Emerson and Michael Holquist. Austin, Tex.: University of Texas Press, 1981.
  Rabelais and His World, translated by Helene Iswolsky. Bloomington: Indiana University Press, 1984.

242 *Select Bibliography*

Jonathan Bardon
A History of Ulster. Belfast: Blackstaff Press, 1992.
Walter Benjamin
Illuminations, edited by Hannah Arendt; translated by Harry Zohn.
London: Fontana, 1973.
Charles Baudelaire: A Lyric Poet in the Era of High Capitalism. London:
Verso, 1976.
One-Way Street, and Other Writings. London: NLB, 1979.
Ernst Bloch et al.
Aesthetics and Politics. London: Verso, 1980.
Elleke Boehmer
Colonial and Postcolonial Literature. Oxford: Oxford University Press,
1995.
Ciaran Brady
(ed.) *Interpreting Irish History*. Dublin: Irish Academic Press, 1994.
Terence Brown
Ireland: A Social and Cultural History 1922–1979. London: Fontana,
1981.
Ireland's Literature: Selected Essays. Mullingar: Lilliput Press, 1988.
David Cairns and Shaun Richards
Writing Ireland: Colonialism, Nationalism and Culture. Manchester:
Manchester University Press, 1988.
Neil Corcoran
Seamus Heaney. London: Faber, 1986.
(ed.) *The Chosen Ground: Essays on the Contemporary Poetry of Northern
Ireland*. Bridgend: Seren Books, 1992.
English Poetry since 1940. London: Longman, 1993.
Tony Curtis
(ed.) *The Art of Seamus Heaney*. Bridgend: Poetry Wales Press, 1985.
Gerald Dawe
How's the Poetry Going? Literary Politics and Ireland Today. Belfast: Lagan
Press, 1991.
Gerald Dawe and Edna Longley
(eds) *Across the Roaring Hill: The Protestant Imagination in Modern Ireland*.
Belfast: Blackstaff Press, 1985.
Seamus Deane
Celtic Revivals. London: Faber, 1985.
A Short History of Irish Literature. London: Hutchinson, 1986.
(ed.) *The Field Day Anthology of Irish Writing*, 3 vols. Derry: Lawrence
Hill, 1991.
Paul de Man
Blindness and Insight. London: Methuen, 1983.
The Rhetoric of Romanticism. Albany, NY: Columbia University Press,
1984.
Terry Eagleton
Marxism and Literary Criticism. London: Methuen, 1976.
Criticism and Ideology. London: Verso, 1978.
Walter Benjamin or Towards a Revolutionary Criticism. London: Verso,
1981.

The Ideology of the Aesthetic. Oxford: Blackwell, 1990.
Heathcliff and the Great Hunger. London: Verso, 1995.
Field Day Theatre Company
  Ireland's Field Day. London: Hutchinson, 1985.
John Wilson Foster
  Colonial Consequences: Essays in Irish Literature and Culture. Dublin:
    Lilliput Press, 1991.
R.F. Foster
  Modern Ireland 1600–1972. Harmondsworth: Penguin, 1989.
  The Oxford History of Ireland. Oxford: Oxford University Press, 1992.
  Paddy and Mr Punch. Harmondsworth: Penguin, 1995.
Thomas C. Foster
  Seamus Heaney. Dublin: O'Brien, 1989.
Jürgen Habermas
  The Philosophical Discourse of Modernity, translated by Frederick
    Lawrence. Cambridge: Polity Press, 1987.
  The Past as Future. Cambridge: Polity Press, 1995.
John Haffenden
  Viewpoints: Poets in Conversation. London: Faber, 1981.
Maurice Harmon
  The Poetry of Thomas Kinsella. Dublin: Wolfhound Press, 1974.
Henry Hart
  Seamus Heaney: Poet of Contrary Progressions. Syracuse, NY: Syracuse
    University Press, 1992.
Eamon Hughes
  Culture and Politics in Northern Ireland 1960–1990. Milton Keynes: Open
    University Press, 1991.
Frederic Jameson
  The Prison-House of Language. Princeton, NJ: Princeton University Press,
    1974.
  Marxism and Form. Princeton, NJ: Princeton University Press, 1971.
  The Political Unconscious. London: Methuen, 1981.
  The Ideologies of Theory: Essays 1971–1986, Vol. 2. London: Routledge,
    1988.
  Late Marxism: Adorno, or, the Persistence of the Dialectic. London: Verso,
    1990.
Richard Kearney
  The Wake of Imagination. London: Hutchinson, 1988.
  Transitions: Narratives in Modern Irish Culture. Manchester: Manchester
    University Press, 1988.
Robert Kee
  Ireland: A History. London: Abacus Books, 1995.
David Lloyd
  Anomolous States: Irish Writing and the Post-Colonial Moment. Dublin:
    Lilliput Press, 1993.
Edna Longley
  Poetry in the Wars. Newcastle upon Tyne: Bloodaxe Books, 1986.
  The Living Stream: Literature and Revisionism in Ireland. Newcastle upon
    Tyne: Bloodaxe Books, 1994.

Blake Morrison
  Seamus Heaney. London: Methuen, 1982.
Mairin Ní Dhonnchadha and Theo Dorgan
  (eds) *Revising the Rising.* Derry: Field Day, 1991.
Richard Pine
  (ed.) *Dark Fathers into Light: Brendan Kennelly.* Newcastle upon Tyne:
  Bloodaxe Books, 1994.
Bernard O'Donoghue
  Seamus Heaney and the Language of Poetry. Hemel Hempstead: Harvester,
  1994.
Michael O'Loughlin
  After Kavanagh. Dublin: Raven Arts Press, 1985.
Richard Rorty
  Philosophy and the Mirror of Nature. Oxford: Blackwell, 1980.
  Contingency, irony and solidarity. Cambridge: Cambridge University
  Press, 1989.
  Essays on Heidegger and Others. Cambridge: Cambridge University Press,
  1991.
Helen Vendler
  The Music of What Happens: Poems, Poets, Critics. Cambridge, Mass.:
  Harvard University Press, 1988.
  The Given and the Made: Strategies of Poetic Redefinition. London: Faber,
  1995.
Robert Welch
  Changing States: Transformations in Modern Irish Writing. London:
  Routledge, 1993.
Raymond Williams
  The Long Revolution. London: Chatto & Windus, 1961.
  Culture and Society 1780–1950. Harmondsworth: Penguin, 1982.
  The Country and the City. London: Hogarth Press, 1985.
  The Politics of Modernism, edited by Tony Pinkney. London: Verso, 1989.
Clair Wills
  Improprieties: Politics and Sexuality in Northern Irish Poetry. Oxford:
  Oxford University Press, 1993.

Index